Bread and Salt

Maria Dziedzan

L T P

LINDEN TREE PRESS

In memory of my beloved father

IVAN SEMAK

1922 - 2017

Bread and Salt

This is offered as a traditional Ukrainian welcome. It may also be included as a part of marriage celebrations, the birth of a child and the move to a new home.

Ukrainians regard the round loaf as a representation of hospitality, a symbol of eternity and evidence of nature's bounty. The salt, as a necessity of life, represents the immutability of friendship.

Important guests are presented with a round loaf of bread placed on an embroidered cloth, a *rushnyk*. A small vessel of salt is placed on, or beside, the bread. The guest takes a piece of bread, dips it into the salt and eats it.

1947

Chapter 1

A village in Western Ukraine

The sisters jerked awake at the same moment. They sat up, hearts pounding as they reached for each other's hands in the darkness.

'Get out!' bellowed a male voice.

They squeezed each other's fingers and held their breath, trying to hear as much as possible from the neighbours' yard.

'Out!' they heard again, followed by a shriek.

'NKVD?' breathed Verochka.

'Who else?' whispered her sister, Lyubka.

Dull thuds followed, interspersed with grunts.

Someone was wailing. 'Please leave him alone. Please don't hurt him. He's done nothing.'

'Shut it, bitch! He should have thought of us when he was helping his son to kill one of ours.'

'But he didn't…'

'Then why hasn't your son come back to clear his name? Because he's playing bandits in the forest.'

'He's not in the forest. He's not a partisan…'

There was a sharp slap and the wailed defence stopped abruptly.

Fifteen-year-old Verochka huddled closer to her older sister.

'We might be alright,' whispered Lyubka. 'They might only be coming for the Kalenkos.'

Their neighbours would not be the only family accused of having connections to the insurgents. However they might be the only ones taken for deportation to Siberia that night.

The sisters listened again, hearing heavy objects being dragged along the ground followed by a crash as if a carcass had been thrown into the back of a lorry.

'Be careful…' begged the same weak voice only to be followed by another dull thud.

'Get up there, you scum!'

The girls strained their ears again, imagining their neighbour climbing into the back of the lorry. It was unlikely they would see the old couple again. Those taken by the NKVD rarely returned, and those taken in the dead of night never came home.

'Let's go,' barked the voice they had heard throughout.

'You can leave me here,' said a new voice, 'since that's the last.'

'Alright. We'll see you in the morning.'

Vehicle doors slammed, an engine started and the lorry drove away.

'Let's try to get some sleep,' said Lyubka. 'There's nothing we can do.'

The sisters lay down again and shuffled about the bed to get comfortable. They had shared the bed in the main room of the cottage since their mother's death in the winter and now they lay close to one another for warmth.

'The poor Kalenkos,' said Verochka. 'They…'

She was interrupted by repeated banging on their door. Both girls gasped and sat up again, hearts pounding. They remained motionless, listening with all their might, hoping they had misheard the summons. But the banging came again.

'Open up! I know you're in there.'

'It's Kripak,' said Lyubka.

The girls shuddered. Kripak was one of the senior NKVD figures in their village. A tall, thin, stooped man with a cowlick of black hair falling over his sallow face, he crept around the village, always appearing when least wanted. In better times, the boys from the forest would have murdered him, thought Lyubka, but now, with no young men left, this crab-like creature terrorised the stranded women.

There was a third bang on the door. 'Open up! Now!'

'I'm coming,' called Lyubka.

'What are you doing?' hissed Verochka.

Seventeen-year-old Lyubka pulled her younger sister by the hand. 'Come on,' she whispered. She tugged Verochka after her, out of the cooling bed and across the room to the table pushed against the bench in the corner. 'Get under there, as far in as you can. Don't move…and don't make a sound. Whatever happens.'

'What are you going to do?'

'Promise me, you won't move or make a sound,' repeated Lyubka.

'I promise but…'

The door rattled. 'If I have to break this door down…'

'I'm coming,' called Lyubka, giving Verochka a final push. As the younger girl crawled under the table and curled up in the farthest corner under the bench behind, Lyubka rattled the lock on the door for as long as she dared before opening it a fraction.

'Who is it?' she whispered.

The door was thrust open, knocking her back into the room.

'You know who it is,' said Kripak, kicking the door shut and reaching for Lyubka's long plait which hung down her back. He wound it round his fist to pull her to him, but he couldn't reach her face with his mouth as she turned away from him.

He yanked her hair again, harder this time, forcing her down onto the floor where he made to kneel astride her. She struggled against him but his slender build belied his strength. He pushed a shoulder into her face, groping for the hem of her nightshirt. She tried to breathe but the stench of his leather jacket sickened her. She couldn't turn her face away, pinned as

3

she was by her plait in his fist.

She crossed her legs and tried to hold them together as he pulled up her nightshirt. She wanted to scream and cry for help, but who would come? Neither she nor Verochka had thought to help the Kalenkos and she did not want Verochka to think she could save her older sister. She would have to fight him.

She held herself rigid, putting all her strength into her legs. He tried to force a hand between her thighs but, grunting with frustration, he reached around to his belt and withdrew a short knife from its sheath. He stabbed the knife hard into her right thigh.

The shock of the pain made Lyubka breathless for a moment as Kripak took immediate advantage, mounting her and riding roughshod until the last gasp of his brief pleasure.

He collapsed onto her and muttered in her ear, 'I'll be back for more.'

Lyubka spoke for the first time. 'I curse you, I curse you, I curse you,' she hissed.

He reeled back from her. '*Ty kurva*!' He slapped her across the face as hard as he could. 'Curse me, would you?' he yelled as he stood up from her. 'Curse me, you bitch?' He kicked her hard before turning to stamp out, leaving the door wide open behind him.

The cottage seemed to hold its breath for a moment. Then Verochka crawled out from under the table and approached a moaning Lyubka. She ran her hands over her sister's face and found it wet with tears. 'Lyubka, oh, Lyubka, my love,' she sobbed.

'Help me,' groaned Lyubka. 'He stabbed me as well.'

Verochka drew back in shock. Then she stood up, slammed and locked the outer door and lit the lamp.

'Verochka, the lamp!'

'Damn them with their rules. If they want to come and see what that bastard has done, let them.'

Lyubka dropped her head back onto the floor. The order to the villagers not to burn lights at night seemed foolish now. They were neither harbouring partisans nor planning rebellion. She lay on her back and felt the tears trickling into her ears while her younger sister brought the lamp to examine her.

Fifteen-year-old Verochka shone the light on her sister's prone figure. Lyubka's breath was coming rapidly but Verochka tried to ignore it as she surveyed the bloody mess. She made up her mind, hoping the wound looked worse than it was.

'It's alright, Lyubka, I'm going to warm some water and wash you. By then it'll begin to be light and I'll be able to go for *Pani* Lazarenko.'

She didn't know if her sister had heard her but she knew there was no point in trying to fetch the village midwife while it was still dark. Even babies waiting to be born had to observe the Bolshevik curfew.

Verochka riddled the remains of the warm embers in the stove and then stoked it up with fresh logs. She placed the large kettle on the hob and fetched some old clean cloths to pack between Lyubka's legs. 'Try to squeeze tight on these,' she said.

'He stabbed my leg,' Lyubka managed to gasp.

'Where?' asked Verochka, frantically trying to see past the blood.

Lyubka tapped her right thigh.

Verochka drew the lamp closer, then wiped her sister's thigh gently with a damp cloth. The blood cleared for a moment and Verochka saw the mouth of the wound. It seemed to pause and then fill with blood again. She tore an old cloth into strips and tied the tourniquet as tightly as she could.

Lyubka was shivering so Verochka drew the feather duvet off the bed they shared and covered her sister up. 'I'm going to fetch *Pani* Lazarenko now. Lie still and don't worry. I'll be back as quickly as I can.' She kissed Lyubka's cheek.

As she opened the cottage door, the sky to the east was

stained scarlet and Verochka hoped the midwife would answer her door at this early hour. She hurried along the still-dark lane, her breath clouding in front of her and tried not to think about the bloody mess lying on the cottage floor.

She reached the midwife's home, which was in a better state of repair than most. Everyone was prepared to support the only person likely to bring them medical help. Verochka rapped on the door and then waited. When there was no reply she knocked again, calling out, '*Pani* Lazarenko, I need your help. It's Verochka from down the lane.' She pressed her ear to the door and held her breath, hoping to hear some movement.

She jumped back when a voice on the other side of the wooden door said, 'What help can you need, Verochka? You're not pregnant, are you?'

'No, *Pani* Lazarenko, I'm not, but Lyubka's bleeding badly. I'm afraid she might die.'

There was a shuffling in the cottage and a few moments later a short stout woman emerged carrying a basket covered in a white cloth. As she joined Verochka she said, 'Come on then, if it's a matter of life and death.'

Verochka followed the woman's rolling gait down the path and they hurried along the lightening lane to the orphans' cottage. Lyubka lay on the floor where her sister had left her, her breathing more shallow now.

The midwife lifted the lamp to examine her patient. She drew back the duvet.

'What happened here?'

'She was attacked,' said Verochka with a sob.

The older woman stared at her. 'Where? Here?'

Verochka nodded then cried out, 'She told me to hide.'

'She did the right thing. Who would have looked after you if you'd both been injured? Get me some hot water and then make her some tea. Do you have any sugar or honey?'

'There's a little honey left.'

'Put that in her tea.'

The woman placed her hand on Lyubka's forehead. 'Don't worry,' she said to her patient. 'I'm here now. We'll soon have you sorted out.'

Verochka brought a bowl of warm water and while *Pani* Lazarenko washed the ruined girl, Verochka held up her sister's head to spoon sweet tea into her mouth.

The midwife shook her head as she cleaned the blood away.

Lyubka whispered, 'He cut me as well.'

'Bastard,' muttered the midwife. She pressed her strong hand into Lyubka's abdomen but there was little reaction from her patient. 'Lyubka,' she said, her voice kinder now, 'I need to examine you inside to see how much damage there is. Can you bear it?'

Lyubka tried to nod but couldn't. She blinked her assent and gave herself up to the older woman's ministrations.

Eventually, *Pani* Lazarenko turned to Verochka. 'Pass me my basket. I'm going to sew up her wounds.'

'Will it hurt her?'

'Not as much as that,' said the woman grimly.

***

Verochka sat in the lamplight beside her sister's bed into which she and Mrs Lazarenko had managed to lift Lyubka that morning. She had slept for most of the day during which Verochka had only left her side to complete the most necessary tasks for their cow and the hens. Now, as night drew on again, she leaned forward to listen to Lyubka's breathing.

'Let her sleep as much as she wants to,' the midwife had said.

Verochka's immediate concern was that Kripak might use his power to have them both deported to Siberia. She doubted whether Lyubka could even survive such a journey at the moment, let alone the frozen horrors of the labour camps far to the north and east. She must find a way for them to remain in the village. She thought of others who had seemed to be in danger of deportation and remembered the muttered gossip surrounding their escape from a fate which everyone in the village feared. There seemed to be only two ways to do that: money or violence. Verochka thought of the hand-to-mouth existence she and her sister shared. They had their vegetable garden and their livestock, but these were the means of survival, not disposable income. And how could she, a puny fifteen-year-old, challenge the might of one of the most powerful men in the village? However, despite his position, he might not want his crime to be generally known. And remain they must. It was their only chance.

Verochka stroked her sister's forehead. In the last seven years of her young life, she had lost all those close to her. Her father had been shot by the NKVD in their own yard when Verochka was eight years old. Her oldest sister, Natalya, had been driven into exile by the Nazis in 1943 to serve as a slave labourer. Her mother had died the previous winter in the typhus epidemic which had hit their village. She dreaded losing Lyubka and resolved to do whatever was needed to keep her sister with her. She hoped Natalya was alive somewhere, but she knew she could not rely on any help from that quarter. She must act alone. She must save herself and Lyubka now.

Chapter 2
The Bay of Biscay

I stroke Taras's hair away from his forehead. He's wet with sweat. He has been sea-sick for so long that when he retches again there's nothing left to vomit.

'Natalya,' he groans.

'It's alright, my love. This will soon be over.'

It stinks in here. There are ten of us in this tiny cabin and all of them have been sick except me. I've tried to help by emptying buckets of vomit and bringing fresh water but they've all suffered. In the meantime I've had double and triple rations along with the crew and the few passengers who, like me, have strong stomachs.

'We'll soon be leaving the Bay of Biscay behind,' I tell Taras. 'The crew say the sea will be calmer then.'

I don't know whether he's heard me or not. I'd like to take him for a walk on deck to get some fresh air, but he's still too weak to move. He's been ill since we entered more open waters. He'd been washing his face in the men's bathroom and, as he'd leaned over the bowl, the ship had heaved and he'd been overcome by the nausea which has remained with him ever since. It's such a pity. He's forgotten the excitement we felt when we saw the coast of Africa in the distance, close enough to see the telephone wires. Then we passed through the Straits of Gibraltar, where the Mediterranean was as smooth as oil, and out into the Atlantic, which has been pouring over the decks. Enough to make anyone sick. But I am whole…apart from the growing gap between me and Mama, Lyubka and Verochka. I try to keep their faces before me but in the five years since the Nazis took me as a slave labourer to Germany and the years in

9

camps for the displaced, their features have begun to fade.

There's no help for it. I need to get Taras well enough to face our new life in England where we'll be expected to work. That's the only reason the British Government agreed to take us from the Displaced Persons camps in Germany and not to hand us over to Stalin.

The day before we land, I finally manage to get Taras to take a little thin soup. I feed him the first few spoonfuls and then he takes the spoon himself and empties the bowl.

I stroke his bristly cheek.

'I must look like a tramp,' he says.

He does but I smile at him. 'Do you feel well enough to be smartened up? We'll be there soon and you want to make a good impression in our new home.'

He smiles too. England, where we will work and live until we can return to our true home.

'How will you do that?' he asks. He's not asking how we'll get back to Ukraine, but how I will smarten him up.

'Wait and see.'

I go to the canteen and peer through a door into the kitchen looking for a friendly face.

A young man in kitchen whites looks over. 'Can I help?'

'Hot water?' I ask, holding up a small pail.

He looks puzzled.

I mime shaving. I know quite a few English words but sometimes I don't have the one I need.

The boy holds out a hand for my pail. 'To shave?'

'To shave,' I repeat after him. I'm like a magpie. I want to store up all the words so I can pour them out later and sound like a native. Or less like a foreigner.

When he hands the pail back, he winks and says, 'For you?'

We both laugh.

'For my man.' I know the word 'husband' but I have no ring to demonstrate my married state and no documents except a certificate which the Ukrainian priest in the UNRRA camp gave us. Will it matter?

I carry the water back to Taras. The towels the Red Cross gave us in Germany have worn thin but they're all we have. I place one under his chin and lather his face with the last of the Red Cross soap. I reach into the secret pocket I had sewn into my coat as the war came to an end, and withdraw the *Sturmbannführer's* razor.

Taras looks shocked. 'Where did you get that?'

'I stole it.'

'Where from?'

'The Kuhn's house. For protection. Besides, the Major didn't need it.'

'So have you carried it all this time?'

'Only two years.'

I can see he doesn't know whether to be glad about my initiative or not, stealing from my German masters. I begin to shave him.

***

As the great ship is guided into port, we congregate on deck with the other passengers and peer into the gloom, trying to make out some recognisable detail of our new home. But all is shrouded in fog.

'I can't see anything of this England,' mutters Taras.

'I think we're somewhere in the north,' says the man next to him.

'The north?'

'That's what one of the crew said. But we'll probably be taken south to the camps,' says the man.

Taras and I exchange a glance and he takes my hand.

'Why don't they tell us where we're going? Why are they treating us like prisoners?' I ask. I can't help it. Soldiers have been marching me away for the last five years but this was supposed to be different. I know we've chosen this. Yet it's a poor choice. To go to work in a foreign land rather than to go home where only execution or deportation to Siberia face us.

'I don't know, but we have no papers, except a card which says we're stateless,' says Taras.

In the end the lack of papers doesn't seem to matter. We're disembarked with hundreds of other Displaced Persons and marched to the train station. We would make the streets ring with the stamp of our footsteps but the English fog encircles us and deadens our noise.

'Where is everyone?' I whisper.

Taras shrugs. 'It's very early,' but I know he feels uneasy too. There have been enough people marched to their deaths, and who knows what might happen in this new country where no one has witnessed our arrival?

I'm glad there are no witnesses. I remember too well marching through Ternopil and the shame of being observed by those who hadn't yet been taken by the Nazis. But there the buildings were white. These blackened edifices fill me with foreboding. The smell of soot is so strong it catches in my throat and the fog seems to flicker before my eyes. I shiver in the cold of the morning and wonder if we'll ever be made welcome anywhere.

We march to the cavern of the station, where the fog begins to diminish but where great clouds of steam rise from the huge locomotives and I can't help shuddering as we stand on the platform beside the hissing trains.

'Are you still cold?' asks Taras.

I shake my head. 'Where are they taking us? Why haven't they explained?'

'These aren't Nazis, Natalya.'

'No, but they're not treating us like people either. And why is it so cold in June?' I know I sound like a child but I can't seem to help myself.

When we're told to board the train, we shuffle forward and mount the steps into a long compartment. At least these steps are manageable, unlike the climb into the German cattle trucks. This time we are European Voluntary Workers and not *Ostarbeiter*. So many trains and so far from home. I wonder how long it will be before we can get a train going east - across the whole of Europe - home to Mama, and my little sisters.

We place our bundles in the racks above our heads and listen to the slamming of train doors. Finally someone blows a whistle so we can start our journey south. Taras takes my hand again and I try to smile at him as we pass the outskirts of the city to enter a harsh and alien landscape. The fog has lifted but the day seems to be no lighter despite the season. I'm sitting with my back to the engine so I see the scenery as we've passed it. It doesn't look much like summer out there. I wonder where the fields of wheat are. Do these people feed themselves with the purple shrub I see growing everywhere? I remember the rolling fields of wheat at home and let my memory stray over the fertile land. I try to see Mama and the girls going out to harvest but the picture won't come. My stomach roils with fear. I wonder how they are. I have had no letter for over two years and can only cling to the hope they might still be alive.

There's a loud screeching of wheels and the train jerks to a halt, throwing us out of our seats and our bundles and boxes from the luggage racks.

'What on earth...?' yells someone.

The carriage door is thrown open by a train guard in a dark uniform. 'Who pulled the Emergency Cord?' he bawls.

'What's he saying?' asks someone else.

No one speaks so I translate loudly enough for them to hear, but I'm not sure what the problem is so I turn to the guard. 'What is Emergency Cord?'

He climbs up into the compartment and stomps over to

where a shabby canvas rucksack hangs by one of its hooks from a chain cord beneath a red sign.

'Whose is this?' shouts the guard.

One of the men stands up to loud jeers from his friends.

'It's no laughing matter.' The guard turns to me. 'You speak English. Tell them this cord stops the whole train, but it's only for emergencies.'

When I translate, the roars of laughter only grow louder.

The guard tears the rucksack down and dumps it on the floor, then leaves the carriage shaking his head and muttering. He slams the door and disappears up the track.

'What did he say?' asks Taras.

'He called us "bloody foreigners",' I say.

Chapter 3

Verochka lifted her face away from the cow's flank and her fingers paused in their work. She held her breath and listened.

The shouts and cries came again.

With a murmured, 'It's alright, girl,' she lifted the bucket of warm milk away from the cow's hooves and went to stand in the barn doorway. She looked across the yard to the chicken pen where Lyubka was also standing, listening. The sisters exchanged a glance and shrugged, but then the cries came again. This time much louder.

Verochka crossed the yard and reached into the pen to take Lyubka's hand.

'Leave that for a moment. Let's go in. It's safer.'

They turned and walked towards the house, Lyubka limping, Verochka taking some of her weight. They entered the cottage, blinking as their eyes became accustomed to the dark interior. Verochka closed the door and the teenagers stood together by the window, their arms around one another's waists, their heads inclined towards each other. They both wore white headscarves but Vera's blonde curls escaped from the edges of hers, while Lyubka's dark, shiny hair framed her face. Despite their difference in colouring, they could only be taken for sisters.

'Who do you think it might have…' began Lyubka, but she was interrupted by the clatter of Militia boots as they ran down the lane past the sisters' house.

The girls drew back from the window until the footsteps had died away and then they peered out again. There was nothing to be seen.

'Wait here,' said Verochka making for the cottage door.

'Don't leave me.'

Lyubka hobbled out into the yard and the pair of them

made their way to the end of the vegetable garden. Here the ground began to fall away into the valley where a tributary fed into the Dniester. They stood on tiptoe to look over the rows of maize, then Verochka said in a low voice, 'There. Across the Tirka.'

Lyubka looked over the open ground to the other side of the stream. Two young men were fleeing uphill towards the trees. 'Looks like the Semenenko brothers…'

'Maybe. They were with the partisans.'

'Run,' whispered Lyubka. 'Run!'

Shots rang out. One of the young men stumbled and fell.

The sisters held their breath as the first man ran back for the second and, taking his arm over his shoulder, hauled up the injured man. They stumbled the last few metres to the trees and disappeared.

Moments later a group of dark-clad Militia splashed across the stream and ran uphill for the treeline.

'Do you think they'll make it?' asked Lyubka.

'I doubt it. There are no partisans left in these woods to help them, so unless they find somewhere to hide I should think those brutes will soon catch them up.'

'What were they doing here, so far from their *kurin*?'

'Who knows? Perhaps they came to see their parents. Or maybe to recruit others and start a new cell.'

'There used to be so many of them when Natalya was at home,' said Lyubka.

'And now so many dead,' said Verochka.

'The Bolsheviks are determined to destroy us.'

Verochka sighed. 'Come on, there's nothing we can do for them. Let's finish our work and take you to *Pani* Lazarenko.'

'There's no need to see her.'

'There is. We want to be sure you're healing and there's no infection.'

And no baby, thought Lyubka with dread. Weeks had

passed since the attack but she had had no sign of a period. Please God, don't let there be a baby.

But Verochka was praying for their continued anonymity. They had not yet been called out in the night to climb aboard a lorry going east. Kripak could easily have included them on the lists bound for Novosibirsk or Krasnoyarsk. Yet he hadn't. She didn't really care why, as long as he didn't come back. There was no one they could report his attack to since the Militia did the bidding of the NKVD and he was one of theirs. She and Lyubka could manage to survive only if they were left alone.

It was late afternoon by the time the girls made their slow way to *Pani* Lazarenko's cottage. Verochka had Lyubka leaning on one arm and in the other she carried a basket with several jars of preserves as the midwife's fee.

Lyubka knocked on the woman's door.

'She'll never hear you knocking like that,' said Verochka as she rapped sharply on the door.

It was opened by the stocky nurse. 'Come in, girls. I was expecting you.'

They entered her warm, stuffy cottage. She pointed Verochka to a chair by the table and led Lyubka to the daybed close to the stove. She helped the older girl to lie down.

'How have you been?' she asked.

'Alright,' said Lyubka, her eyes stretched wide.

'And the pain? Still as bad?'

'No, it's easing.'

'Good.' She turned to Verochka. 'Is she doing any heavy work?'

Verochka shook her head. 'Not if I can help it.'

The older woman turned to her patient. 'You mustn't lift anything for a while yet. You don't want to risk a rupture.'

'But Verochka…'

'Verochka what?' asked the nurse.

'She can't do it all alone.'

'She can,' said Verochka. 'I've told you. I only want you to get better.'

'I don't want to be a burden.'

'You're not a burden. You're the only person I have left.'

'Verochka's right. You have to let her do most of the work for now. Your time will come again. Now, is there anything else worrying you?'

Lyubka looked up with something like terror in her eyes.

'Have you had your monthlies since the attack?'

Lyubka shook her head.

The midwife lifted Lyubka's skirt to examine her. 'I don't think you're pregnant,' she said at last. 'You may not have had your period because of the trauma you've experienced. We just need to wait and see.' She smiled a rare smile at the girl. 'And then we'll do whatever we have to do.' She stood back. 'You've been brave, now you have to be patient and let your body heal.'

She turned to Verochka again. 'Have you kept up with the salt bathing?'

'Yes.'

'Of course you have,' she said as she saw the tears well up in the younger girl's eyes. 'You're a good nurse.'

A shot rang out.

All three women jumped at the sound. They listened again. They could hear a man shouting but could not decipher what he was saying.

'I'm going to see what's happened,' said *Pani* Lazarenko. 'Someone might need my help. You two stay here until we know it's safe.'

She hurried from her cottage and Verochka watched her take the lane towards the centre of the village.

Lyubka joined her sister at the window. 'Do you think they caught the Semenenko boys?'

'I don't know but I want to have a look. Can you wait here?'

'Don't go.'

'Wait here. I'll be back.'

But as Verochka moved towards the door, Lyubka took her arm. 'If you're going, then I am too.'

'Alright but be careful. We can't show any emotion whatever they say or do.'

'I know.'

As the girls entered the lane, they could see their neighbours being drawn inexorably to the village green to witness another horror.

And it was yet another horror. At the foot of the village cross lay the crumpled bodies of two young men.

'Try not to look,' murmured Verochka as they drew closer.

The boys' bodies lay broken and bloodied while around them stood black uniformed men holding clubs in their hands.

The sergeant of the Militia, Bakay, addressed the crowd. 'These bandits were caught this morning. They were Enemies of the People who could not be allowed to live.'

Verochka remained stony faced at the back of the crowd while she wondered why the brothers could not simply have been shot rather than beaten too. She gripped Lyubka's hand and risked a glance at her sister. Lyubka was poker-faced, but she raised her chin just a fraction to Verochka who followed the direction of her sister's eyes. Opposite them stood Kripak.

'Bring them forward!' bellowed Bakay.

The crowd craned their necks to see an old couple being led towards them at gunpoint, except Kripak whose eyes raked the onlookers for their reactions. When he saw the sisters, his glance slid over them like oil.

Verochka watched the Semenenkos advance and her heart burned for them. Their sons had been murdered and now the old couple would have to deny any knowledge of them to try to save themselves.

'Who are these bandits?' demanded Bakay, pointing to the bodies at his feet.

The old pair trembled as Mr Semenenko stuttered, 'I don't know.'

'What about you, old woman?'

The woman stared at the ground. 'I don't know either,' she said.

'Look at their faces!' yelled Bakay.

Neither of the old people obeyed this order.

The sergeant strode forward, pistol in hand. He pointed it at the old man's head and fired. *Pan* Semenenko collapsed like a fallen puppet.

'Look at their faces, old woman!' bawled Bakay.

But the mother of the dead boys knew she had nothing left to live for. She stood, head bowed, awaiting her fate.

The sergeant pressed the barrel of his gun against her forehead but before he could fire, Kripak stepped forward.

'Leave her,' he said. 'Let her live as a reminder of what happens to Enemies of the People.' He paused and looked again into each of the faces of the watching villagers. 'Fire the house.'

His men hurried to carry out Kripak's order, the sergeant directing them around the Semenenko cottage which stood on the edge of the green. They fired the roof on all four sides and stood back to watch their work. The flames licked the straw, finding gaps and tunnels beneath the surface until, with a shout, they erupted over half of the roof, reaching up into the blue sky. The smoke darkened the day as the villagers stood rooted.

Kripak did not move either but stood with his hands behind his back watching every movement. Mrs Semenenko knelt beside her dead husband and sons keening their loss, oblivious to the destruction of her home.

Verochka took Lyubka's arm and led her wounded sister away. They spent the afternoon out of sight of the burning cottage, but none in the village were able to ignore the acrid smell as the fire roared on.

Later, as she lay in bed trying but failing to sleep, Verochka remembered Mama talking about an old wise woman called *Baba* Chara. When the letters from Natalya had stopped after Stalin's defeat of the Nazis, Mama had agonised about where Natalya might be…even whether she still lived. The Bolsheviks had boasted on the radio about their destruction of German towns and Mama had ached to know what had happened to her eldest daughter. But her fear of *Baba* Chara's reputation for spiteful revenge was greater than her uncertainty regarding Natalya and, after all, she had two more daughters to raise, so she had never gone to seek help from the old woman. However, Verochka needed to protect herself and Lyubka from the forces in the village who did exactly as they pleased. It might help her to know whether her older sister still lived and whether she might return to add strength to their numbers.

The following morning, taking a jar of their best cream, she walked along the valley bottom trying to ignore the stale smell of yesterday's fire. She knew the old woman was said to live alone in a shack by the stream which fed into the Dniester. When she came to the stream, she crossed the stepping stones turning towards the supposed location of the old woman's hovel.

As she approached the almost derelict structure, she saw, by the rocks beside the water, an old woman, bent almost double. She was leaning into the stream and appeared to be trying to wash something.

'Can I help you?' called Verochka as she approached.

The woman straightened up with a snarl. She stared at the girl while pulling up some kind of wet fabric from the water.

'Can I help you with that?' repeated Verochka, trying to keep the tremble out of her voice.

'Why?'

'It looks heavy.'

'Go on then. Wring it out.'

Verochka put down the jar of cream and took hold of the

coarse fabric. She tried to squeeze as much water out of it as she could, but the prickly material stung her palms. She knew the old woman was watching her closely, so she did not complain. Instead she squeezed along the length of the fabric again.

'Hang it over the post,' said the old woman.

Verochka hauled the dripping cloth over to some split rail fencing and laid it across the top bar. 'Is it alright here?'

The woman ignored her question and said, 'I dreamt of her last night.'

Verochka started back. 'Dreamt of whom?'

'Who did you come to ask me about?'

'My sister, Natalya.'

'That's who I dreamt of.'

Verochka's heart was pounding in her chest. She swallowed and waited.

The old woman jerked her head towards the hut. 'Let's go inside.'

Verochka felt even more afraid of being closed in with *Baba* Chara but she had come this far, so she picked up the cream and followed the woman through a curtained doorway into a dwelling big enough to hold one animal. She breathed through her mouth as the stench of old clothes assailed her.

'Sit,' said the woman.

Verochka made out a low stool in the gloom and sat down.

Baba Chara knelt on the hard-packed ground beside a small fire over which hung a metal pot. The woman dipped a cup into the pot and sprinkled some dry leaves into the hot liquid which she stirred with a bony finger.

'Drink,' she said, giving the cup to Verochka, who tried not to think about the old woman's filthy fingernails.

She sipped the tea and then said, 'Natalya…'

'I know. Your sister. A partisan.'

'No…'

'I see many things,' the old woman interrupted her. 'Do not

22

assume I'm a fool.'

'Of course not except…'

'Except you don't want anybody in the village to remember that about her.'

Verochka shook her head, trying to hold back her tears.

'She went with the Germans,' said the old woman.

'She had to,' cried the girl. 'They'd been betrayed. She wanted to protect us, Mama and my sister.'

'So where is she now?'

'I don't know. We haven't had a letter in more than two years.'

'And you think a little cream will find her?'

'I have no one I can ask.'

The old woman began to rock back and forth, humming to herself. Verochka wondered if this was a show for her benefit or if the old witch was trying to reach some trance-like state.

'I can tell you nothing if you do not believe,' she said without opening her eyes.

Verochka jumped.

The old woman continued to rock herself and hum but after a time she shook her head. 'I can't see anything except the colour blue.'

'Blue?'

'Does it mean anything to you?'

'No, I don't think so.'

The woman shrugged. 'Well, that's all. Bring me some meat next time.'

'Yes,' said Verochka, knowing she would not come this way again.

'If you're not going to come again,' said *Baba* Chara, 'then I may as well tell you now. Be very careful when you handle the black berries.'

'I will,' said Verochka.

'I mean it,' said the old woman.

'I will be careful,' said Verochka again as she bent to go through the doorway into the green dappled light of the wood. 'Thank you,' she called over her shoulder.

'Don't thank me. It's going to be a long time before you step into the sunlight.'

Verochka shuddered and hurried across the clearing to the stepping stones over the stream. It was as she had thought. She and Lyubka were alone.

Chapter 4

Our train arrives at another large station and we're told to get off. I read a sign which says "Lincoln" but it means nothing to me. I still don't know where we are. The station echoes with announcements which are barely understood, so we stand, stretching and yawning. A man with a loudhailer calls for our attention.

'Ladies and gentlemen! We would like you to line up, please. We are going to be moving off shortly and we need to do this in an orderly fashion.'

He doesn't seem to realise that most of his listeners speak little English so his announcement is met with a wave of talk. He looks about him and fixes on one of our number he seems to think might speak English. He's chosen well. Our translator might have been a teacher in a past life – he has that look – and he explains to us what we're to do. As we shuffle forward to the exit I take hold of Taras's hand. There are hundreds of us and I don't want to lose him.

Outside the station there are several buses parked at the kerb and we're directed to board them. I try to peer around the heads of those in front of me. All I can see are fresh home perms on the heads of the women and the headgear of the men – the precious caps and homburgs acquired in Germany. But then I notice that as people reach the buses, the women board one bus, the men another. My heart thumps in my chest.

'I think they're separating us,' I say to Taras.

'What do you mean?'

'Look. The women are going to the left…'

Taras tries to see past those in front of him. 'It's alright. We'll tell them we're married.'

'But so are some of these.'

25

'Don't worry, it'll be alright.'

We shuffle forward and I have a sudden urge to pee. I remember the couples separated on Ternopil station who probably never saw each other again. I turn to look at Taras but he seems as calm as ever, blue eyes looking straight ahead at what's going to happen next, his blond fringe flopping forward over his forehead. I want to stroke his hair back but squeeze his hand instead. He squeezes my fingers back but doesn't take his eyes off the crowd in front of him.

As we draw closer to the buses, I see young women in military uniform with the initials WVS on the breast directing the females. What do the initials stand for? I know SS and NKVD. I know UNRRA too. The man directing the males is also in military uniform. When our turn comes, I'm directed to one bus, Taras to another.

'No! No!' I say. 'We married.'

'Yes, but you're going to be housed temporarily in separate hostels,' smiles the young woman. 'It won't be for long.'

'I'll find you,' says Taras, giving my hand a firm squeeze before he lets go.

And that's it. We are parted. I see his back as he gets on the men's bus. That's all.

I get on the women's bus fighting back tears. I can't believe that these English, of whom I've heard only good things, would behave in this way. I sit down in the nearest vacant seat.

'Don't worry,' says the girl sitting next to me. 'I'm sure they'll explain everything to us.'

I can't speak.

'I'm Lesia,' she says.

'Natalya,' is all I can manage. I can only see the SS officer's long black leather coat, the peaked cap with its eagle and *Hakenkreuz*, the pistol in its holster at his waist as he separated the men and the women in Ternopil station five years ago. There were women in the UNRRA camps who had never seen their husbands again. I bow my head. Let that not happen to us. I have lost so many of my own.

'Do any of you speak English?' asks a voice at the front of the bus. I make myself look up and see an attractive young woman in a navy blue uniform with her beret tipped over one ear, blonde hair in fat rolls, red lipstick. She's smiling at us.

I sit still while another woman offers her translation services.

'You will be taken to a women's hostel in the town where you will be given a shared room. Tomorrow you will be processed and we will be allocating you your work places.'

'What about our husbands?' a woman calls.

Yes, what about them?

'The men will be taken to a former military camp not far from here.'

'Why? They're not soldiers,' calls the same woman.

'Because you will be working in hospitals and the men will be working on farms.' She pauses. 'For the time being.'

A cloud of protest begins to build.

'You'll be able to see each other at the weekends. It will only be temporary. But the Ministry of Labour needs you in these two areas of employment at the moment.' She pauses again and then adds, 'You will be paid for your work.'

No promised land then. I feel angry with myself for allowing my hopes to be raised. We're homeless and stateless – why would anyone give us anything? We're the detritus of war and anyone who has a mind to, can make use of us. I resolve to expect nothing from anyone. Even Taras who quietly got on the other bus. Why didn't he protest? I learned to be independent when I was living at the Kuhns. There was no one to protect me so I managed. There were even times when I protected my mistress and her children. Being with Taras has made me soft, vulnerable. I will have to learn to stand up for myself again. Neither of us has the power to change our situation, so I must learn not to be cowed by it.

The bus draws up in front of an old building bearing the letters YWCA. More initials. It doesn't matter what they stand for. We're led into a wide hallway and the WVS girl stands on the stairs to address us.

'You must be tired after your journey,' she says.

I wonder which journey she's referring to. Does she mean the cart I had to take from the village to get the train to Germany as a slave labourer? Or does she mean the journey we've just made across Europe as Displaced Persons, doubling the thousands of miles we are from home?

'We'll get you settled in your rooms first. You'll be four to a room so perhaps you'd like to choose who you want to share with as we go up. When you pass the front desk, you will be issued with a Welcome Pack.'

There's lots of comment on this.

'Just a moment. Let me explain a couple more things…'

The noise dies down a little.

'There are bathrooms on each floor if you want to freshen up. Supper will be at seven o'clock this evening here on the ground floor behind me and then you are free until breakfast at seven tomorrow morning. We need you up bright and early because we will start to process you in the morning. Oh, and one more thing, please do not leave the premises until then.'

No one pays much attention to 'process' or not being allowed to leave the premises. Most of the women just want to know where their rooms are. People begin to clatter up the stairs, manoeuvring to be beside those they would like to share with. I follow them.

We climb up to the third floor. There are faces at the doors on the first and second floors so others like us are already here. Women slip into the rooms as we shuffle along the corridor. The crowd thins in front of me and I'm tugged by the sleeve.

'Come in here with me,' says Lesia. I look at her properly for the first time. She gives me such an open smile my heart shrinks.

She looks just like my friend Olha whom I've left behind in an UNRRA camp in Germany.

I follow her into a room and drop my bundle onto the last free bed. I sit down and watch the others making themselves at home. They're opening the wardrobe and looking in the chest of drawers, dividing up the storage space.

'What's your name?' asks the smallest woman. 'I'm Maryna.'
'Natalya.'

'Well, cheer up. This is better than the camp, isn't it?'
'We'll see.'

'She's been separated from her husband,' explains Lesia and I look again at this echo of my dear friend whom I have left behind…just as I left my mother and sisters behind.

'Oh, you'll soon meet up with him again,' says Maryna. She turns to the fourth girl. 'This is my friend, Paraska. We were in an UNRRA camp together.'

'I'm Lesia,' says my self-appointed guardian angel. 'I don't remember any of you. We must have been in different camps.'

I can't seem to make myself budge. I sit and watch them unpack. Maryna and Paraska chatter to one another as they hang up their meagre supply of dresses. Maryna is brisk and her smile never falters. Paraska, too, seems to smile a great deal. Maryna's dark glossy hair is neatly parted in waves while Paraska's fair hair is teased up into a flattering halo. I feel old and drab beside them…but they're probably twenty years old like me. Maybe they haven't already held a dying husband in their arms, although they've almost certainly left their families behind. Lesia is quieter than the other two. A cloud of dark hair frames her serious face. I feel the loss of Olha more than at any moment since I left her and wonder how she and Dmitro and their baby, Levko, are faring.

Lesia waves her Welcome Pack at me. 'Aren't you going to have a look at what they've given us?'

She's right. As I'm here I might as well unpack my things. I set aside the soap, towel and cutlery from the Welcome Pack and they are welcome. I place my *rushnyk* with its photo of Roman under my few belongings in what is now my drawer. I take the last letter I received from Mama from my bundle but resist the temptation to re-read it. I also close my mind to the image of Lyubka and Verochka waving to me as the cart drew away from the village. The worn three-year-old letter goes under the pillow. When I unroll my old towel I see I still have the *Sturmbannführer*'s razor hidden in it. I'd intended Taras to have it but while we were together it hadn't mattered. I put the razor back in the secret pocket in my coat. It won't hurt to keep it there.

'What's this booklet about?' says Paraska, waving around a small brown and beige booklet which we have all received. Its purpose is self-evident, I would have thought, as it's entitled 'To help you settle in Britain'. However, it is written entirely in Ukrainian apart from some tiny letters on the back telling the reader it has been issued by the Ministry of Labour.

Maryna flicks it open and reads out the chapter headings: '*Where to turn to*…presumably when we get into trouble,' she says. '*You must learn English*…Can anyone already speak any?'

'I can, a bit,' I say. 'We had lessons in the UNRRA camp.'

'You can help us then,' says Lesia.

'I'm sure there'll be lessons here,' says Maryna. 'They want us to work so we'll need to understand instructions at least.'

'It's almost time for supper,' says Lesia.

'Let's go down and see who's here,' says Maryna.

'Don't forget your new cutlery,' says Paraska, waving the utensils in the air.

As we enter the already crowded canteen, I'm amazed to hear someone calling my name across the room. When I turn round I see a dark-haired beauty wearing a tight red sweater which matches her lipstick. She's standing on a chair waving to me. Marichka. It couldn't have been anyone else.

Turning to Lesia I say, 'My friend from the camps.' I take Lesia's hand and we make our way through the crowd to Marichka who stays on the chair waving whilst directing those below her to make space for two more. When I reach her, she jumps down and flings her arms around me.

'Natalya! I was hoping they'd send you here.' We kiss each other on both cheeks then she peers at Lesia. 'No Olha?'

'And no Taras.' Seeing my beautiful friend brings tears to my eyes. Not only because she's here, but because Taras and Olha aren't.

'Oh, you'll see him on Saturday. We've arranged a dance for the newcomers. Look at all these women needing husbands.'

'Well, it won't do them any good. They won't be able to stay together.'

'They will. This is only temporary.'

'Everything's temporary,' I say.

'Oh dear, we are grumpy.' Marichka turns to Lesia. 'Have you had to put up with this for very long?'

Lesia smiles. 'No. I think she'll get over the shock of the separation soon.'

'Let's get some food then you'll feel better,' says Marichka leading us to the front of the queue. 'Excuse me, excuse me, but my friend is feeling ill,' she says as she pushes people aside. So no change there.

We collect our supper, which features potatoes and cabbage more than anything else, and sit down among Marichka's friends, who, having been in the hostel for the last month, consider themselves to be old hands.

'Tell me all your news,' says Marichka, after we've eaten.

I tell her briefly about Olha and Dmitro, left behind in Germany with their baby, and about Taras being who knows where. 'Tell me about the set-up here,' I say. If anyone knows the system and how to use it, Marichka will.

'Well, you'll be given a medical tomorrow…'

'Again?'

'They want to know you're healthy and not pregnant.'

'Why?'

'You can't work if you're pregnant. They send you back to Germany.'

I think about this.

'You're not, are you?' she asks looking at my abdomen.

'No, I'm not.'

'Sure?'

'Yes.'

'Good.'

'Any DDT this time?' I ask.

Marichka pulls a face. 'No, thank goodness.' She looks at me. 'I know we're being organised by others again, but it really is better here than in Germany. They want Taras and the men on their farms so they've put them in the old military camps, but he'll be able to come into town at the weekends.'

'How long is that going to go on for?'

'They say we can change our jobs after a year.'

'A year!'

'Yes, but they pay us in the meantime. You'll be able to save a bit for a place of your own.'

'Is that what you're going to do?' I ask, knowing Marichka's plans will be anything but domestic.

'God, no. I'm going to America just as soon as I can.'

'America? Why?'

'No rationing and rich men.'

I can't help grinning at her. 'Marichka.'

'That's better. I don't like this gloomy Natalya. The most important thing this week is to find you a nice dress for the dance on Saturday.' She glances across at Lesia. 'And we'll have to do something about your hair.'

As I lie alone on the thin mattress that night, I count back more carefully to my last period. To be sent back to Germany, away from Taras would be even worse than the few kilometres which separate us now. But I also think of the half-stories we've been told…that we could come to England to work and start a new life. We hadn't been told the British Government would control the detail of where we would work and where we would live…Still, what choice do we have? To go home would spell disaster, not only for me, but for Lyubka and Verochka too.

Chapter 5

Verochka walked down the stony track to the river. It was a warm sunny day and she itched with sweat from her work in the vegetable garden. She looked across the pasture which bordered the river but could not see the other girls yet. However, they would be there soon enough. They would come to bathe after their work in the fields. All but one.

Lyubka still kept to the house. She continued to limp from her injuries, but worse, she feared the open spaces in which a dark-haired man might suddenly appear. Verochka sighed. Kripak had not approached either of them since that terrible night and, as the weeks became months, she had to try to suppress the seed of hope that they might not be deported to Siberia after all.

She turned from the track towards the stand of willows beside the Dniester. Their drooping foliage provided a screen for the women to bathe out of sight of prying eyes. More shelter was provided by a mound of large rocks which formed a natural harbour; somewhere to spread their clothes to dry while the girls rested and gossiped.

Verochka climbed over the rocks, ignoring the longer path around them, and chose a spot to undress. She stripped off her heavy cotton blouse and stepped out of her dark skirt to stand naked in the dappled shade. She shivered but then crossed the mossy slabs at the river's edge which bordered a deeper pool. She plunged into the cool water and rose up again, sparkling and gasping. She reached around to draw her plait over her shoulder and undid its binding. As she bent to untangle a knot, she heard the distinct crack of a twig from behind the rocks. Her heart lurched, but she did not look up from her task. Her fingers appeared to be busy while her ears were alert to every sound. She peeped from the corners of her eyes but saw no movement. She thought she could hear someone trying to remain motionless, but wondered if it was just her imagination. It might have been an animal, but it might also have been a man. The only men left were the very old, the very young, and those who served Stalin.

She turned away from the bank and threw herself into the flood. With several strong strokes she was in the middle of the river. She trod water, now able to admit to the certainty that she had seen a dark head disappear behind the rocks. There was someone there, but had he come to spy on all the girls...or had he only followed her?

She breathed a sigh of relief as she heard the chatter and laughter of the approaching girls. Whoever the peeper was, he would not attack a group of young women.

She swam towards her friends as they began to strip off their hot garments. She stepped out of the water calling a greeting to them, and approached her own discarded clothing. She held her blouse against her body.

'No Lyubka?' asked one of the girls.

Verochka shook her head. 'She's still not feeling well.'

The girls began to call to one another to come in, the water was lovely.

Verochka scanned the shady spots behind the rocks before joining her friends in the water. Her heart lurched again. She had been right. A dark figure crouching in the deepest crevice lifted his face. It was Kripak.

Verochka shuddered but then felt a spurt of anger. How dare he plague them?

'You'd better scarper,' she muttered through clenched teeth, 'before I tell them there's a pervert spying on us.'

She swallowed her desire to spit on him and turned back to her companions who were splashing each other in the cool river. As she walked away from her sister's attacker, she heard the mournful cry of buzzards. She looked up and saw two of them circling and riding the air currents above the river. When she joined the other girls she glanced back. Kripak was slinking away between the trees.

Verochka thought of him again as she returned home. Her footsteps took her past the piece of land where the church had once stood. It was here the priest had been hung but the NKVD had made him witness his beloved church being razed to the ground before they had pulled the rope. His had been a slow and painful death.

She did not dare to cross herself as she passed the hallowed ground but she bowed her head briefly. Her prayer was silent, yet she hoped God would hear her plea that she and Lyubka might survive this terrible time with no further injury. Neither did she look across at the overgrown graves. The villagers were forbidden to tend them. If God is dead there can be no afterlife was the logic forced upon them now. But she hoped Mama was still looking down on them and protecting them.

She heard a skirling shriek and looked up to see the sky was full of swallows, swooping and diving for insects in the overgrown cemetery. She envied them their freedom. It did not matter how bleak and dangerous people's lives became, nature continued to mock them.

***

As the summer reached its zenith, Verochka found herself having to grit her teeth to bear her apparent haunting by Kripak. It seemed wherever she went he was hovering in the borders of her vision. In the balmy dusk of a July evening, she went to fetch water from the well. She lowered the bucket and waited for it to change its tempo and slacken, then she began to turn the handle in the opposite direction, feeling the weight of the water immediately. Although slim, the fifteen-year-old was strong from the work in the fields and she turned the crank confidently.

But she almost lost the bucket of water when she felt another hand clamp itself over hers. She let out a shriek and looked around to see Kripak's sallow face.

'It's heavy,' he said. 'Just thought I'd help you.'

'Do I look as if I need help?' asked Verochka, recovering herself.

'No, but there's no need for you to work if I can help you.'

Verochka remained motionless, still holding the handle firmly. After a moment she shrugged. 'Have you got it?' she asked before relinquishing it. If she let it go, the weight of the full bucket would tear the rope down into the depths of the well taking a hand or an arm with it. She had no objection to the rapist having a hand torn off but she did not want to lose her own.

Kripak nodded and brought up the full bucket. He lifted it off the hook and turned to the young beauty by his side. 'Shall I carry it back for you?'

Verochka stared at him. Either he'd been drinking too much vodka or he'd been listening to sentimental love songs. Who did he think he was? A Cossack accompanying her into the orchard to make love to her? How had he made the leap from peeping at her beside the river to open courtship?

'I don't think you should come to my house.'

He had the grace to flush. He opened his mouth as if to offer an explanation but Verochka shook her head and took the bucket from him. Where did he think she'd been on the night of the attack? She turned away from him and walked towards her home, letting herself into the garden by the little gate. As she entered the house, she turned to close the door. Kripak was standing where she had left him.

She said nothing of the encounter to Lyubka but, as they lay down for the night, she tried to find an explanation for it. He must know that she knew he had violated her sister. Why would he rape one sister and imagine he could court the other? Verochka knew he could rape her too, so why tiptoe around her?

Verochka had heard Lyubka curse him and she knew the men in the village gave *Pani* Lazarenko a wide berth, not quite trusting where her power to heal came from. But surely those things would drive him away and not draw him to the younger sister? If only Mama were alive, she could ask her. But if Mama had lived, he would not have attacked Lyubka. She wished Natalya would come home. The war was over but she had not returned. Perhaps she was dead. She wondered again about the significance of the colour blue which *Baba* Chara had mentioned. Verochka turned on her side. She had not spoken to Lyubka about her visit to the wise woman. Her sister needed kindness and love at the moment, not doubt and anxiety. She closed her eyes and tried to sleep.

***

The sisters' garden was burgeoning. They gathered the ripe tomatoes, beans and peas knowing they could preserve some, but also knowing they should take advantage of summer's bounty to trade for things they could not provide themselves.

'I'll take them to market myself,' said Verochka.

'Alone? How will you carry everything?' In the past both girls would have taken their produce to sell.

'I'll manage. What do you want me to bring back?'

Lyubka ducked her head. 'I can't come,' she said eventually.

'I know. It's much too far for you to walk yet.' It was almost ten kilometres to the market town.

'And it's too far for you to carry all this,' said Lyubka pointing to the produce they had selected for trading.

'I'll take the little cart.'

'It's awkward to pull.'

'It'll be alright. Besides I don't have to take a mountain of stuff. I'll take what I can this week and then, I'll take some more next week.'

Lyubka still looked doubtful. 'I feel bad. I wish I could help.'

'You can. You can start preserving the things I don't take. We have those jars we managed to salvage. Do that instead. You can come to market with me when you're stronger.'

'I would have died without you.'

'Well, you didn't and we're both going to live. What shall I buy? Sugar? Salt?'

***

Verochka rose before dawn and left the house just as the sky cracked open. She manoeuvred the full cart onto the lane and, taking both handles, pulled it behind her. She tried to avoid the ruts but, until she joined the wider road beyond the village, the full barrow did its best to wrench her arms from their sockets. She hummed to give herself courage and, finding it helped, began to sing loudly as she passed the last houses in the village. She marched along, her young heart lifting.

The sky lightened and, as Verochka drew nearer the market town, she was joined by other women with their wares, all united by their grim determination to make good exchanges. As they hurried along the last length of road before the town, a car sped past them, throwing up a cloud of dust in their faces.

'Bastard,' muttered one old woman.

Verochka nodded. Bastard indeed. She had seen a sallow face peering out of the car's window. But she cast Kripak from her mind as she approached the market which was already bustling with bigger traders. She chose a spot on one of the side streets leading to the market, where other smallholders stood selling either small livestock like rabbits and pigeons, or fruit and vegetables from their own gardens. She had begun to unpack her goods when a voice at her elbow said, 'I thought it was you.'

She looked up at Kripak. 'Yes, it's me.'

'No, I mean on the road. Did you walk all the way from the village with that cart?'

'Yes. How else would I get here?'

'Well, don't walk back. I'll give you a lift.'

'You can't. I have my cart.'

'We can squeeze it in.'

'I don't think so,' and she turned away to serve her first customer.

Verochka did well. By late morning she had sold all the vegetables which the town dwellers did not have the space to grow. Leaving her cart with a neighbouring stallholder, she walked through the market pricing the items she and Lyubka could not provide for themselves. She made her purchases, collected her now light cart, and made her way home. There was only one indulgent item which she had bought: a pair of second-hand gloves to protect her hands when pulling a full cart. She felt light-hearted as she walked home. She had triumphed over the weight of the goods she had pulled to market and she had done their trading alone. She had done it once and she knew she could do it again.

Chapter 6

I urinate into the small metal bowl they've given me, hoping neither Lyubka nor Verochka will ever be subjected to this kind of invasion of privacy. But then I think Mama would not allow it. It's warm today and I imagine them walking to the fields with their hoes over their shoulders. The morning would be misty, whiteness in the hollows of the land. They'll spend the day weeding the crops to ensure a good harvest and then come back, singing with the other girls to mask their weariness. I dreamed of them last night. This morning they seem almost close enough to touch. They were crossing the garden to the house and although I called out to them they couldn't hear me. I called for Mama too but she wasn't there. I wonder where she was…

Someone raps on the toilet door. 'Have you finished, love?'

Love? What's this got to do with love? I pull back the bolt and offer the bowl to the waiting nurse.

'Thank you. Take a seat over there and wait till you're called.'

I follow her instructions and sit in the queue, looking around to see if any of my roommates have reached this stage. I wonder if the doctor will inspect my mouth, as if I were a horse he was thinking of buying. Lesia comes out of the toilet, hands over her urine sample and sits beside me. We raise our eyebrows at each other.

'It could have been worse,' she says in Ukrainian.

'Yes. But what's next?'

'Only questions apparently.'

'No more tests? No dusting us for fleas?'

'It's not likely. This is England.'

'And the last lot were American. It didn't stop them disinfecting us.'

We sit in silence, waiting for our interviews with the doctor.

***

Lesia was right I think as I swab the wide corridor, trying to ignore the scent of disinfectant in my nostrils. Just questions. What illnesses have I had? What illnesses have my parents had? What did *Tato* die of? I wonder if the doctor has a column for 'Shot by the NKVD' on his checklist.

Still, I passed their scrutiny and have been assigned a job. They call me a 'domestic' but that just means I'm a cleaner in a hospital. A hospital for the mentally insane. I swab left to right across the chequered floor of the corridor, glad of the tiles which help me to be sure I have been thorough. I move forward a couple of tiles at a time. It's quite restful. The length of the corridor stretches away from me to the double doors at the end. No doubt I will be told what to do when I reach them.

A young nurse clatters through those doors from what I assume is a ward beyond. She hurries past me and disappears into an office, not hearing my, 'Careful! Wet floor.'

But I hear her.

'Sister, Captain Tillyard is trying to leave the ward again.'

The big ward Sister marches past me, the little nurse following.

'Bring a straitjacket, Hobbs,' barks the Sister.

What is a 'straight jacket'? This English language has some tricks. I have learned 'Sister' does not mean a female sibling. I swish forward and reach the ward doors. There's no one to tell me what to do so I push the bucket inside with my foot. I may as well carry on but I peep at the disturbance going on around the third bed on the right.

A man in pyjamas is being held down by a nurse on each side of the bed. They must be strong. He's thrashing about and trying to kick them with his bare feet. He's also shouting. 'Let me go, you bitches! Let me go!'

'Now then, Captain,' says the Sister, 'we won't have any of that language on my ward.' She hardly turns around when another nurse arrives carrying a thick padded white garment. She just takes it from her. Is this the 'straight jacket'?

'Hold his feet,' says the boss. Then she looks up and catches me peeping. 'You! Come here and close these curtains.'

I look behind me, but there's no one there. She means me.

'Yes, you, mopping the floor.'

I lean my mop against the wall and hurry towards the group by the bed. What does she mean, 'curtains'? Then she says again, 'Draw those curtains,' nodding her head at the fabric hanging by the wall. I take hold of the fabric and pull. It follows me the length of the bed and across its foot. Behind the Sister is another such length of fabric. I draw it towards the foot of the bed, enclosing myself in the tight world of the yelling man and the four struggling nurses. I'm not sure whether she meant me to be in here with them but then she says, 'Hold his feet.'

I do as I'm told and relieve the nurse who's been trying to hold his legs still. She goes to help the other nurses put him in the jacket with its strange long sleeves.

I struggle to hold on to the patient's bony legs, while the four nurses cross the sleeves across the man's front. They roll him onto his side and begin to buckle the jacket behind his back. His pyjamas have ridden up so I shift my grip on him. I want to tell him to relax, that everything will be alright, but he's kicking and thrashing harder than ever. I lean towards him. Before I can speak, he manages to wriggle one leg out of my grip and kicks me in the face, just below my right eye. I feel shocked and stunned.

The Sister glances over. 'Keep a tighter hold on him.'

Thanks for the sympathy. How am I going to explain a black eye to Taras?

She leaves the cubicle and returns moments later with a

kidney-shaped enamel dish containing a syringe. She picks up the syringe and, while she holds it up to the light and ejects the first drops of liquid, one of the nurses pulls down the man's pyjama trousers showing the rest of us his skinny backside. The three nurses and I continue to hold him down while the Sister administers the drugs.

Within moments I feel the tension go from his legs and watch as his eyes close and his mouth droops open.

The nurses check his position on his side and cover him up with a sheet.

'Curtains,' says the Sister.

Assuming she wants them opened, I push the folds of fabric towards the walls.

'Carry on,' says the Sister to her nurses and then she turns to me. She looks at my cheek which must be red and says, 'You'll live. Change the water before you clean this ward.' Then she marches back to her office.

I do as I'm told and once I've got over her rudeness I think about the men lying in these beds. What have they done that they should be kept almost comatose? None of them speak to me as I work between them. Some watch as if from far away, others appear not to see me at all. They make me feel uneasy and I'm reminded of the rumours about Stalin's hospitals for those whose politics he didn't like. But these men are not mine. I keep on mopping, making sure I don't miss any corners.

I reach the end of the ward and begin to mop down its second side, trying not to see the man in the straitjacket. I've learned a new word but hope it won't be of any further use to me. I peer at his face as I mop beneath his bed. He seems to be sleeping but his eyes are moving beneath their lids. What nightmare is he reliving? I wish I hadn't held him down. He doesn't look like a criminal.

As I reach the end of the ward, one of the nurses holds the door for me. She smiles. 'Are you alright? We soon learn to keep well back of feet and fists.'

'What is wrong with him?'

'War neurosis.'

'War neurosis?'

'He saw some terrible things and can't forget them,' says the nurse closing the door behind me.

I walk up the corridor, the bucket knocking against my leg. I try to ignore the image which has flashed up in my mind but it won't budge…

I had been returning from the air-raid shelter with *Frau* Kuhn and the children when my mistress had muttered my name and had crossed the rubble-strewn street. I followed, holding six-year-old Jutta by the hand but I couldn't help glancing into the collapsed house we had been about to pass. Among the charred remains of what once had been someone's home, an arm pointed at the sky with the fingers of the hand curled into a black claw. Someone who had decided against going to the shelter had paid the price for believing in their own immortality. We had hurried the three children home and had tried to distract them and ourselves for the rest of the day.

My mistress and I didn't go crazy. Nor did any of the others. We all saw terrible things. We just got on with what we had to do. Like now. I have to clean the spaces occupied by these damaged men.

I repeat the English words I've learned for the rest of the shift, mopping and murmuring to myself. I can't let images of the dead and dying take me over. I especially don't want to feel the lifeless weight of Roman's head in my arms. I sweep the mop vigorously to and fro.

When I'm free from work at last, I walk off some of my anger rather than taking the bus back to the hostel. I mean to save every penny I can for a place of our own, even from this one pound they gave us on arrival, to tide us over until we get our first pay packets. I seek out Marichka, who is in her room, plucking her eyebrows.

'What happened to you?' she exclaims as I appear in her doorway.

'A patient kicked me.'

'In the face?'

As I tell her the story, I am furious with myself because I begin to cry.

'I don't want to see their sick men,' I say. 'I don't want to have to care for them. Nobody cares for us.'

'It's alright. Calm down. I can mend this.'

'How?'

'I'll get you a job with me in the kitchens at the hospital.'

I wipe my eyes and blow my nose. 'What? Just like that?'

'Natalya, a man runs the kitchen.' She grins at me, forcing me to smile back. 'Leave it to me. I'll speak to him tomorrow.'

'It's that easy?'

'Well, no. It might take him a little time but he'll do it.'

'What will I do in the kitchens?'

'Whatever's needed. We're almost all foreign girls in there. Ukrainians, Latvians, Lithuanians. We peel potatoes, wash saucepans, you know.'

'Very exciting.'

'We don't get kicked in the face.'

'Alright then. Thank you.'

She leans over and kisses me. 'No need. I thank you every day that I'm here in England and not in Siberia.'

'Oh, Marichka.'

'Oh, Marichka, nothing. I knew what you were risking to lie for me.'

It's my turn to kiss her.

'Come on,' she says. 'We're survivors.'

Marichka is as good as her word. Within days, she has me up to my elbows in dishwater at the biggest sink I have ever seen, but at least I don't have to see the patients we cook for.

And she's right. We are survivors.

But I still have to explain my bruised face to Taras.

Chapter 7

The short nights did not allow the Bolsheviks enough time to gather their victims in darkness so it was almost dawn when the village was woken once again by shrieks and cries. The sisters lay terrified, clutching one another.

'When is this going to end?' asked Verochka.

'When they've deported the lot of us.'

'Who do you think it is this time?'

'Could be anyone,' said Lyubka.

The sisters lay listening, knowing their locked door was an illusion designed to comfort them. They knew better than most that if Kripak wanted to enter their cottage, then he would, lock or no lock.

The following morning, the sisters took their laundry to the washing stones by the spring in the village where the women gathered. Lyubka was still limping but she knew Verochka would struggle to fold the wet bed linen alone.

'Good morning, girls,' called one of their neighbours.

There were no questions asked about Lyubka's absence as the women made room for them at the scrubbing stones. These had been set at waist height in two rows facing one another and a pipe led directly from the spring into the channel between the stones. This primitive laundry had been built by the menfolk before the successive waves of killing had robbed the village of most of its male population. Here gossip was traded with the flow of fresh water.

Lyubka and Verochka worked side by side, scrubbing their white cottons.

Another elderly matron approached, her bundle tucked under her arm.

'You're late,' called one of the older women.

'It's not surprising,' grumbled the matron as she reached them. 'I got almost no sleep last night.'

Several pairs of eyes looked up and then down again at their washing.

'Be careful…' someone began.

'Careful!' muttered the latecomer. 'It doesn't matter if you're careful or not. They'll still come for you.' She paused as she undid her bundle. 'Last night's excuse was that their daughter hadn't come back from Germany. That means the whole family must be traitors.'

Lyubka leaned a little towards Verochka until their elbows were touching.

'But a lot of girls went,' said the first woman.

'Some came back,' added another.

'Maybe the others couldn't.'

'Or wouldn't.'

The sisters remained silent.

'Are they clearing those families out then?'

'Who knows?'

Verochka tried to keep her breathing even as she and Lyubka wrung out their washing. They clambered up the stream to the flat rocks where the laundry was laid out to dry in the sunshine. Then she and Lyubka sat close enough to hear the talk of the other women.

They didn't discuss what they had heard until they were safely inside their own cottage.

'They're going to come for us too,' said Lyubka.

'Not necessarily.'

'They will. Natalya hasn't come back either.'

'That doesn't mean she's a traitor. She might not be able to. She might even be dead,' said Verochka.

'I don't feel as if she's dead.' Lyubka paused. 'At least I hope she's not.'

'We can't know what's happened to her and we can't be

held responsible. We were only girls when she had to leave.'

Lyubka wanted to say, we're still only girls now, but she knew loss and violation had made women of them prematurely. Instead she said, 'I'm not sure how we can keep out of danger.'

Verochka looked up. 'There has to be a way.'

***

Once again, on the eve of market day, Lyubka and Verochka harvested the vegetables in their garden.

'If I could manage it, I'd take flowers too,' said Verochka. 'Some people had them last week and they sold well.'

'Difficult to carry without damaging them.'

'Yes,' said Verochka, eyeing the marigolds and roses. They were lovely and brightened up the garden but worth it if they could be traded for jars to preserve their other produce. Not for the first time she regretted the loss of Mama's hoard of jars during the bombing after Natalya had left. Such a waste. They had very few of them now.

As she turned back to the rows of beans, she heard a voice calling from the lane. 'Hello!'

She looked across the garden and sighed. What did he want now? He was like a dog returning to his own excrement, she thought.

'*Dobroho dnya*,' she replied. Out of the corner of her eye she saw her sister slip down the garden to disappear behind the maize.

Kripak either hadn't noticed Lyubka or didn't want to reveal he had. He stepped across the garden delicately as if he really cared about not damaging any of the plants.

She watched him, trying not to let her lip curl.

He stopped a couple of metres away from Verochka who had no idea the sun behind her was making a halo of her blonde hair.

50

Kripak gazed at her and only remembered himself when she said, 'Did you want something?'

'Yes. Oh yes. I came to tell you, Balanchuk is taking his cart to market tomorrow. He's agreed to take you and your produce.'

Verochka stared at him. What did he want? She had seen his works in her own house and in the village so she was sure he wasn't troubled by a guilty conscience.

'I can manage on my own. I did it last week.'

'I know you can manage, but you don't have to. Accept the lift. You'll be able to take as much produce as you like without the trouble you had last week.'

'Why should you care what trouble I have?'

Down amongst the maize, Lyubka crumbled the drying leaves between her fingers as she too listened for his answer.

He dropped his eyes. 'You're young and it's heavy work to pull that cart all the way.' He paused. 'Take the lift.'

'Alright, but I'll walk back.'

'As you wish. Balanchuk will be here at first light.'

'I'll be ready.'

He turned crab-like to cross her garden just as an old woman stumbled down the lane, muttering to herself.

Verochka badly wanted to cross herself as *Pani* Semenenko went by, oblivious to any living creature, only haunted by her murdered husband and two sons, but Kripak barged past the old woman, not caring whether he knocked her over or not. Verochka watched until he was out of sight and then called, 'It's alright. He's gone.'

She felt like a fist was squeezing her heart when she observed Lyubka's broken gait as she came back up the vegetable garden.

'What did he want?' asked Lyubka and then wondered at herself. Why didn't she want Verochka to know she'd been eavesdropping?

'To offer me a lift to market.'

Lyubka waited.

'I know. It's odd. I don't know why he's trying to help us either,' said Verochka.

'Not us. You.'

'Me?'

'Yes. He looks at you differently.'

'What do you mean, differently?'

'As if he wants you.'

'Well, we know nothing prevents him from taking what he wants.'

Lyubka blushed. 'No, not like that. I think he may be in love with you.'

Verochka felt the bile rise in her throat and she had to swallow to control the gagging reflex. 'I don't think he knows how to love,' she said at last.

'Hmm,' said Lyubka. 'I think he does. In his own way. You need to be careful.'

Verochka began to gather the ripe beans. 'I'll be careful,' she said. As she worked she made herself replay her memories of that day by the river and the evening by the well. What if Lyubka was right?

***

Balanchuk came as promised just as the light began to shoulder its way over the rim of the valley. Verochka stood at her gate flanked by her wares, holding a basket of flowers.

The cart creaked to a halt.

'*Dobroho dnya*,' said Verochka quietly, aware of her sleeping neighbours.

Balanchuk climbed down to help her stow her goods safely. 'Get up then,' he said.

He climbed back up onto the cart, muttering, 'No wonder,' as he took in the picture of loveliness by his side. Verochka's

52

blonde curls were escaping from her white headscarf, her cheeks rosy despite the early hour, the bright blooms in her lap adding to her radiance. He clicked his tongue to the mare and the wheels began to turn.

The pace became a trot as they passed the last house but Verochka was able to catch a glimpse of the end cottage with its door and windows swinging open, the front gate hanging askew.

'Searched last night,' said Balanchuk, in answer to her unspoken question.

'What for?'

'Huh! What for?' He paused. 'You're right though. It could have been for anything. UPA propaganda this time.'

Verochka looked up surprised. 'But I thought the Semenenko boys were the last of the partisans.'

The old man shrugged. 'Who knows? They'll use any excuse to get rid of someone they don't want. Even insurgent leaflets in the house of someone who can't read.'

Verochka felt herself shrivel. The NKVD had cleared all the villages, not only theirs, of any suspected members of the *Ukrainska Povstanska Armiya* or their sympathisers. There had been no quarter given. No soft option of deportation, but instant execution. However, if someone still had propaganda leaflets did that mean the partisans were active or was it just a bogus reason for destroying another household?

The old man looked across at her. 'No point in trying to make sense of it.'

She nodded and let her gaze rest on the fat ears of corn which stretched away to the horizon. That was another thing the Bolsheviks wanted.

Perhaps she and Lyubka had nothing to fear. Their mother had been adamant her remaining daughters would not go the way of Natalya. They had been given no opportunity to help the partisans, so no suspicion could cling to them now.

But the old man would not let her have the luxury of trying

to convince herself she was safe. 'Doesn't matter who you are,' he continued. 'Doesn't matter who you think your friends are.' He took a quick glance at her again. 'Nobody's safe.' Then he hawked and spat onto the dusty road.

**

As she had done before, Verochka swiftly sold her stock of fresh produce and, taking her empty baskets, she wandered the market, trying to decide which might be the best purchases to make. She had just bought some honey when she felt a tug on her sleeve. She knew who it would be.

'Good day,' she said, turning to face Kripak.

'Good day,' he said. 'I assume Balanchuk met you as planned this morning?'

'Yes, he did. Thank you for arranging the lift.'

'My pleasure. Have you finished your shopping?'

'Not quite.'

'Come,' he said. 'I saw a trader with a supply of fine flour.'

She followed him, wondering why he would want to point out the finer flour to her when she could buy coarse milled flour in her own village.

'I'm sure it would be excellent for baking,' he said as they reached the stall.

'Yes, it would,' she agreed. She was to buy the flour, bake him a cake, ask him in to sample it…What on earth did he think he was doing? She tried to step away from him, the smell of his cheap hair oil in her nostrils.

'Are you going to buy some?' he prompted.

'Yes, I am,' she said and purchased a kilo of the flour. She placed it in her basket where it lay like lead.

They turned away from the stall.

'Have you got all you need now?' he asked.

She nodded. 'Yes, thank you.'

'Then let me give you a lift home.'

'Oh, there's no need. I like to walk.'

'I insist. The car's parked through here,' and he turned away towards an alley which ran from the market place towards the station.

Verochka sighed and followed his dark figure down the narrow alley which after a hundred metres opened up into the marshalling yard of the station.

As she came out of the alley, Verochka saw a train being loaded with people. She looked from left to right but the cattle trucks filled her vision. The marshalling yard in front of the trucks was crowded with bedraggled figures. She could not estimate how many of them there were. There was little sound. The people stood with their heads bent, then climbed obediently into the trucks as their turn came. The Red Army soldiers simply pointed, not needing to shout or prod. Verochka's breath came short and fast as she realised what she was witnessing.

'Are you alright?' she heard Kripak ask.

'Just a little hot.'

'Better to be warm than freeze to death,' he said and paused to let her absorb the sight of hundreds of men, women and children clambering up into the wagons which would take them to almost certain death in the frozen wastes of Siberia.

The baby's cry made Verochka look along the crowd to focus on a family group of a woman surrounded by four or five children, all under ten years of age, the youngest a protesting bundle in her mother's arms. How would she keep them alive? Verochka wondered, but she knew the answer. The mother wouldn't be able to. They would all die, the youngest first.

'Come. The car's over here.'

She followed him dumbly to the black car with its unnecessary NKVD initials on the side. He held the door for her and she climbed in, sitting as if paralysed, her heart still pounding in her ears. She stared through the windscreen, not seeing what lay beyond it as he started the engine and began to drive out of the town towards the village. She was grateful that he did not speak on the journey home. She tried not to remember the figures sweating in their winter clothes, which all too soon would prove inadequate on the taiga. She wondered at Kripak's courtship methods. He wasn't simply a rapist, but a bully who wanted to pretend to himself that he was charming too. She thought of the young men who had left the village during the war. All the decent ones, gone as soldiers and slave-labourers. Why had none of them returned to marry and protect girls like herself and Lyubka?

As they drew closer to home she saw the fat green wheat through the windows and the verdant hedgerows where soon she and Lyubka would collect blackberries…if they were allowed to forage. She swallowed hard as her home came into view, the little cottage flanked at the moment by hollyhocks in a riot of colour.

'There you are,' he said.

Verochka half-turned back to Kripak. 'Thank you for the lift,' she said and then hurried away from him without waiting for his reply.

Chapter 8

I'm torn between going down onto the pavement to wait for Taras or standing on the steps so I can see him first. But either way, the steps are full now and I'm caught in the middle. Each of us is wearing the best dress we could find and everyone has fixed their hair in curls or waves. I seem to be the only person to have kept my hair long in plaits. My *kosi* are wound in a bun at the nape of my neck despite Marichka's best efforts to persuade me to cut them off. But I gave in over the dress. She has managed to find me a sky blue dress with a wide white collar and a circular skirt. It will swing and sway as we dance. She has dabbed some powder over my bruised face, but Taras will notice it, I'm sure.

There's excitement and jostling as we wait for the men's bus to arrive. Because there are far more Ukrainian men than women, my single friends will be able to pick and choose. But I don't envy them. I have missed Taras's quiet calm over the last few days.

A bus draws up at the kerb and every window frames smiling faces. The men disembark quickly, smoothing back their hair, straightening the collars of their newly laundered shirts. Taras comes down the steps of the bus, checking to see where I am and he gives me his slow smile as soon as he sees me.

'Excuse me, excuse me,' I say to the girls on the steps below me and hurry towards my handsome husband.

He doesn't speak but embraces me, then steps back to look at me.

'You look...what happened to your face?'

The dress gets barely a second glance.

'A patient kicked me.'

'In the face?'

'It's not as bad as it sounds.'

'Tell me.'

So I do.

'And what did the chief nurse say?'

'The Ward Sister? Not a lot.'

'Did he kick any of theirs?'

'We were all struggling to hold him down.'

He strokes my face.

'And anyway, I don't need to go back.'

'Why not?'

'Marichka wangled me a job with her in the kitchens.'

'She's here too, is she?'

'Yes. She got me this dress.' I twirl for him to admire it.

He smiles. 'You look beautiful.'

'Despite the bruise?'

'It matches your dress.'

We laugh, but before we go into the dance I want to know what has happened to Taras since I last saw him.

'Tell me everything,' I say as we link arms and stroll up the street. 'Where are you living?'

'It's an old army camp. We're sleeping in barracks.'

'Oh dear.'

'Better than tents,' he says. 'We've been working for English farmers, hoeing their crops. Apparently, next week we start on the potato harvest.'

'Is it hard work?'

'No harder than at home. They pick us up early in the morning in lorries and we're taken where we're needed. Then they bring us back at night.'

'What? All of you together?'

'No. About twenty of us with one English ganger to each group.'

'To make sure you do the work?'

'Of course.'

'Are they feeding you?'

He nods.

'Enough?'

'Enough,' he says. 'You know how men are. They could always eat more.'

I know he's glossing over it. He didn't have to work hard in the UNRRA camps so the small portions we received mattered less. Now that he's labouring, not only will he be more hungry but he'll be more tired too.

'It's alright,' he says. 'Don't worry. We'll get through this time.'

'A year.'

'Yes, a year before we can choose to work elsewhere. We'll manage,' he says again and kisses my cheek. He turns us back towards the hostel. 'Now, let's go and dance.'

The canteen has been transformed into a dance hall. Someone must have carried a flag with them across Europe because there is the blue and yellow *prapor* draped above the stage. The musicians have already set up and begun to play their first set. Taras twirls me round in a waltz and we sing along with the band.

'*Nich yaka misyachna, zoryana, yasnaya…*' The familiar love song invites the dancers to the same romantic thoughts of lovers walking out at dusk, the man intent on protecting his girl from the freshly fallen dew. I forget my recent troubles and lean back to spin round and round with my husband.

As the dance ends, someone taps my arm.

'You found him then?' says Lesia.

'Yes! Lesia, meet my husband, Taras. Taras, this is my room-mate, Lesia. She rescued me when we were separated.'

They shake hands and grin in complicity. Apparently, I need saving from myself.

'Pleased to meet you,' says Taras. 'Thank you for keeping an eye on her.'

'It was a pleasure,' says Lesia. 'I was alone too. We can look after each other now.'

'Does she remind you of anyone?' I ask Taras.

He looks at Lesia for a moment and then says, 'Olha.'

'Who's Olha?'

'Natalya's dear friend in Germany.'

'Where is she now?'

'She's still there,' I say. 'She has a baby so it will be difficult for her to come here.'

'She'll come,' says Taras. 'Even if her husband has to come alone first, they'll get here.'

'I hope so,' I say.

'Come, Lesia,' says Taras. 'I have some handsome friends for you to meet. You won't be alone for long and,' he turns to me, 'there's someone I want you to meet too.'

He has also made new friends. We join a table of lively young men who already have several young women amongst them and Taras introduces us.

'This beautiful woman is off limits. She is my wife, Natalya. This other beauty is Lesia.' Taras turns to me. 'I found an *odnoselchan*,' he says. Someone from his own village.

I stare at Taras. 'That's marvellous.' And it is. It's like finding family.

A dark-haired man stands up from the group at the table.

'This is Stefan,' says Taras.

Stefan gives me a handsome smile and says, 'You must be the beautiful wife.'

I smile in wonder at this living representation of Taras's former life. At home. In the little village at the foot of the pine-clad mountain, a river rushing past.

Stefan leans forward and I offer him my hand but he kisses me on both cheeks. '*Sestrichko*,' he says. I suppose I must be like a sister-in-law and, for a mad moment, I want to search through the other faces in the canteen for my beloveds too.

Taras puts his arm around my waist and I pull myself back to the present. 'You must be thrilled to have found one another.'

'We are,' says Taras.

We sit down with them and I'm glad to see Lesia happily chatting to the men on either side of her. I lean against Taras and feel his warm arm against mine. This is what I miss. The physical comfort. Around us, the talk whirls as everyone searches for this comfort too. The men lean towards the girls in their eagerness to find a Ukrainian wife. If our new lives are to begin, we need partners to do it.

A figure leans between us. I look up into a cloud of perfume and see Marichka. Taras tries not to scowl.

'Hello, you two. Lovely to see you again, Taras.'

'You, too.' He tries to smile but it's too much for him. He does remember his manners though. 'Thank you for helping Natalya this week.'

'You're welcome,' she says. 'As you know, I owe her a lot.'

'I do know that.'

'Where are you sitting?' I ask before hostilities can go any further.

She grins at me. 'Oh, here and there. I'll see you later. Have fun.' As she steps away, she waggles her fingers at the only man wearing a silk tie at our table. He stands up immediately and takes her to dance. I watch her whirling and smiling. Marichka, who always seems to get what she wants.

I look at Taras. 'It was good of you to thank her. I know you don't like her but she has done me a big service this week.'

'Not as big as the one you did for her.'

'Let's not go over it again. You know I couldn't let her be sent to Siberia. And in the end I didn't even have to lie.'

'No, but you coached her.'

'I only told her about my village.'

I think back to the terrifying time in the UNRRA camp when we were afraid we would be sent home to face Stalin's wrath. He was either deporting or executing the slave labourers who returned home, making no allowance for the German guns which had forced us to leave. Those of us from Western Ukraine had pleaded to the Allies that we had never been Soviet citizens so should not be returned, but for people like Marichka, from Eastern Ukraine, who had lived under Bolshevik rule in 1939, Churchill had agreed to Stalin's demands that they be repatriated. I had made Marichka familiar with the geography of my village and some of its more important characters so she could answer any questions put to her during the screening of DP's. She could pretend to be my neighbour, rather than a girl from a village near Odessa.

'She let you take a big risk,' said Taras.

'Which I was willing to do. Besides, we both survived. We're here and we're safe.' I kiss his cheek. 'Don't be grumpy. Come and dance with me.'

He forces himself to smile and stands up, but the smile reaches his eyes again as we spin around the dance floor.

I feel cheated though when the last dance is announced. How is it that minutes crawl by with the swish of my mop and yet tonight the hours have fled to the tunes from home? Taras and I should be able to return to our own room at least. To have a little privacy. But like children, he is to be taken back to the barracks while I must sleep in this hostel. We're not alone in feeling like this as the men climb the steps of the bus and the girls stand on the steps of the hostel to wave them off.

Lesia wriggles in next to me and takes my arm. 'He'll be back tomorrow.' There has been talk of a park in the town where many of the couples plan to meet, including Taras and me.

'Yes, he will,' I say. I watch the bus disappear as it turns the corner at the far end of the street. A year is a long time.

As we turn to go into the hostel, Lesia can't resist asking: 'What did you think?'

'Of what?'

'Of Stefan.'

I drag my thoughts away from curling around Taras and look at my new friend properly. Her eyes are sparkling and her cheeks are flushed.

'Taras's *odnoselchan*? Or was there another Stefan?'

'Oh, you!' She nudges me with her elbow but the smile does not disappear.

'Which one was he?'

'The tall, dark, handsome one.'

'Tall?'

'Well, alright, not tall. My height. But you have to admit he's handsome.'

'He is.'

'And he's coming back tomorrow.'

'What for?'

'Natalya!' she shrieks.

I can't help smiling at her. 'He's keen then?'

'I hope so.'

I hope so too. We all deserve a little happiness.

***

Fate has another trick up its sleeve for my absent friend, Olha. Returning to the hostel from my new job in the hospital kitchen with Marichka, I'm startled to be told I have a letter.

'Want me to wait with you?' she asks.

I nod. My heart is pounding in my chest as I wait to be given the letter but when I have it in my hand I see the postmark is German. Not Mama or the girls then.

'It's from Olha,' I tell Marichka as I open it.

Dearest Natalya,
I hope you are settling into your new home with Taras and I

know you will be making the best of everything, as ever. It is only a few weeks since you left yet I feel as if I saw you in another lifetime. I am trying to be strong like you and can say that, thanks be to God, my Levko and Dmitro are both well. Levko is growing quickly and is trying to walk.

I, however, have had a little accident. I fell down the concrete steps at the door of our building. You remember how uneven they were. That would have been bad enough but I have worse news. I was pregnant again but I hurt myself so badly in the fall that I lost our second baby. I was in the Medpunkt for a while but I am now recovered enough to be back in our room with my husband and my little boy. This is a relief to Dmitro because Levko was very upset to be without his Mama.

Don't be sorry for me, dear Natalya. I have survived although my baby did not. I do miss you though and I would have been very glad to have had you here. The doctor says I will recover with time and rest. I plan to be a lady of leisure while you and Taras pave the way for us to join you in England in the not-too-distant future.

I kiss your cheek, my dear friend, and Levko sends a baby's kiss to his Chresna. Dmitro sends his best wishes to both of you.

Take care of yourself and write to tell me about your new home. Your dear friend, Olha.

'Bad news?'

'She's had a fall and miscarried.'

'Was she pregnant again? So soon after the other one?'

'I suppose so. She didn't say anything about it before we left.' She might not have wanted to worry me, I think guiltily, as I remember the excitement I felt as Taras and I waved them goodbye at the camp.

'Dmitro will have to be patient for a while, won't he?'

I look at Marichka. I try not to show how little faith I have in Dmitro putting others first. I shrug.

'I'll have to write to her,' I say.

'And tell her all about the fun of the hostel and the crazy patients who kick you in the face.'

'I know. I'll have to try to think of some cheerful things to tell her,' I say as we go up the stairs to our shared rooms.

Chapter 9

The girls stood at the edge of their vegetable garden, looking into the sun setting fire to the tops of the trees across the valley. The swifts were shrieking above them as they caught their last meal of the day.

Verochka looked up. 'I've thought of a way we can survive.'

'How?' asked Lyubka as if there had been no pause in their discussion.

'You said Kripak was interested in me,' began Verochka.

Lyubka reared back.

'No, don't worry. I'm not going to seduce him. I'm going to get him to marry me.'

Lyubka couldn't speak. She stared at the baby of the family.

'If I were his wife, and if you, my disabled sister lived with us, then we would be untouchable.'

'Untouchable?'

'Yes. I know what you're going to say. Kripak might not be powerful forever but he is now. We could use that.'

'But if you marry him he'll expect…'

'I know. That would be our agreement. He could have me as long as he kept us both safe.'

'Why didn't you tell me you've been thinking about this?'

'I needed to be sure.'

'And are you now?'

'Yes. We're alone, Lyubka. No one will help us. Our neighbours won't and there are no partisans left in the forest. We have to help ourselves and we have to use whatever we can.'

Lyubka moved towards her younger sister and took her in her arms. 'Verochka, you're a virgin so you can't imagine what it will be like. I can't bear the thought of you having to go through it with him.'

'Yes, but if I don't sell myself to him, we know he could just take me.'

There was a pause as both girls tried to wipe the image of Lyubka's rape from their minds.

'We can't afford to be sad about this,' continued Verochka. 'There will be no handsome Roman for me. I know he was killed by the Nazis but Natalya was so lucky to have had a lover, even for a short time. There are no young men left for us. We only have these *Moskali*.' She paused. 'The chances of us surviving in Siberia would be very slim.' 'I'm going to do this,' she said with determination in her voice.

'People will hate us.'

'You mean those hordes of people banging on our door to help and protect us? Let them hate us. We can survive hate. It's starvation and cold and being worked to death that worry me.'

'I'm your older sister and I can't let you do this.'

'It's not your decision. It's my body. I know it'll be difficult for you to have him in the house but he's only a man. We'll make the house ours. We'll be stronger than him.'

'But what if…'

'What?'

'…there are babies?'

'Then they'll be our babies, not his. They'll love us, not him.'

Lyubka shook her head.

'You think about it,' said Verochka. 'I've given it a lot of thought and there doesn't seem to be any other way. If you can bear to live in the same house as him, I can bear the rest.'

***

Verochka held the paper cone she had made from an old torn poster in one hand while she snapped off the seed heads from the dill growing by the roadside. As the cone filled up, she poured the seed into a linen bag which hung from her waist. Dill grew in her own garden, scattered among the neat rows of vegetables, but since the attack on Lyubka, she had got into the habit of making an infusion for her sister to drink at bedtime. As she rubbed the seeds between her fingers she marvelled at the herb's magical properties. It not only helped Lyubka to sleep but Verochka also believed *Pani* Lazarenko's wisdom that it would eventually help Lyubka to have a normal menstrual cycle again.

She stepped further onto the verge as she heard the sound of a car approaching. She didn't turn to see who it was. No one but the NKVD or the Militia rode in cars…although sometimes the passengers were prisoners being taken to Buchach for questioning. But she had not seen Kripak since he had shown her the deportees. She knew he had been giving her time to think.

As the car drew to a halt beside her, the fist of fear squeezed Verochka's heart tight. She turned around as she heard a gruff greeting.

'*Dobroho dnya!*' Kripak's sallow face looked out of the driver's window.

'Good day,' she replied and waited.

'What are you doing?' he asked.

She shrugged. 'Collecting seeds.' She waited again, offering no explanation.

He shifted in his seat, his leather jacket creaking a little. She saw the sweat on his upper lip and wondered at the vanity of wearing such a garment on a sunny day.

'How have you been?' he asked.

'Fine.'

'Did you get a lift to market again this week?'

She nodded.

'Good. I told Balanchuk to look after you.'

She threw him a bone. 'Thank you.'

When he said, 'Glad to help,' she realised he would not

mention the threat of deportation again but would pretend theirs was a more conventional courtship.

'It has been a help.'

'Is there anything else I can do?'

'I don't know.' She raised her eyes to his and saw him flinch. 'Perhaps. We're just two girls and I'm the only one who can do the heavy work at the moment.'

A flush began at his neck and stained his cheeks.

'We need to work on our woodpile for the winter.'

'Of course,' he said. 'I'll sort that out for you.'

Verochka gave him the benefit of a wide blue-eyed stare, pretending not to notice his deepening flush.

'Thank you,' she said again.

'Well, I'd better get going. Work to do in Buchach.'

She nodded but did not comment on the interrogating or torturing which might be waiting for him. She watched the black car drive away.

The following morning, Lyubka called her sister out of the barn. Verochka placed the bucket of milk she had just drawn in a safe corner and came out into the yard.

'Do you know anything about this?' asked Lyubka.

A lorry was parked on the lane, its rear at their gate. A man had undone the backboards and was beginning to unload logs.

'Have you got a wheelbarrow?' he called to the sisters. 'It would make my job quicker.'

'Yes,' said Verochka and, as she turned to fetch the barrow, she mouthed to Lyubka, 'Kripak.'

The man unloaded the logs and then stacked them neatly under the eaves of the cottage. Meanwhile, the sisters harvested their beans. The pods had dried and the girls ripped them from the withered plants onto an old sheet. Then they sat in the sunshine separating the beans from the pods and spreading them to dry.

'We'll be warm and fed,' said Verochka with a little smile.

Lyubka shook her head. 'Is he courting you or apologising to me?'

'Both I hope.'

***

The neatness of the stacked logs beside the sisters' cottage drew no comment from the other women, neither at the laundry nor at the river but Verochka detected a widening rift between herself and the others as September approached. They drew their water at the same well but…

'What?' asked Lyubka as Verochka brought a pail of water into the kitchen.

'Nothing,' said Verochka, putting down the heavy bucket.

'There is.'

Verochka sighed. 'It's just as we thought it would be.'

'We're *syksoti*? Traitors?'

'We could be. They're taking no chances. Polite helloes but no gossip.'

Lyubka watched her sister carefully. 'We don't need his help. We can manage on our own.'

'Yes, but we can't control the decision to deport us. Besides, we don't need gossip,' said Verochka, holding the memory of the deportees close to her chest. She knew she would not confide Kripak's threat to Lyubka. She would carry that fear alone.

Later, after they had eaten supper, Lyubka said, 'I'd like to go and see *Pani* Lazarenko tomorrow.'

Verochka looked up sharply. 'Of course. Are you in pain?'

'No. I'd like to ask her advice.'

'Is there anything I can help with?'

Lyubka shook her head. 'It's alright. Don't worry.'

'Do you want to go alone?'

'No. I think we should go together.'

The following day Lyubka took a clay pot of soured cream

and covered it with a linen cloth. 'You don't mind, do you?' she asked Verochka.

'No, it's a good idea.'

They set off in silence down the dusty lane.

Pani Lazarenko had been collecting mushrooms and had just returned with two large baskets full of *pidpenki*. She stood, her feet apart, sleeves rolled up, squinting into the sun, watching their approach.

'Hello girls, just give me a hand with these baskets and we'll go indoors.'

Lyubka took the proffered basket, holding it aloft as they entered the cool dimness of the midwife's cottage. Verochka followed with a second shallow basket which she laid on the table.

'Sit down, girls,' said *Pani* Lazarenko, taking in their anxious faces. 'A little drop of *sik*, I think,' and she bustled about pouring cool birch juice into three cups. 'Here you are. Refresh yourselves. It's hot today.'

Lyubka placed the pot of soured cream on the table. 'We thought you might like this,' she said.

The older woman lifted the linen cloth. 'Does she give good milk, your cow?'

Lyubka nodded. 'Yes, but Verochka milks her.'

'They often have a preference, don't they?'

Verochka nodded. What could she add to the conversation? She didn't know why they were there.

Pani Lazarenko went to fetch three large needles and then cut some lengths of fine string which she passed to the girls. They began to thread the mushrooms onto the string.

'So…' she said looking up from her task and from one serious face to the other.

Lyubka cleared her throat but continued to thread mushrooms.

'Lyubka, has anything changed since we last spoke?'

71

prompted *Pani* Lazarenko.

'No…Yes.' Lyubka swallowed. 'The firewood.'

Pani Lazarenko looked at the two young women and then down at her work.

Verochka threw a glance at Lyubka, who gave her sister an intense stare and then said, 'We have no one else to ask.'

Verochka flushed. 'We don't need to.'

Pani Lazarenko waited.

Lyubka swallowed again and then said, 'We were afraid we'd be deported…because Natalya didn't come home from Germany.'

Pani Lazarenko looked at Verochka. 'You struck a deal?'

'Not yet.'

The older woman looked at her hands doing the work which would flavour the winter's meals. 'I can't give you absolution,' she said at last.

'I don't want it,' said Verochka.

'No, but Lyubka does.'

'Lyubka doesn't need it.'

'Do you?' asked the older woman.

Verochka shrugged.

The three women continued to thread the mushrooms in silence.

***

In the twilight, Verochka was closing up the hens for the night. They spent their days foraging around the yard and sometimes in the lane, but the hens were more than glad to avoid the foxes at night as they enjoyed the safety of their hut. It was tucked, with its wire enclosure, behind the cottage against the border of the sisters' property. Verochka turned the wooden paddle to close them in and thought of the supper Lyubka was making. She tried to catch the scent of it on the air as she turned towards the house, but instead she smelt leather and hair oil. She looked up and saw Kripak waiting for her by the woodpile. He was leaning against the stacked logs, a look of expectation on his thin face. Verochka reached into her apron pocket for her only weapon. Two fresh eggs.

'What have you got there?' he asked.

'Eggs.'

She tried to walk past him but he took hold of her wrist. She paused and looked down at his hand.

'Put them down.'

'What for?'

'I don't want you to break them.' He took them from her hand and laid them on one of the logs. He had not let go of her wrist and he drew her towards him.

She stood stiffly, determined not to let him sense her fear.

'Where's your gratitude?'

'Is that what you think I am? A whore?'

'No. Of course not.'

'You do. You think I can be bought.'

His hold on her wrist slackened but he put his other arm around her. When he pushed his nose into her neck, Verochka tried to lift her face away from him.

'Come on, Verochka.'

'Come on, what? Sex in return for a load of wood?'

'And lifts to market,' he whined as he tried to push his foot between hers.

'No. I won't be bought. Take your wood back. And in future I'll walk to market.'

He drew his head back. 'Don't be such a child. You knew what was happening.'

'Who's the child? It was you who thought I could be easily bought.'

He sighed. 'Alright. How much do you want?'

'Not how much. What.'

'What then?'

'A marriage certificate.'

'What?' He stepped back and stared.

'A marriage certificate.'

'Who from?'

'You.'

'Me?'

'You want me, don't you?'

He spluttered.

'Well, you can have me as long as we're married.'

He continued to stare so she took advantage of his shock to step past him. 'Think about it,' she called as she marched into the house. She slammed the door shut and shot the bolt home. She was panting a little as she leaned her weight against the door.

Lyubka turned to her from the stove but Verochka put her finger to her lips.

The sisters stood listening until they heard their gate slam.

'Who was it?'

'Kripak. I think I just proposed to him.'

'Verochka! What would Natalya say?'

'She'd say I was only doing what she did.'

'What do you mean?'

'I'll be hiding right in amongst my enemies in order to survive.'

Chapter 10

Taras and I walk arm in arm towards the Arboretum, as we do every Sunday. It seems every Ukrainian man from miles around cycles or walks to be here with their fellow countrymen and to flirt with the remaining single girls. Most of them have been taken, although some are still locked in shyness or wartime caution and some, like Marichka, are looking for Mr Rich. As we reach the park and take the path downhill towards the terrace and the bandstand we see them all around us, the men in their dark suits they have been acquiring with their EVW earnings, and the women in every bright colour they have been able to find. I am happy to be with my Taras and I know how foolish I look with a wide smile on my face. Sunday, the best day of the week.

We stroll along the wide terrace, passing a couple of men playing chess on a bench. They are surrounded by a circle of silent watchers while the two players contemplate their next move. I see Lesia ahead of us strolling arm in arm with Stefan. We smile and wave at one another, then Taras and I take the steps down to the lawn to catch the words of a vociferous speaker addressing a group of men around the bandstand's steps.

'Look,' he's saying, 'it stands to reason. They've taken us in, here in England. How many of us? Tens of thousands, I'm told.'

'About sixty thousand,' adds a helpful listener.

'About sixty thousand then. Do you think Stalin was happy about that? Of course he wasn't. And Churchill – would he have taken us in if he was frightened of Stalin? He'll stand up to him and he'll fight for us.'

'He won't,' says a cynic. 'Why should he? He let the Cossacks be taken back to certain death.'

'And those from Eastern Ukraine,' adds another voice.

'He understands the situation,' persists the first speaker. 'He said no one should be subjected to tyranny. We should have the same liberty as the English.'

'Yes, but he also said an Iron Curtain has descended across Europe.'

'From the Baltic to Trieste,' says another.

'They will fight for us,' resumes the speaker. 'They want everyone in Europe to have the same freedom.'

'They won't! Everyone is out for himself. You've seen the English. They're sick of war too. They've still got rationing. They're not going to fight for us. They don't even know who we are. When I say I'm Ukrainian, they ask me if it's in Russia.'

'Or Poland.'

'Yes, but they don't like the Communists.'

'No one likes the Communists.'

I feel sick to my stomach as I listen to them arguing back and forth. This 'Iron Curtain' which they say divides us – how will I ever be able to go home, or even write a letter to Mama and the girls?

'Listen,' says a new speaker, 'I'll tell you how much they like us here. Last week four of us were sent to a small farm. We worked hard all day as usual, every day, until Friday. On Friday, this one just gone, the farmer comes out at dinner time and says, 'Boys, my wife has cooked a meal for you.' Very kind, we say, hoping for some decent food. 'Come with me,' says the farmer. We follow him up to the farmhouse. We can't help our mouths watering and I'm feeling glad someone cares a little bit about us. When we get there, he points to an outside tap and we wash our hands and faces. Then he tells us to sit on a bench outside the kitchen door. His wife brings out four plates of food and hands one to each of us. She gives us a fork each out of her apron pocket, smiles and the two of them go into the farmhouse and close the door. We're a bit stunned so I stand up and look through the kitchen window. The farmer and his wife are sitting at the table eating.'

He pauses. I look at him and see him struggle to hold back his humiliation. In the end, he turns aside and spits. 'That's what they think of us. Beasts to be fed outdoors.'

I tug at Taras's arm. 'Let's go.'

We take the path under the huge beech trees.

'It won't be forever,' he says.

'I hope not. That man's right. They feel sorry for us but not enough. We're on our own here.' I sigh. 'If only I could have one little letter to tell me Mama and the girls are well. Just a note. It would put my mind at rest and I could put up with everything else.'

'We'll write to them just as soon as it's safe,' he says.

He doesn't mean safe for us but safe for them. Under the Bolsheviks, a letter from abroad would spell death for those who received it.

Taras squeezes my arm and I tuck myself tighter into his side.

'And as for what the English think of us, it doesn't matter. We know who we are,' he says.

'I know.'

'They're not all bad. Look at my customers.'

I smile. His customers. He has canvassed the houses in the little village close to his camp for extra work and he does the gardening for three old ladies who live together in one cottage.

'How are the Misses?' as we call them. Taras thinks none of them ever married.

'Very well. They had me pruning and clipping yesterday.'

'Did they pay you?'

'Always.'

'With a cup of tea and a piece of cake?'

'Yes, that too.'

'Outside?'

'We sat in their orchard together.'

'They sound lovely.'

'They are. And it was another ten shillings into the savings.'

'I wish I could find a job for a Saturday,' I say. 'It would help with our savings and it would give me something to do while you're busy.'

'Don't worry. We don't spend much of the five pounds we earn each week. By the time our year is up, we'll have some money to set up home with.'

'I'm also a bit worried about Olha and Dmitro.'

He squeezes my arm. 'I know you are but it has to be one thing at a time. They can't come yet with a baby and we have to stay in the accommodation given to us. We just have to be patient.'

'I hope Dmitro is looking after her.'

'I think he is. You know I wrote to him.'

'Yes, but that doesn't mean he'll take your advice. He'll still put himself first.'

'He's not that bad. He loves Olha and he needs her to care for Levko so I think he'll pay more attention now.'

'I hope so.'

We cross the bridge between the ponds and take the path uphill. The tall trees shade us and then we take the gate out of the park onto a piece of land nobody seems to be using. A thick border of trees surrounds a tiny meadow. We make our way to the only private spot we have.

***

As the weather becomes colder and the leaves fall from the trees, our private place becomes less welcoming and less private.

'What will we do when it snows?'

We are still many months away from being able to have a home of our own. I dream of a room entirely to ourselves, a luxury we have never yet had. Somewhere warm and dry where we can be at our ease. But since there is little choice, we walk through the autumnal park, huddled against one another.

'Natalya…'

I turn to Taras knowing he has bad news. 'What is it?'

'They're sending us to Suffolk.'

'Where's that?'

'Further south.'

'How much further?'

'About two hundred and fifty kilometres.'

'Why?'

'There's no more work here at the moment. We're to go south to do some logging.'

'Logging? I didn't know they had forests in this country.'

'Woodland, I think. Anyway, we must work wherever they send us.'

'Will you be able to come to see me at weekends?'

'It's too far, my love.'

'So they're taking you away for good.'

'No. Just a few months.'

'Months?' I feel as if I can't get my breath for a moment. 'Months?'

He puts his arms around me and rocks me. 'This is the price we have to pay to be here, to be safe. It won't last long.'

'It always seems as if a parting is just for now, because it can't be helped. It's easy to leave but it seems impossible to come back.'

'Natalya, we'll see each other again. There's no question of it.'

'I was sure I'd go home again. I was only going to Germany for a little while to keep Mama and the girls safe from the Nazis and look what happened. I haven't seen them for four years and I haven't had a letter from them for three.'

'Natalya…' he tries to interrupt but the floodgates have been opened. I open my mouth and howl like a baby. 'Natalya.'

He holds me tight and doesn't let go until we both feel my sobs subsiding. He reaches into his coat pocket for a large cotton handkerchief and starts to mop up my face.

'It won't be so bad,' he says. 'We'll be able to write to one another.'

I want to howl again at the uselessness of letters when I want him to be here, to hold me.

'At least we'll know what's happening.'

He's doing his best I know, but letters…Then I remind myself that what seems a paltry means of communication for Taras and me is a precious luxury I don't have with my family in Ukraine. As he says, we'll know what the other is doing…and whether we're alive or not.

Ever the pragmatist, he says, 'I have to leave the bicycle here.' His precious bike which he bought second-hand as soon as he had saved twenty-five shillings. But it has been precious. He has been able to reach me more swiftly and more frequently than would otherwise have been possible.

'Where can you leave it that's safe?'

'With you.'

'With me?' I remember there are a couple of girls at the hostel who have bicycles and are allowed to keep them in the yard at the back of the hostel. 'What will I use it for?'

'You can go for bike rides in the countryside.'

'Or find a job for the weekends.'

'Yes, but don't work too hard, Natalya. Your job in the kitchens is hard enough.'

'I'd be able to save more.' Which reminds me. 'What about the Misses?'

'I've tidied their garden for the winter and yesterday I finished the pruning in the orchard. They've said they'll have me back if I'm here in the spring.'

'If?'

'We haven't been given a return date yet.'

'Or a departure date?'

'This week,' he says apologetically.

So he has been building towards this. This is the last time I will see him and I have no idea when I'll see him again. I bow my head and he pulls me close. 'One day we'll look back on this time and laugh,' he says.

I doubt it.

We walk back to the hostel in the darkening afternoon. He has already left his bike in the yard of the hostel when he came to meet me. Now he must walk the slow miles back to the camp.

'There,' he says, 'your means of freedom.'

'Can I cycle to Suffolk?'

'I should think it's too far in one weekend.'

So that's that, I think. 'You'd better go,' I say. 'You've a long way to walk and it's getting dark.'

'I'll send you my address as soon as I know it,' he says. He holds me tight and, with a final kiss, turns and walks away down the street. I wait until he reaches the corner knowing he will turn and wave. We wave to one another then I climb the hostel steps alone.

Chapter 11

Kripak had taken to riding around the village on horseback. He found he could reach places the car could not get to and a horse gave less warning of an unwelcome visitor. Besides, hay was more plentiful than petrol. He paused now at the top of a field where the women formed a line across its width. He watched the sisters working as a pair, the younger, stronger one protecting the older girl who would be forever marked by her limp. He called the foreman over to him.

'Those two.' He nodded towards Lyubka and Verochka. 'Do they always work together?'

'Yes. Is it a problem?'

'I don't know. Do they both work hard?'

'Yes. The older one limps but she's strong.' The foreman didn't quite meet Kripak's eye and the NKVD man wondered how many in the village knew what he'd done.

'And the younger one?'

'She's a hard worker too.'

'Alright. Not a word.'

The foreman nodded. He didn't need to be told.

Kripak also watched the sisters take their turn to lead the cows to pasture. Like every other group of neighbours, the small herd made up by the individual cows from their lane would be grazed together, taking up the time of only one human being as each household took a turn on the rota. He waited until he was certain it was Verochka's turn, then he rode down to the meadow beside the river. The cows were at the foot of the hill rather than on the plain, the autumn weather having made the lower ground more boggy. Kripak walked his horse towards the girl who stood bundled in her shawl, her back to the wind.

'You don't need to be out in the cold,' he called.

She turned to watch him approach.

'I said you…'

'I heard you.'

'Well, you don't need to be out.'

'It's my turn.'

He halted the mare beside her. Verochka stroked the mare's cheek.

'You could ride her,' he said, looking down at her from the saddle.

'If?'

'Not tempted?'

'No.'

'Sure?'

'You know my price.'

'Well, I do and I don't.'

She looked up at him and waited.

'There's your sister…'

'You've already had her.'

Kripak flushed. 'I didn't mean that. I meant, she lives with you.'

'Yes, she does.'

'And if we were to marry?'

'She would still live with me.'

He looked at Verochka's face, blown pink by the wind, then shook his head. 'You want too much.'

'How do I want too much? You'd have two women to do the work in the house and garden. What man would turn that down?'

'I don't have to marry you for what I want.'

'No. I've seen you take what you want.'

His flush rose again.

'You could live at your ease,' she said, 'instead of camping out above your office. You'd have a wife to take care of your needs and Lyubka's work would make us comfortable.'

Then she made herself wait. She knew pleading would not be the way to win him. She pursed her lips and turned to see his small brown eyes watching her.

'Where would she sleep?'

Verochka wanted to cheer. 'In the back room.'

'Alright. Come to the *Silrada* tomorrow morning at ten.'

Her heart lurched and for a moment she feared she might vomit. She nodded.

'Good.' He shortened his reins, clicked his tongue to the mare and rode away.

Verochka let out her breath. She knew he was testing her. To see if she had the courage to appear at the village council's office to be formally married to the man who held the lives of villagers and partisans alike in his hands.

***

The following morning at five minutes to ten, Verochka walked along the lane from her house towards the *Silrada*. She wore her usual work clothes and a warm shawl around her shoulders. She walked at a steady pace, looking neither to right nor left, but she did try to loosen her jaw. Her upper and lower teeth were gripped against one another. She swallowed the saliva which had gathered in her mouth. There was no going back. If she refused him now, Kripak would be certain to have her and Lyubka deported. She must keep her bargain…and keep her balance over the years to come. She acknowledged the fear roiling in her stomach before quietly putting it aside. There could be no wavering. She must hold her nerve and then she and Lyubka might survive.

She entered the office without knocking. Kripak was sitting at a desk untidy with papers, a portrait of Stalin above his head. Two men lounged against the wall to her left. The witnesses.

'*Dobroho dnya*,' she said.

'And it is a good day,' said Kripak standing up. He waved a piece of paper at her. 'I've filled in the details,' he said pointing to their names and places of birth. He had filled in his own date of birth but he now tapped the gap under her name. 'Write your date of birth here.'

She did so and saw he had also filled in the date and place of their marriage. He took the form from her, signed his name, and then passed both the pen and the form back. 'Sign here below my name.'

She picked up the pen and prepared to sign.

He touched her arm. 'Remember, you are mine now,' he said.

She realised she was to sign in her married name. His name. And with no childish diminutive – she would no longer be Verochka but Vera. She looked into his pointed face but merely nodded.

'Vera Ivanovna Kripak,' she wrote, thinking, it's only a name. But a name which will protect me.

He picked up the stamps on his desk, rolled each in turn on the ink pad and pressed their impressions onto the bottom of the certificate. He gestured to the taller of his henchmen. Zladko shook his head and pointed at his partner.

He can't write his name, thought Vera.

The second man signed across the rectangular stamp with a flourish and then wrote the date across it too.

'There you are, wife,' said Kripak, handing her the marriage certificate.

'Thank you, husband,' she said. She turned to leave the cold office but Kripak wanted more.

'A kiss from the bride,' he said.

She tried to peck him on the cheek but he was having none of that. He put his hand around the back of her head and pulled her face towards him. He kissed her on the mouth to the guffaws of the two witnesses.

'Now you're married!' cried Zladko.

Vera looked her husband in the eye. 'See you later.'

'Oh yes, I'll see you later,' Kripak grinned.

This time he allowed her to leave the office, holding the certificate between her finger and thumb and resisting the temptation to wipe her other hand across her mouth. She walked back to the cottage looking straight ahead and speaking to no one. She went into the kitchen of the home she had shared with the women of her family since the NKVD had shot her father in the yard six years before. Lyubka was by the stove. She turned as Vera entered.

'Where've you been?'

Vera let the certificate slide from her fingers onto the table. Lyubka picked it up, glanced at it, and then looked at her sister in horror. 'You did it.'

Vera nodded. 'Yes, it's done.'

'Where is he?'

'In his office.'

'Is that it?'

'What else would there be? You welcoming us with bread and salt into our marital home? A celebration with feasting and dancing which might last several days?'

'Verochka, no,' said Lyubka putting her arms around her younger sister.

Vera drew back. 'Lyubka, it had to be done and now it is done, I have to stay strong. I need you to help me. If you're too kind to me I won't be able to do it. I don't want you to sympathise with me. I want you to be my ally.'

Lyubka drew back. 'Of course I will, just as I will always love you, no matter what. Shall we start with the beds?'

Vera nodded.

The sisters set about airing and sweeping out the second room of their home which they had once shared with Natalya. Lyubka would now sleep in it alone, acknowledging that Kripak would come and go at all hours of the day and night, so the married couple would sleep, as the girls' parents had, in the marital bed behind the stove in the main room of the cottage. The sisters aired linen and made both beds up with fresh sheets, then Vera swept out the kitchen. Lyubka finished off the pot of soup she had been making and baked the bread to accompany it.

'Do you want to kill a chicken for dinner?' she asked Vera.

'No. Not today. He can eat what we would eat.'

She knew she needed to be at home whenever he might choose to come but she could not sit and wait. 'I'm going to dig over the end of the vegetable garden,' she said.

'I'll help you,' said Lyubka and together they cleared the ground and turned it.

'We can spread some manure tomorrow,' said Vera. 'There'll be plenty of it.'

***

By the time Kripak came it was dark and Lyubka had withdrawn to her own room. He lifted the latch without knocking and entered the kitchen.

'Boots please,' said Vera.

He stopped by the door and looked at her.

'Your boots. Take them off and leave them by the door, please.'

As he bent to take off his boots, Vera approached him. 'Sit on the bench.'

He did as he was told and sat back onto the bench behind him. She bent down and tugged off one boot after another and placed them neatly by the door.

'Are you hungry?' she asked.

He looked as if he wanted to say something else but after a pause said, 'Yes.'

She served him with bread and soup, then sat and watched him eat. He tore at the bread with his yellow teeth and used it to mop his chin when he dribbled the soup. He slurped and chewed until the bowl was empty, then he pushed it away.

'Would you like some more?'

He shook his head and burped.

'Is there anything else I can get you?'

He looked at her from the corner of his eye. 'Yes, there is, wife.'

'Very well.' She rose from the table and approached the freshly made bed. 'We will sleep here,' she said.

He stood up and walked towards her. He began to tug at the waistband of her skirt.

'Wait,' she said and undid it herself. She let it fall to the floor and then she took off her heavy cotton blouse. He stared at her like a starved man as she stood naked before him in the lamplight and then he fell on her, gripping and biting, unable to hold himself back.

Vera pushed him away. 'That is not how we are going to behave,' she said in a low voice. 'Like animals. I will respect you as my husband and you will respect me as your wife. Now take off your clothes.'

Mouth open, he removed his clothes, hopping about to take off his socks and trousers.

Vera lifted the feather duvet and slid into the bed. She lay on her back waiting for him, while he blew out the light and climbed in beside her.

Chapter 12

I am wiping some saucepans when the head chef enters the kitchen accompanied by a tall woman with an iron grey perm and wearing a purple tweed suit. I wonder if she is the boss of the hospital and whether this is an inspection, but I carry on with my work.

The head chef nods at me. 'Natalya, come here please.'

'Is this the one?' asks the woman.

My stomach lurches. Have I done something wrong? Has she come to give me bad news? Then I think, whatever it is I'll deal with it. I put my shoulders back and wait to see what she will say.

'Is she a good worker?'

'Yes, very good.'

As is my hearing, I think.

'Does she speak any English?'

'Yes, I do, madam,' I say.

She looks at me with a raised eyebrow. 'Can you cook,' she demands, 'or do you only do the washing up?'

'I can cook, madam.'

'I need some help this Saturday at my house,' she says. 'One of my staff is ill. Can you come?'

'Yes, madam, but where?'

'Oh, William will explain everything.'

I smile at "William". He has only been Mr Drake to us.

'I need a presentable girl for waiting at table too,' says the woman.

'My friend Marichka is very good at table,' I say quickly.

Again she looks surprised I can hear and speak. 'Where is she?'

'I go fetch her.'

89

I hurry to the pantry where Marichka is sitting on a huge can of oil turning the pages of a magazine left behind by a patient on one of the women's wards.

'Marichka, come. There's the chance of a job with a grand English lady.'

'Rich?' asks Marichka.

'Yes. She wants you to wait at table.'

Marichka looks doubtful.

'Think who might be sitting at the table,' I say.

She grins and follows me, straightening her overall but ducking her chin.

'This is Marichka,' I say as we approach the woman and Mr Drake.

I watch my friend assess her potential employer from her three rows of pearls to her patent leather shoes.

'Can you wait at table?'

'Of course, madam,' replies Marichka.

'Very well, then. I'll expect you both at eleven o'clock sharp on Saturday morning.'

'Thank you,' I say but she has already turned away to leave the kitchen.

Marichka turns to Mr Drake. 'Who's she?'

'She is Mrs Bough-Smith, a very important patron of this hospital.'

'Buff?' repeats Marichka and I want to laugh. She always knows how to puncture someone.

'Yes, Bough-Smith.'

'Is she rich?'

'Very.'

'Why does she want us? Hasn't she got servants already?'

'Of course she has. She explained someone was ill. Now, you need to get back to work. I'll write down her address and how to get there later.'

As we return to our work Marichka says, 'I bet she's short-staffed because she bullied her workers.'

'I wonder how much she'll pay us,' I say.

'Didn't you ask?'

'Not in front of Villiam.'

We both laugh.

'Villiam,' she says. 'But rich guests.'

'And extra wages.'

***

Villiam also gives me directions to the city library. The Ministry of Labour booklet, which we received on arrival in England, says these places can be used by anyone, although I don't really believe it. I approach the domed building and creep into the doorway under the clock. A man is coming out of the library and when he holds the door open for me, I enter. There is a woman at the desk opposite the door. She looks up at me and smiles.

'May I come in?' I ask.

'Of course,' she says. 'Are you looking for something in particular?'

'Maps,' I say.

'Maps? Of Great Britain or the world?'

'I want to see where is this Suffolk.'

'Suffolk. Oh, that's easy,' and she leads me to a stack containing large tomes. She pulls one out and shows me what she calls the index and how to find the right page, then she takes the book to a table and lays it open for me.

'There you are. If you need anything else, just ask.'

Taras's letter was postmarked Bury St Edmunds. I look for the town on the map and then I try to measure how far it might be…Roughly one hundred and twenty-five miles from Lincoln. I look at the towns between us and wonder what they look like. I also try to imagine what Taras's new home looks like.

I look around me and see other people at tables like mine. Some are reading and a few are writing – so it must be allowed. I take the notepad I have bought from my bag and begin to write…

My dear husband, Taras,

Thank you for writing to me so quickly. Would you believe it, I am writing to you in an English library. I have been allowed to look at a map to find you! You are more than two hundred kilometres away, my love, but I am telling myself it is not very far. But, as you said in your letter, train tickets are very expensive. You are better than me at being patient but I know you are right – we must wait out this period and hope it does not last long.

My only news here is that I have an extra day's work for a rich English woman. I am to cook in her kitchen on Saturday. I got work for Marichka too. She will be waiting on table. I know you don't approve of Marichka but she is like a sister to me and I miss my little sisters so much. Besides, she makes me laugh when there is very little to laugh about.

Otherwise, all is the same – the hospital, the hostel. I miss you every day but as each day passes I know it brings you closer. Try to look after yourself. I worry that I cannot see whether you are doing this or not.

I send you my love, dearest Taras. Write to me soon.
Your Natalya

I fold the letter and put it in the envelope I bought. My only extravagance. I seal the envelope and address it. I'll buy a stamp on the way back to the hostel. I take a last look at the map and put the heavy book back on the shelf.

As I leave the library, the woman behind the desk calls me back.

'Do you live in Lincoln?' she asks.

'Yes. I live in YWCA. With other EVW's.'

'If you're resident in the city, you're allowed to take books out of the library.'

'Any books?'

'Yes. You're allowed three books for three weeks, then you have to change or renew them.'

'How much?'

'Oh, you don't have to pay,' she smiles.

'And I can read anything I want to?'

'Yes, of course.'

'Of course.' This lovely woman has no idea there might be places where some writers are forbidden and it could be death to the reader to be caught reading their work. And free. We had a little lending library in our village and each family paid a small fee to use it. But the Bolsheviks came and burned the books.

I realise I must be staring at her when she says, 'Your English is good but reading in English would help you to improve it.'

I blink back tears. 'Thank you. You are very kind.'

'Would you like me to show you how the books are arranged?'

'Yes, please,' I say and she begins by showing me the riches of stories and poems.

She leaves me enthralled among the shelves, wondering how I am ever going to choose one book.

***

On Saturday, Marichka borrows a bicycle and we cycle out of town to the residence of Mrs Bough-Smith. And it is a residence. We pull up at the end of a tree-lined drive to look at the square house ahead of us. I count the bedroom windows. Eight across. And how many more behind?

'Are you sure this is it?' asks Marichka.

I check Villiam's piece of paper and look at the nameplate

on the brick gate post. 'Yes, it is.'

'Good. It's big enough,' says Marichka and I know she intends to be more than a waitress tonight. Mrs Bough-Smith has no idea.

We cycle up the drive and I know enough to go around to the back of the house where we're met by a tall thin man wearing a black waistcoat and trousers with a white shirt.

'Leave your bikes there and follow me.'

He turns and disappears into the house. We have to hurry to follow him. He points out a cupboard where we can leave our things and says to Marichka, 'We'll tidy you up in your uniform later.'

We raise our eyebrows at one another as he marches off again down a long corridor in the direction of the kitchen. We're given aprons by a round woman with red cheeks who points at a sack of potatoes which are waiting to be peeled.

'No, I waiting at table,' says Marichka.

'I don't know about that,' says the woman, 'but there are twelve for dinner so get peeling.'

Marichka purses her lips but we set to. We have almost finished when Mrs Bough-Smith comes into the kitchen.

'Ah, they've arrived, Ellwood.'

'Yes, ma'am.'

'Keep them busy.'

'Will do, ma'am.'

'Will you have time to make the Major's apple pie?'

The woman, Ellwood, sighs and says, 'I'll try but there's a lot to do.'

'Maybe one of these could help,' says Mrs Bough-Smith. She looks at me. 'You. You said you could cook. Do you know how to make an apple pie?'

'Apple pie? Yes,' I say although I'm not sure what she wants.

'Good. Get on with it then.' She turns to go.

'Madam,' calls Marichka taking a step towards her.

Mrs Bough-Smith turns slowly.

'Our money,' says Marichka. 'What will you pay us?'

Mrs Bough-Smith almost rears back and then says, 'Jackson will see to it.'

'Jackson?'

'The butler. He brought you in,' says Ellwood.

'No, madam,' says Marichka. 'We must know now before we work what you will pay us.'

Mrs Bough-Smith sighs. 'Very well.' She looks at Ellwood. 'Very demanding,' she says. And then to us. 'You'll get ten shillings.'

'Ten shillings?' repeats Marichka. 'No, is not possible. We get one pound every day at hospital. So we must have one pound here.'

'A pound?' says Mrs Bough-Smith.

'Yes, madam. One for me and one for Natalya.'

'I'm afraid that's not possible.'

Marichka looks at me. 'Natalya, *idem.*'

She's right. This woman thinks she's going to get us cheaply but we can walk away. I put down my peeler and we both take off our aprons.

Mrs Bough-Smith watches us but then says, 'Now, there's no need to be hasty. I'm sure we can manage something.'

'Manage nothing,' says Marichka. 'One pound for day.'

'Very well,' sniffs Mrs Bough-Smith, 'but your work had better be good.'

'It will be,' I say and Marichka and I put our aprons back on.

When our employer has gone, I say to Ellwood. 'Apple pie?'

She makes a noise like 'Humph' in her throat and gets up from her chair. 'Come on then,' she says and makes for a door. It leads to a pantry in which the shelves are crowded with tins and packets and the floor is covered with wooden boxes of fruit and vegetables. She begins to hand me my ingredients and I take

95

them back to the long kitchen table. I check through them but there are no raisins. However, I don't know the English word.

'Something is missing,' I say to Ellwood.

'Missing?' she says.

'Yes.' I look at her hoping she knows what I mean but she looks blank. I'm to understand there'll be no support from this quarter. 'I don't know word. I show you?'

She gets up and bangs her chair against the table. We go into the pantry again. I look along the shelves and then see what I want in a large jar.

'This,' I say.

'Raisins?'

'Raisins,' I repeat.

'For apple pie?'

'Yes, for pie.'

She gives me a long look and then shrugs before passing me the jar of raisins.

'And *Zimt*,' I say.

'*Zimt*?'

I don't know its English word, or its Ukrainian word for that matter, since my only acquaintance with this lovely spice was in *Frau* Kuhn's kitchen. I look along the shelves, smelling the air. There are some smaller jars so I lift them one by one, taking the lids off to sniff their contents. Then I find the unmistakable scent of it. 'This,' I say.

'Cinnamon?' she asks, even more surprised than last time.

'Yes. The word please?'

'Cinnamon.'

'Cinnamon,' I repeat and smile.

She doesn't smile back.

I take the jar to my station at the kitchen table. Marichka is nowhere to be seen. I get to work peeling the apples for 'apple pie'. The only 'pie' I have ever made is *Apfelstrudel* with *Frau* Kuhn so I make it again now. More than two years later. As I fold the knobs of butter between the layers of pastry, I wonder if she and her three children are safe and whether the *Sturmbannführer* made it home from the Eastern Front. But I will probably never know. I feel a twinge of regret for the woman who taught me a lot, not least that to be German did not necessarily mean to be a Nazi. But I am snapped back to the present by Ellwood peering over my shoulder at my pastry.

'Apple pie?'

'Yes,' I say. I think the English must make their pie differently but I have no fear. I know this pie to be delicious.

And it is. At the end of the evening when the dinner has been served, Mrs Bough-Smith comes into the kitchen.

'Natalya?'

'Yes, ma'am?' I don't know why the English drop the 'd' in 'madam' but it's another thing I've learned today.

'Your apple pie was a great success. My guests enjoyed it very much, especially Major Peterson,' and she actually smiles at me.

'I'm very happy,' I say.

'You can leave when you have helped Ellwood to clear the kitchen.'

'And our money?' asks Marichka.

Mrs Bough-Smith looks past her. 'Jackson,' she calls, 'please pay these young women when they have finished their work,' and she sweeps away to return to her guests.

Marichka grins at me. 'Thank you, ma'am,' she says.

Around midnight, we receive our one pound notes and go out into the dark to fetch our bicycles. We wheel them forward to the drive but then Marichka stops.

'Natalya, I'm not going back to the hostel,' she says in a low voice.

'Why not?' I ask, guessing the answer.

'I have also been a great success this evening. With Major Peterson.' She grins at me. 'An American Major.'

I can't help grinning back. 'We have to make use of every chance we're given,' I say as I mount my bike. I leave her standing in Mrs Bough-Smith's garden while I cycle through the flat empty lanes back to the hostel wondering if the Major realises Marichka will want more than nylons.

1947-48
Chapter 13

Vera leaned her forehead against the cow's warm flank. The milk spurted into the bucket and the girl relaxed into the rhythm she and the cow knew well, their breath clouding the cold air. The cow huffed as she gave up her milk and Vera felt her own breasts tingling in sympathy. She knew she was carrying Kripak's child and was probably three months into her pregnancy. She rejoiced that she had caught this baby so quickly. It would tie Kripak to her more securely because he would want to protect his own child…but the baby would be hers, hers and Lyubka's, to love.

When Vera had finished milking the cow, she walked across the icy yard with its banks of snow which she and Lyubka had cleared. She went into the warm house and saw Kripak's tousled black hair still on the pillow. He had come home late and would sleep late. He seemed to be able to sleep through any domestic noise she and Lyubka made. She turned to the stove, ignoring the portrait of Stalin which now hung where once their icon had been. Kripak had come home in the days shortly after their marriage and demanded the icon be removed. He had carried a framed picture of the Bolshevik leader under his arm. The sisters had switched the images without comment. It was only a picture. Lyubka hid their family's icon in her room along with the Bible and the women had continued their lives unperturbed.

It was Christmas Eve, but Vera and Lyubka were not busy in a frenzy of cooking and baking for the holy feast. Like the rest of the villagers, they behaved as if God was dead. It certainly felt like it. There might be families who would celebrate the birth of Christ secretly but Vera and Lyubka would not be able to do that. Kripak would be able to see what was on the stove although he would not be able to divine what was in the minds of his wife and sister-in-law.

He bestirred himself when it was almost midday and went outside to urinate in the snow. Vera had not been able to break him of this habit. He would not use the earth closet, he had told her, simply to piss. She comforted herself that at least he didn't do it in the house. He returned to the kitchen, frowsty and scratching. Silently she placed a bowl of *kasha* on the table for him. He sat down to eat it without acknowledging her and shovelled the food into himself. When he had finished, she passed him the clean shirt she had been warming for him by the stove.

She busied herself at the sink while he put on his shirt and sweater under the leather jacket he always wore. She wondered that he clung to it so. It was too hot to wear in the summer and in winter gave no warmth. As he pulled on his boots, she turned to look at him. He had never yet told her where he was going when he went out, for which she was grateful. Nor did he ever tell her when he might return.

He stood up from the bench, lifted the latch and left the cottage.

'He's gone.'

Lyubka came out of her room. 'How are you feeling?' she asked her younger sister.

'Fine. My breasts are prickling and I think they're getting bigger.'

'Do you want to go to see *Pani* Lazarenko?'

'No, I don't think so. Do you think I need to?'

'Well, we haven't got Mama here to tell us if your pregnancy is progressing normally. And it's not a secret, is it?'

'No, of course not. But should we go today? She might be busy.'

'She might also like to know about a new baby today.'

100

'Alright then. I'll bake a honey cake and then we'll take her some.' Vera put her arm around her sister's shoulders. 'It won't be forever. One day we'll be able to celebrate Christmas again.'

Lyubka nodded but could not speak.

'We haven't lost all those memories,' Vera went on, 'they're still there. We have a future with our baby. And even though we can't pray openly, we can pray in our minds – for Mama and *Tato*, and for Natalya, wherever she might be.'

Lyubka tried to smile.

'Come on, let's do it now. Not out loud – in case he comes back.'

The girls stood together, their heads bowed, silently praying for the absent members of their family.

Later, they took half of the aromatic cake Vera had baked to *Pani* Lazarenko. They knocked at her door and waited on the snow-cleared path. Vera stamped her boots nervously.

Pani Lazarenko opened the door to them. 'Come in, girls. Don't let the cold in.'

Feeling relieved at her welcome they entered the midwife's warm kitchen.

'Come and get warm by the stove.'

'We brought you some honey cake,' said Vera making the offering.

'Thank you,' she said, looking into Vera's face, 'but I don't need it yet. How far along are you?'

Vera looked at the midwife startled. Were the men right? Was she a witch?

Pani Lazarenko smiled at her. 'A woman's face and skin begin to change when she's pregnant. Sit down and tell me what's happened so far.'

Vera related the physical changes she was experiencing and when she had had her last period.

'You must be about twelve weeks pregnant then. Which means you'll have the baby about the middle of July.'

Vera nodded.

'Are you well otherwise?'

'Yes, thank you.'

'Would you like me to examine you?'

'Is it necessary?'

'Not really but it might reassure us.'

'Alright,' said Vera, knowing the older woman would also be checking her for bruises. However, having submitted to the examination, she couldn't help feeling a weight lifting when *Pani* Lazarenko pronounced everything was in order.

The midwife turned to the older sister. 'You're looking better, Lyubka. How are you managing?'

'I'm alright, thank you. I just wanted to know Verochka was alright. And I thought it better for you to know about her condition.'

'Of course. Whenever you need me, you know where I am.'

The sisters left the midwife's cottage but as they stepped into the icy lane, they were almost knocked over by three men running towards the western end of the village.

'Where are they going?' asked Lyubka, holding on to *Pani* Lazarenko's fence.

Women began to come out of their houses.

'What's happening?'

'They're going towards the shrine.'

Vera and Lyubka followed their neighbours as they hurried towards the tiny chapel which marked the entrance to their village. It had been derelict since the NKVD had vandalised it in 1944. As a result it seemed to pose no threat to Stalin's policy of atheism so had not been burned down as the village church had been. But now there was a hue and cry as men in dark clothing surrounded what was left of the shrine. They were shouting across one another and pointing at something in the shrine itself.

The sisters drew closer, trying to see over the shoulders of the gathering crowd. Lyubka could not help gasping when she saw what the fuss was about. Someone had placed a plaster figurine of the Christ child in a manger in the centre of the shrine. It was flanked by two lit candles. Vera glanced at her sister before scanning the faces of those in the crowd. Immediately opposite her stood her husband. As Kripak ordered the men to gather more kindling, she recognised the witnesses from her wedding. The hulking men now gathered together sticks and twigs, pulling them in a heap around the figure of Christ. When the pile was compact enough, Kripak took one of the candles and threw it into the dry straw. Then he turned to address the crowd. 'Whoever did this,' he shouted, 'needs to pack warm clothing because they will be taking the next train east.' He stared at the faces in the crowd and then turned away.

The villagers began to disperse but Vera and Lyubka seemed mesmerised by the flames. Vera looked up. Kripak had approached her through the crowd.

'Go home,' he said quietly.

She met his eyes and then took Lyubka's arm. The sisters walked back down the lane into the village and to their own cottage.

He came home as the afternoon was darkening. 'What were you doing out in the village?' he asked.

'I'd been to see *Pani* Lazarenko.'

'What for?'

Vera blushed then looked at her husband. 'I'm having a baby.'

He stared at her. 'Mine?'

'Of course yours.'

He did not speak, but continued to stare at her.

'I'll get you something to eat,' she said at last.

He shook his head as if trying to clear it. 'A baby.'

'Yes, a baby.'

'Did that old witch Lazarenko say you were alright?'

'Yes. Everything is as it should be.'

She thought he might try to embrace her so she turned to get some *holubchi* out of the warm oven. She served him the cabbage-wrapped parcels and poured some mushroom sauce over them. Let him eat at least one course of the Christmas feast, she thought. This burner of shrines.

Before he began to eat, he said, 'Be careful when you go out.'

'I will be, but I still have to do my work,' she said, thinking he was concerned about her physical well-being.

'Not just your work. Be careful who you talk to.'

She turned to look at him. 'Did you find whoever had been to the shrine?'

He shrugged. 'Someone has paid.'

Whether they had done it or not, she thought. Their disaster would remind everyone else that God was dead but that Stalin wasn't. It would also teach her not to ask him any questions about what he did outside the house.

Chapter 14

I rest my forehead against the dark wood of the *prie-dieu* and hope the Blessed Virgin can hear my prayers. I try not to doubt. God may exist despite the horror of the last few years. Our priest always used to say that Christ's mother, Mary, would intercede for us when we were in need. I am in need. I need to be sure my husband is telling me the truth and that he is safe and well in Suffolk, and I need to know that Mama, Lyubka and Verochka are also safe and well. There is no news from them but neither has any other stateless Ukrainian here in England had any news from home. So this is all I have. I kneel in the Lady Chapel where I have lit candles for them. Perhaps my prayers will float up to God from this beautiful cathedral which sails like a galleon above the city where I live.

Hail Mary, full of grace…

I say the words of the prayer I learned as a child to make my mind still. I can't let my imagination wander to the disasters which might have befallen those I love. I can only hope and try to trust in God that they are well. My mind skitters away again but I trap it in the rhythms of prayer:

Holy Mary, mother of God…

After a while, I get up from my knees and walk slowly around this soaring vastness of stone so bare of ornament. Anyone can come in here to pray, to wonder at the exquisite work of medieval stone masons. No one is prevented from entering by soldiers, or the Militia, or a dictator's edict. This England. They have no idea how lucky they are.

I step out of the cathedral into the snowy courtyard to return to the hostel, deciding to walk back through the Arboretum which looks beautiful in the snow. The great old trees stand stark against the white ground and there's a skirt of mist clinging to the lower levels of the park. I shiver and put my hands in my pockets where I touch Taras's last letter. It is too much of a temptation. I walk along the Terrace to a bench where I sit down to read my husband's letter.

Dorohenka moya Natalya,

I send you all my love as we approach Christmas and I hope you are well and strong.

The work here continues just the same. We are still clearing the dead and damaged trees from the woods where the British Army used to do much of their training. They made a terrible mess but we are gradually putting these lovely old woods back in order. I have to admit the work has reminded me of home. Remember I told you that in my village the forest came down the mountainside right to the river? With the Ukrainian voices here between the trees, I can almost imagine myself back there.

They feed us reasonably well but the work and the cold make us hungrier than ever. Sometimes we are lucky, though. Like the other day. We were coming back from work and had to pass through a town. The English ganger, Tom, stopped the lorry by a bakery and went in to ask them if they had any leftover bread. The baker gave Tom what he had left at the end of the day. Such luxury. We ate white bread, Natalya, like kings!

So you see, I am managing. We do not know yet when this work will end but just looking at where we are working there is much more to do. Do not lose heart, my love. I am saving my wages and have found a local publican who also keeps horses. He doesn't have much time to look after them so I'm helping him.

I hope you are not working too hard in the hospital. If Mrs Bough-Smith has you to work for her again, make her pay you by the hour. Don't work till midnight for a day's pay!

My love, I kiss your eyes and your mouth. I dream of you every night. Stay well and it won't be long until we're together. Try not to be sad over Christmas. It is only another day and we will have many Christmas days together. Perhaps in Ukraine with those we love.

I send you all my love,
Taras

I fold the letter and hold it against my breast. Sometimes they are not hungry…But he sounds contented and I must accept that as the truth.

I walk back to the hostel and as I enter its busy hallway one of the WVS girls calls me over. 'Natalya, there's a message for you.'

My heart thumps. Who might have tried to contact me?

She hands me a note.

No terrible news, just Mrs Bough-Smith asking if I can work for her again.

'She'd like you to telephone her if you're able to help her.'

'How do I telephone?' I ask.

'I'll do it for you if you like. Come into the office.'

We make a telephone call. She would like me to work for three days. Christmas Eve, Christmas Day and what they call Boxing Day here. I already know I don't have to be at the hospital on two of those days so we agree I will come on Christmas Day and Boxing Day.

'Tell her I want to be paid by the hour,' I tell the WVS girl.

'How much?' she asks.

'Two and sixpence.'

She smiles. 'Mrs Bough-Smith, Natalya says she would like to be paid at the hourly rate of two and sixpence.'

Even I can hear Mrs Bough-Smith's outcry from the black receiver. 'That's outrageous!'

'Well, it is Christmas,' says the WVS girl. 'Any worker would expect double pay and I don't think Natalya's asking for quite as much as that.'

As she listens she grins at me and puts up her thumb. I give her a nod.

'Yes, she'll do it. When would you like her to come?' She takes down the details, finishes the call and turns to me. 'You're to be there for eight o'clock in the morning on Christmas Day.'

'Alright,' I say.

'Are you sure you want to work on that day?'

I shrug. 'What else would I do? My husband is hundreds of kilometres away and my mother and sisters are thousands of kilometres away.'

She looks at me sympathetically. 'I'm sorry. But things will get easier for you.'

'So everyone keeps saying. But thank you for the phone call.'

'My pleasure. If there's anything else I can do to help…'

But what can she do, this sweet English girl? Change the law of her country so I can live where I want to with my husband? Depose Stalin so I can go home and kiss Mama's hands? I shake my head and try to smile. They mean well here. They just don't understand.

However, Lesia does. On the feast of St Nicholas we exchange presents as we would have at home. I have bought her the prettiest headscarf I could find and she has given me the gift of remaining sane…

'Oh, Lesia,' I say as I open the parcel. Inside is a long narrow piece of white linen and, among its folds, a skein of black embroidery silk. 'Thank you,' and I hug her to me.

'You'll need a *rushnyk* for your home with Taras and it'll help you pass the time until he comes back. But I'm sorry there's only one skein of silk…'

'Oh no,' I say, knowing how expensive they are. 'I can choose whatever colours I like to go with the black.'

'And you can get started straight away.'

'You are thoughtful,' I say, wishing I had given her present more thought.

'We must be sisters to one another now,' she smiles.

'We must.'

'And thank you for my present. I have wanted a lovely headscarf for ages but it seemed too much of an extravagance.'

'Don't tell Marichka that,' I say and we both laugh.

***

Our guardian angels, the WVS, arrange a celebration for us on the sixth of January, Ukrainian Christmas Eve. The announcement is made one evening after dinner.

'A fund has been set aside to help you to celebrate your own Christmas. We will arrange for your special meal to be cooked for you…'

But there is an outcry at this.

'No, no, we'll do it ourselves.'

And we do. We volunteer for different tasks and Lesia and I are in the *vushka* group. We'll make enough mushroom dumplings to go in the *borshch* for the couple of hundred women who live in this hostel. Maryna and Paraska, our room-mates, are on the decoration detail, while Marichka works with the entertainment committee.

The hostel rings with the cries of young women who have not eaten the traditional Christmas meal since they left home five, or even six years earlier. Our hearts are full of excitement and love for the life we left behind while our hands are busy pinching *varenyki* and folding *holubchi*.

On *Svyat Vechir* itself, as the evening draws on, Marichka takes a couple of other women out onto the steps of the hostel to wait for the appearance of the first star. As soon as it appears, they run indoors calling out to us that we may begin.

The only man in the room, our Ukrainian priest, begins the proceedings. We stand to pray and when he says, 'Let us remember those who cannot be here at this table with us,' many a tear is wiped away. He passes around the *prosfora,* the blessed bread, and then we sit for the first course, my favourite, *kutya.*

'My mother used to use sugar as well as honey,' says Lesia.

'Oh no,' says Maryna. 'My mother only ever used honey…'

A discussion begins which will continue through each course, right up to the cakes and pastries at the end of the meal, how each mother's recipe was the correct one…or the best one. This talk of our mothers brings them closer to us in this English hostel where the table has been set with straw under the tablecloth to remind us of the Christ child, just as it would have been at home.

The carols remind us too. Two hundred female voices pour out between every course. There will be no carol singers crunching through the snow carrying their bright star to sing at every villager's door. But we can comfort ourselves with our own singing in this brightly lit hall.

'*Oy, raduysha zemle, syn Bozhi narodyvsha.*'

'Rejoice, o earth, the son of God is born.'

1948
Chapter 15

Vera felt a sudden warm rush of liquid run down her legs as she pushed the spade into the loose soil around the beetroot. She knew what it signalled. *Pani* Lazarenko had warned her what to look out for. She took the spade with her in case she might need to lean on it and began to make her way between the lush green rows of the vegetable garden. The huge leaves and corkscrew vines of the marrows and squashes tried to impede her progress but she batted them aside with her free hand as she made her slow and heavy way back to the cottage. When she reached the fence which protected the crops from the hens, she had to stop. A wave of pain rippled through her abdomen then squeezed her in its fist. She held onto the fence and tried to let her breath out in small spits as the midwife had taught her. She knew she could reach the house before the next wave so she waited until the pain receded. She leaned the spade against the fence and made her way along its palings to the gate. As Vera was contemplating the open ground of the yard, Lyubka came out of the cottage.

'Verochka!' She hurried over. 'Has it started?'

Vera nodded. 'My waters.'

'We'll get you inside and then I'll go for *Pani* Lazarenko.' She took Vera's arm and the sisters shuffled across the yard, Lyubka shooing the hens from under Vera's feet. 'Go away! She hasn't got any food for you. We're busy.'

At the door, Lyubka stood back to let Vera enter and then she hurried past her to pull back the duvet on the bed.

'Take it away,' said Vera. 'We won't need it.' She sat down carefully on the side of the bed holding her abdomen.

'Do you want to lie down?'

'I don't know. I'll decide while you're gone.'

'Are you sure you're alright?'

Vera nodded with her eyes closed.

She heard Lyubka's footsteps leave the cottage and then gave herself up to another wave of pain. For a few moments she did not know herself, only the pain in which she swam. She gripped the straw mattress until the dizziness passed.

'What are you doing?' demanded a gruff voice.

She tried to speak but could only whisper, 'The baby.'

She did not know whether he had heard or not and found she didn't much care. She held the round heaviness of her abdomen and wondered how the baby was going to manage to get out of her body.

A shadow fell across her and Vera tried to look up. She could smell the sharpness of his sweat. He always stank, however often she washed his clothes and heated water for his bath. She breathed through her mouth, not wanting to vomit now.

'What's wrong with you?'

'Nothing's wrong with her,' said a woman's voice. 'The baby's coming.'

Vera could still feel him standing before her. Immobile. He would probably be staring with his mouth hanging open, she thought.

'Come along,' said *Pani* Lazarenko. 'There's nothing to see yet. Let's have you outside and off to your work.'

'I'm hungry,' he said at last. 'I want my dinner.'

'Well, there'll be no dinner here today,' said the midwife.

Kripak started to growl in his throat and Vera managed to say her sister's name. 'Lyubka…'

'I know. I'll feed him.'

As the sudden wave overtook her again, Vera cried out in surprise.

'What's wrong with her?' asked Kripak again.

'Come on,' said Lyubka. She tried to usher him away but he

would not move and it was more than she could do to touch him.

It was *Pani* Lazarenko who took him by the arm. 'This is no place for a man and we have work to do. We'll call you in when we're done. Lyubka, give him a bowl of soup outside and then boil some water.'

Kripak allowed the older woman to propel him out of his own cottage and then he perched on the chopping block outside. When Lyubka brought him a bowl of soup and a hunk of bread, he took them from her, snarling, 'Make sure the boy lives.'

She did not bother to say that none of them knew yet whether it was a boy, but returned to the house and closed the door.

He slurped his soup in the sunlight. When he had finished he placed the bowl on the ground beside him, rolled a cigarette and smoked it hunched over his crossed legs. Finishing the cigarette, he ground it out under his foot and immediately rolled another and lit it. The smoke curled around his nostrils as he waited for his son. He showed no curiosity when a woman's cries came from the house. He simply waited through the afternoon. A small boy came along the lane with several cows, each of the beasts recognising its own home as they approached. Vera's cow came clattering into the yard, full udders swinging. Kripak turned his head to watch her and then he sauntered across the yard to shut her into the barn. He heard her lowing as dusk fell but he ignored her.

The door of the cottage opened and Lyubka walked across to the barn, bucket in hand. 'You can go in now,' she muttered.

He stood up and stretched the stiffness from his skinny limbs before walking into the hot, stuffy cottage. Vera was sitting up in bed, nursing something swaddled in white cloth. He looked at her across the room.

'He won't bite,' said *Pani* Lazarenko. 'He's only a baby.'

Kripak approached the bed.

Vera closed her nose to the stale cigarette smell. The baby withdrew from her nipple, his rosy mouth partly open as he drifted into the bliss of his first milky sleep. Vera lifted him toward Kripak and said, 'Michaylo.'

'Michaylo?'

'Yes. It's what I want to call him. Do you want to hold him?'

Kripak seemed to nod.

'Sit down then.'

He sat on the extreme edge of the bed.

'Hold your arms out,' said Vera. As she placed his son in Kripak's arms, she said, 'Make sure you hold his head. You mustn't let it flop.'

He took the tightly wrapped bundle from her and held it with his arms still outstretched.

Vera watched him and shook her head. 'Not like that. Hold him against your chest.'

When he drew the baby towards him, she saw a shiver go through him and knew they were safe…for now. While Kripak was in awe of his baby, she and Lyubka could breathe a little more easily. She sat back against the pillows and watched Kripak sitting motionless with his sleeping son in his arms.

She looked up as *Pani* Lazarenko approached. 'Thank you,' she said. 'Thank you for everything.'

'You're welcome.'

Vera prodded Kripak with her foot.

He looked up. 'What?'

'*Pani* Lazarenko's going.'

'Oh, bye.'

Vera prodded him again.

'What?'

She glared at him and then rubbed her thumb against her fingers.

114

'Oh, yes,' he said.

Pani Lazarenko took the child from him and laid the baby beside his mother. 'She needs to rest,' she said.

He stood up to fumble in his pockets. He withdrew a few crumpled notes and glanced up to see Vera nodding her head towards *Pani* Lazarenko. 'Here.' He put the notes uncounted into the midwife's hands. 'Is it enough?'

'For now,' said *Pani* Lazarenko. 'And I mean it,' she repeated, 'your wife needs to rest.'

Kripak looked up in surprise as if he had forgotten he had such a thing as a wife, but then said, 'Yes, she must rest.'

At that moment Lyubka came into the cottage with a pail of milk from the cow. Kripak's confusion seemed to fall away from him. His sister-in-law would look after his wife.

'I have to go out,' he said after a moment.

Pani Lazarenko tightened her lips and turned to the sisters. 'I'll be back tomorrow but don't hesitate to call me if you need to.'

'Thank you,' said Vera again.

Lyubka followed the midwife to the cottage door and said in a low voice, 'Thank you. I'll look after her.'

'I know you will,' said the older woman. She patted Lyubka's arm and left the house.

Lyubka returned to Vera's side. 'Are you comfortable or do you want me to fluff your pillows?'

'I think I'm alright.'

'Wriggle down a bit,' said Lyubka, making sure mother and baby were held in the warm nest of feather pillows and duvet. 'Close your eyes,' she said and leaned over to kiss the warm cheeks of her sister and her nephew. She turned from the bed and approached Kripak who seemed to have washed up in the middle of the kitchen. 'Do you want something to eat before you go?'

He nodded.

Lyubka gave him another bowl of soup from the same pot as before but he did not complain. He ate the food, fuelling up for his night's work. She closed her mind to where he might be going and to what he might be doing. He could, and would, go to hell as far as she was concerned. She only cared what happened to her beloved family. She had two to love now.

Chapter 16

It's a lovely summer's evening as I walk arm in arm with Taras along a tidy row of Edwardian terraced houses. When we reach number 84, he points out a large display of portraits, alongside advertising material for a well-known photographic company, in the front window.

'Is he a photographer?' I ask.

'Yes. Apparently he runs his business from here.'

Apart from the display which sets it apart, the house is like the others on the street with its recently mowed front lawn bordered by hollyhocks as high as a man. After more than a year in England, I am still amazed at the time the English spend on their beautiful gardens.

Taras raises the knocker.

An apple of a woman opens the door. Kind eyes twinkle at us from behind rimless spectacles and her shiny grey hair is smoothed back into a knot at the nape of her neck. My hopes soar. She looks as if she might be willing to rent a room to two displaced persons.

'Good evening, madam,' says Taras. I can hear him trying to straighten out his Ukrainian accent as much as possible.

'Good evening,' she says. 'How can I help you?'

We still haven't recovered from the constant politeness of these people. A knock at the door in either of our villages might mean deportation to Siberia or summary execution. Here, people expect to be able to help others.

'You have room?' asks Taras.

'Oh, you've come about the room. Come in.' She turns to lead us into the house, calling, 'Albert! There's a young couple come about the room.'

A slender man appears from the front room. He is smartly

dressed in a charcoal grey waistcoat over a white shirt. His tie is held in place by a gold pin. Like his wife, his grey hair is swept back from his forehead but his spectacles have round black frames. They look more like brother and sister than man and wife. He puts out his hand. 'How do you do?'

We shake hands repeating the phrase, 'How do you do?' It makes no sense but the English like it.

'I'm sorry,' says the man, 'but I think there's been a mistake. We do have a room for rent but it's only a single room.'

Taras looks at me and I take over. 'Excuse me, sir, my English is bit better than my husband's.'

He smiles and nods.

I go on. 'We live separate. I live in women's hostel. Taras lives in barracks at Warby. For one year since we came to England.'

'That's a bit of a distance. Why do you live separately?' asks the wife.

'It is the English law. For one year we must live where they say and work where they say.'

'It seems a bit harsh doesn't it, Albert?' she says.

'It does but that room is very small.'

'We very much want to live together,' I say.

The old couple look at one another and after a silent discussion, the man says, 'I suppose you'd like to see it?'

Taras nods. 'Yes, please.'

We both already knew the room was only a single but when Taras had heard about it from his ganger, we had hoped to be able to persuade the landlord to take us in. It's worth a try. There are so few rooms available for rent we're prepared to take anything to live together.

'Come this way then,' says the old man and we follow his thin legs up the stairs, at the top of which we go along a narrow corridor to the back of the house. The man opens a door and shows us into a bedroom with a single bed, a narrow wardrobe, and a wicker armchair.

'There you are,' he says. 'I warned you it was tight.'

'We sleep here,' says Taras.

We can barely see into the room and the old woman is on the corridor behind us. When I realise they are going to say it won't be possible, I tell them: 'This is good. In camp in Germany we had small room for four people and on boat we were in room for ten people.'

'That may be,' says the man, 'but this is England, not Nazi Germany.'

I turn to look at the wife. She stares back at me. 'This is good,' I repeat trying not to sound as desperate as I feel. 'Please. For one year we cannot live together.'

'But there's only a single bed.'

'Is all we ever had,' I say.

'Oh dear,' she says. 'Albert, perhaps we should go downstairs and have a cup of tea and talk about it.'

'Are you sure, Rose?'

'Yes, dear.'

'Very well, then.'

'Come,' says the woman and she turns back towards the stairs. She leads us down to the ground floor and into a room with a table in the centre covered with a chequered cloth.

'Please sit down,' she says and she bustles into the kitchen next door. She brings in cups and saucers and a large brown teapot which she places on a wooden stand on the table.

'I suppose we should introduce ourselves,' says the man. 'I'm Mr Burrows and this is my wife, Mrs Burrows of course.'

Taras stands and says, 'I, Sidorenko Taras and this my wife Natalya.'

'Pleased to meet you,' says Mr Burrows.

Mrs Burrows spoons tea leaves from the caddy into the pot, then pours in hot water from the kettle on the shining black range.

'How do you like it?' she asks me.

'No milk please.'

'No milk! How unusual.'

'In Ukraine we do not put milk in tea.'

'We always drink it with milk. But you'll take a little sugar?'

'Just a little,' I say, guessing she will have less of this rationed commodity than Mrs Bough-Smith.

When we're settled with our tea, Mrs Burrows asks, 'Did you know each other in Ukraine?'

'No. We meet at end of war in Germany,' I explain. 'We were in camp – UNRRA – you know, United Nations.'

The old couple nod.

'We married there. Then we come to England to work but we must live apart.'

'Where did you learn to speak English?' asks Mrs Burrows. 'You speak it very well.'

'Thank you. I still learning,' I say. 'I had lessons in camp in Germany and here with WVS.'

'Can I ask a question?' asks Mr Burrows.

'Of course,' I say.

'Why didn't you go home at the end of the war?'

'Germans take us to work in 1943 so Russians think we are traitors. If we go home, we sent to Siberia for punishment.'

'Or maybe shot in village,' adds Taras. He points at his temple with his forefinger.

'That's dreadful,' says Mrs Burrows with a shudder. 'No wonder you didn't go home. Did you know about this, Albert?'

'No, Rose, but perhaps the Allies didn't want to tell us what the Russians were up to.'

'But Russia was our ally too.'

'Exactly,' says Mr Burrows.

Just as I'm thinking he might be sympathetic to us he asks another important question.

'Do you have any children?'

'No,' says Taras. 'No children.'

'Not until we get own house,' I say.

'Oh, you'd like your own house?'

Taras looks at me and I know he hasn't the words.

'Yes. We save. We have two jobs and try to save money for house one day,' I say.

Mrs Burrows smiles at me. 'I'm sure you'll get your own home,' she says.

I smile back but have a terrible feeling this is a polite rejection of the idea of two lodgers in her house. I don't know what I can say to persuade them we would be little trouble and I can't help looking at Taras who has also heard the dismissal. I look down at my hands while I get my face in order and swallow the tears of disappointment which have risen of their own accord. How much longer must we wait, I wonder, to make our lives in exile more bearable?

I feel, rather than see, the old couple exchange a glance.

Mr Burrows coughs. 'We have an attic,' he says.

'Attic?' asks Taras.

'Up under the roof,' says the old man.

'*Horyshche*?' I say to Taras.

'Perhaps you should show them, Albert,' says Mrs Burrows.

He rises from the table. 'Come with me,' he says, 'but I warn you now, it's a mess up there and will need some work doing to it.'

He leads us up two flights of stairs and opens a door onto a room which is a large space under the roof and, although the walls slope down, a large skylight makes it light and airy. At the moment, though, it is a palace of lumber and dust for which the Burrows are keen to apologise.

'We've neglected this a bit. As you can see we'd have to clear it out and give it a clean.'

I look at Taras and he says, 'We help?'

'That would be useful,' says Mr Burrows, 'especially as we're not getting any younger.'

'We glad to help,' I say.

'Alright then,' says Mr Burrows. 'We'll need to empty this out. There might be some useful bits of furniture but there's no bed. Do you think you could provide a bed yourselves?'

I check with Taras and then say, 'Yes, we get bed ourselves.'

'I suppose you'd like to move in as soon as possible,' says Mrs Burrows.

'Yes, please,' we say together so quickly that we all burst out laughing.

'How do you feel about making a start this Saturday?' asks Mr Burrows.

'Yes, good,' says Taras.

'What time?' I ask.

'As early as you like,' says Mrs Burrows. 'We don't sleep in late.'

'Thank you. Thank you very much,' I say.

'Don't thank me yet. We've this lot to clear first.'

We go down the stairs and Taras and I leave the house, passing the loaded blossoms along the path with lighter hearts. We turn at the gate to see the old couple standing in their doorway watching us. We smile and wave as we set off up the road. When we are out of their sight, I take Taras's hand.

'A room of our own!'

'Next we'll save for our own house.'

It seems like an impossible dream and we look at each other in an agony of hope.

'A house of our own…'

Chapter 17

When Kripak was absent, Lyubka slept with the door of her room open, alert to any summons from mother or baby. She woke hearing the rustling of the straw mattress and got up at once.

'Are you alright?' she whispered.

'Yes,' Vera whispered back. 'He's hungry.'

Lyubka got up and putting a shawl around her shoulders went into the main room. She lit a single candle. 'Can I get you something?'

'Some water. I'm really thirsty.'

Lyubka filled a cup with water and passed it to Vera as she nursed her baby. Vera drank most of it then gave the cup back to her older sister. She stroked the baby's dark hair. 'It's like silk,' she said and they smiled at one another conspiratorially, thinking of the greasy black locks of the baby's father.

'I need you to take a message in the morning,' said Vera.

'I know,' Lyubka replied.

'You know where to go?'

'Of course.'

'Will you be able to manage the walk?'

Lyubka stroked Michaylo's cheek. 'For him, I could walk to the sea and back.' She paused. 'When shall I ask him to come?'

'As soon as possible. Tomorrow night. Tell him the hours Kripak is usually out but warn him we'll have to be very careful.'

'I will.'

The following day, Lyubka left her home and set off while Kripak slept. She took the path beside the stream, down past the laundry and across the sloping meadow where the thyme was in full flower. She reached the wood and climbed up through the trees for about twenty minutes. Her gait was still uneven but the muscle in her leg had regained most of its strength, although she knew she would be sore the following day. She reached a small cottage perched on the hillside surrounded by a vegetable garden. When she knocked on the door a boy of about ten answered.

'Good morning, Yurko. Is your father at home?'

He nodded.

'May I speak to him, please?'

'I'll see,' said the boy. 'Please wait here.'

Lyubka turned to look at the view while the boy slipped back into his house. The approaches to the cottage were open and visible, despite its position. The ground had been cleared on all sides so the dwelling stood surrounded by neat beds of leeks and potatoes, beetroot and carrots. There would be a few moments' warning if anyone approached. The cottage door opened and a man emerged pulling up his braces. His hair was dishevelled and his eyes puffy with sleep.

'I'm sorry to disturb you, Father,' she said.

He glanced around immediately and said, 'No, no. I'm not that now.'

'I'm sorry,' said Lyubka. 'It's difficult not to.'

'Of course it is,' said the man, 'but I don't want to be shot for a little mistake.'

Lyubka hung her head, ashamed of her childish error.

'It's alright,' said the priest, 'but I have Yurko to protect too.'

Father Antin had once served a neighbouring parish but he had given up the priestly life when the Russians had arrived in 1939. For the last nine years he had lived quietly, providing for himself and his family on their smallholding, denying God and any connection with him…and he had survived. Like all Ukrainian priests he was married. He and his wife had had three children but he had lost two of them and his wife in the typhus epidemic which had killed Lyubka and Vera's mother. Now his only concession to his old life was the service he secretly provided to new mothers. He was willing to baptise their babies. For all other services a priest might render, the community had to manage as everyone else did under Stalin's rule. Since God was dead, there was no need for Mass or the sacraments. Despite the threat of execution or deportation, Father Antin's conscience would not allow babies to face the threat of limbo if they remained unbaptised so he was willing to perform the christenings in secret, at the dead of night.

'Is it your sister's baby?' asked the priest.

'Yes. He was born last night.'

'When shall I come?'

'Kripak goes out every night, usually as it gets dark. Perhaps just after that?'

'I'll come up through the garden at the back of your cottage.'

Lyubka nodded. 'I'll meet you there. Can you wait in the maize if I'm not there?'

'Yes. We'll wait till you come.'

'I can't tell you an exact time.'

'I understand. But let's be as careful as we can. You'd better go now.'

'I will, and thank you,' said Lyubka, biting back 'Father'.

***

Vera dozed in bed with the baby tucked in beside her. If she had opened her eyes she would have seen her husband sitting hunched over the stove. He always seemed to be cold yet carried with him the acrid smell of sweat. She would also have seen Lyubka sitting at the table sewing another small white garment. There was nothing she could do until Kripak went out so she dozed on, the tingling in her breasts telling her that soon enough her son would be demanding to be fed. But for now, she

125

allowed herself to drift.

There was a clatter of the stool as Kripak rose. He stepped over to the bed and peered at his son. He glanced at Vera then went to the cottage door to put on his boots. He left without a word while Lyubka continued to sew and Vera to doze. They let half an hour pass and then Vera opened her eyes. Lyubka looked up and they nodded to one another. Lyubka blew out the candle before slipping out of the door and going round to the woodpile behind the cottage. If he were watching, or if he came back, this was her excuse. She had failed to bring in enough wood to keep mother and baby warm. She stood in the darkness and held her breath, the better to listen for any movement, but she could only hear the wind rustling the leaves of the walnut tree. She walked through the gate into the vegetable garden as if it were the middle of the day and went down to the end where it bordered the field of maize. In the head-high crop, a man stood perfectly still with his boy. No words were spoken, but three silent figures returned to the cottage. Lyubka closed the door behind them.

Father Antin approached the bed and Vera shifted to sit up.

'No, don't get up,' he said as Lyubka re-lit the candle.

Lyubka took the baby in her arms and stood ready with Yurko to answer the priest's questions as the child's godparents. Vera looked at her baby and thanked God for Lyubka who would help her to keep this boy safe and she knew the other boy, only ten years old himself, understood the promises he was making as Michaylo's godfather. He had had plenty of practice as the godfather to many of the region's children born under Stalin's yoke.

Father Antin took his stole from an inner pocket, kissed it and placed it around his neck. From another pocket he took a bottle of water and a small jar of ointment which he placed on the bed. He glanced at Vera. 'I'm going to be as quick as I can, but have no fear. Your child will be properly baptised,' he said

126

in a low voice.

'I know, Father. I'm very grateful.'

The priest began the ritual of the baptism and Vera found herself comforted by the cadence of the familiar words and responses which had been denied to them for the last four years since the Communists had taken power again. But she shuddered as he said,

'Drive out from him, O Lord, every evil and unclean spirit…'

thinking of Kripak who must, at that very moment, be carrying out some heinous act of cruelty on behalf of his master.

'Make of this creature, O Lord, a spiritual lamb of Christ, a child of light…'

Vera bowed her head, fervently echoing the priest's words. Let her child not be seduced by his father's evil. She looked up to see the godparents turn away from the priest in the ritual denial of the devil.

'Do you reject Satan and all his works and all his angels and all form of service to him?'

'I do reject him,' replied Lyubka and Yurko in unison.

The formula was repeated three times and then followed by the *Credo* for good measure: *'I believe in God, the Father Almighty, Creator of Heaven and Earth…'*

There was a clatter in the yard and a stutter in the prayer as the sisters stretched their ears for more sound. If Kripak found the priest in his house he would not hesitate to cut his throat. And the boy's too. But Father Antin and Yurko finished the prayer in low tones. Lyubka handed the baby to Yurko while she tiptoed to the cottage door and listened for more sound. She stood holding her breath for a few moments and then, shaking her head, rejoined the group by the bed. The priest asked her for the *kryzhma* to bind the baby in the symbolic cloth of light. He took the single candle they were using and passed it to Yurko saying,

'Take the light of this candle to shine brightly throughout your life with the light of faith and good deeds…'

Father Antin unscrewed the cap from the bottle of water, tipped some drops onto his right thumb and drew a cross on the baby's forehead. Then he dribbled some of the water over the baby's head, saying, 'I baptise you…'

He paused and glanced at Vera.

'Michaylo.'

'…Michaylo, in the name of the Father, the Son and the Holy Ghost.'

The three watchers murmured 'Amen' in reply and the sisters shared a smile that Michaylo had not howled in protest.

Father Antin screwed the top back on the bottle. In accordance with the rites of the Ukrainian Catholic Church, he would now give Michaylo the sacrament of Confirmation. He opened the small jar and dabbed a finger in the ointment. He made the sign of the cross on the baby's forehead, eyes, nostrils, lips and ears. Lyubka opened up the baby's clothing and the priest dipped his finger in the ointment again. He leaned forward to make the sign of the cross on the baby's chest as there was another rattle beyond the windows.

Vera and Lyubka held their breath as they listened beyond the priest's words, 'The seal of the gift of the Holy Spirit…' to any possible movement of an unholy spirit outside their home to which there was only one entrance. Father Antin continued with the ritual reaching the concluding words, 'Deliver him from the Evil One and preserve his soul in purity…In the name of the Father, the Son, and the Holy Spirit, now and forever…'

'Amen,' said the sisters and Yurko on an outbreath of relief.

Father Antin took off his stole, folded it carefully and placed it in an inner pocket of his jacket. The jar and bottle went into another pocket and he and his son were ready to leave.

'Thank you, Father,' said Vera taking a small bundle of notes from under her pillow.

128

'There's no need for that,' said the priest. 'It is God's work we do.'

'I know but we must all live.'

He took a small note from the bundle and left the rest on the bed. 'We must go,' he said.

The candle was blown out and Lyubka went to the cottage door. She opened it a fraction and listened. The wind was still in the walnut tree but she could hear nothing beyond it. She opened the door and stepped out into the yard. She gave an infinitesimal nod and turned away while the priest and his son slipped into the shadows behind the cottage and down to the field of head-high maize beyond the vegetable garden. Lyubka withdrew into the cottage and closed the door behind her.

Chapter 18

This time as we walk up to the Burrows' house it is early morning, not quite seven o'clock. I yawn widely and Taras leans into me.

'Couldn't you sleep for excitement?'

'Partly. But I dreamt about Verochka and then I couldn't get back to sleep.'

'Was it a bad dream?'

'I don't know. It was such a jumble. I heard her crying out but then she was laughing. I couldn't see what she was doing though.'

'Was she on her own?'

'No. I had the sense that Lyubka was there. I don't know where Mama was.' I pause and then admit, 'I haven't dreamt of Mama for some time.'

Taras squeezes my arm. 'Try not to worry. Think how pleased they'd be for us today.'

'I know they'd be happy for me…but it would be nice to have some news.'

'I know,' he says as he leads me up the tiled path to the Burrows' front door. He knocks and the door opens almost immediately.

'My, you are early birds,' says Mr Burrows.

'Early birds?' I ask.

'Catches the worm.'

I tuck the saying away for later. I'll have to look in the dictionary to make sense of that one.

'And you've come dressed for work.'

We refuse Mrs Burrows' offer of tea and set to, carrying the lumber down from the attic. Amongst the old furniture is a chest of drawers with a battered top, and a couple of dining chairs with broken seats.

'We use?' asks Taras pointing to the articles.

Mr Burrows appraises them doubtfully. 'They're damaged but if you want to repair them, you can have them.'

'Repair?' Taras looks at me.

'*Vypravlyaty.*'

'Yes, I repair,' says Taras.

We fetch and carry until the attic contains only dust and cobwebs. Mrs Burrows and I carry up a bucket of hot water, a mop, a brush and dusters. The old woman starts to sweep the floor but I stop her.

'Please, I do.'

'I'll help you, my dear. It's very dirty.'

'No, no. My room, I work.'

'Alright then. I'll go and put the kettle on.'

I sweep and dust our first home, then I wash all of the surfaces including the windows. The room smells of disinfectant but at least it's clean.

'Tea's made,' calls Mrs Burrows.

In the dining room Mrs Burrows has laid the table with sandwiches as well as the promised tea.

'Sit down,' she says. 'You must be hungry. Tuck in.'

'No, thank you…' I know about British rationing and they're old. They should not be feeding us.

'Now, don't be silly,' says Mrs Burrows. 'Help yourselves, please.' She offers the plate first to Taras and then to me. She won't accept our refusal but waits until we've submitted and taken a sandwich each before offering the plate to her husband.

'Thank you, my dear,' says Mr Burrows. 'Perhaps if we show them the photograph, they'll understand.'

Mrs Burrows leaves the table and goes over to the sideboard where she picks up a framed photograph of a young man in Air Force blue. She returns to the table and holds the silver frame so we can see him.

'This is our son, Mike. He was killed in the skies over Europe.' She pauses to swallow while I wonder if he flew one of the bombers which came over Bavaria.

'Very sorry,' I say.

'We would like to think that if he'd survived - needed help - someone would have taken him in.' She reaches up with her fingers under her spectacles to wipe her eyes.

Taras says, '*Vichna yomu pamyat.*'

I translate for the Burrows, 'We have saying when someone dies – may he be remembered always.'

'That's a good saying,' says Mr Burrows. 'He will certainly always be remembered in this house.'

'Of course.'

'Now then,' says Mr Burrows, 'let's eat Mrs B's delicious sandwiches.'

When we have eaten, Taras says to me, 'Ask them about the painting.'

'Taras want to know if we may paint the room.'

'Paint it?' says Mr Burrows.

'Yes. White paint. Taras have friend who come to help.'

'I'm not sure,' says Mr Burrows. 'I haven't got any paint.'

'Taras friend – he have paint. They do good job,' I say.

The old couple look at each other.

'It would brighten up the room for them,' says Mrs Burrows.

Mr Burrows sighs. It is his home after all.

'No matter…' I begin.

'Yes, my dear,' he says. 'Rose is right. It would look much better for a lick of paint.'

A lick of paint. I'm reminded of a cat and smile at the image. 'They do good job,' I say again.

'I'm sure they will. When do they want to start?'

'This afternoon.'

'This afternoon?'

132

'Yes. Then dry for next week when we move here.'

Mrs Burrows places a hand on her husband's arm. 'Albert, they've had to live apart for the last year,' she reminds him.

It's agreed we'll move in the following Saturday and will pay two weeks' rent in advance. We also discuss how much we'll contribute to the food bill. There are no facilities for us to cook in the attic and no running water up there. Mrs Burrows's kitchen is too small for two women, so we will eat our meals together. One day I will be able to cook in my own kitchen...but not yet.

Taras and I leave Monkton Street and hurry away to carry out this afternoon's plans. Taras will meet his *odnoselchan* Stefan who has commandeered some paint from the back of a disused shed in the camp and they will paint our room. Meanwhile, I have my own surprise to carry out...

I go to meet Marichka at her hairdressers. She's seated under the dome of the hairdryer and even here she manages to look glamorous, a cigarette held between fingers which end in long red nails, her legs crossed, one stiletto sandal hanging off her toes, the nails of which are similarly painted. As I approach she holds out the magazine she has been looking at.

'What do you think of this?'

I glance at the page she is holding towards me. The model is wearing a white feather hair band over her tight dark curls...and a fitted satin wedding dress. I look at Marichka.

'Has he?'

She nods, grinning.

'When?'

'Last night.'

She waggles her left hand at me. She is wearing a diamond ring.

'Is it real?'

'Of course.'

So she has led the Major up the primrose path and achieved

one of her goals.

'When are you getting married?'

'Soon. Here. Before he's posted home and then he'll send for me.'

'Are you sure?'

'Yes.' She looks serious for a moment. 'I'm making sure of him.'

'Oh, Marichka, I hope it works out for you.'

'It will.' She smiles. 'Now what about things working out for you?'

I shrug. 'I don't know.'

'Shirley.' Marichka calls over a young woman who has been washing the clients' hair. 'Please tell Mrs Marshall my friend is here.'

The girl goes to a room at the back of the salon while Marichka explains, 'Mrs Marshall is the owner. It is she who will buy your hair.'

I touch my braids.

'Have you changed your mind?'

I shake my head.

'I told you, she'll pay good money for your *kosi* and then you can buy your precious bed.' She winks at me. 'Natalya, my love, you and Taras should have a big bed. It is the future!'

I can't help smiling although I still feel nervous.

A woman of about forty approaches us. She is well-corseted under her smart black dress. Her own hair is set in luxurious blonde waves.

'This my friend Natalya,' says Marichka.

'How do you do,' says Mrs Marshall.

'Well, thank you.'

'I understand you want to sell your hair.'

'I think so.'

'Could you sit over here, please?'

She places me in a chair before a mirror and begins to undo

my plaits from the bun they are wound in at the nape of my neck. Then she unbraids my hair, spreading it across the back of the chair. My scalp tingles and I can't help shuddering.

'Hmm,' she says, lifting my hair.

'How much?' I ask.

She names a price.

'*Za malo*,' calls Marichka.

She's right. It's not enough; the bed costs more.

'No,' I say to Mrs Marshall, 'I would like…' and I name the price of the bed with bed linen and blankets.

She tuts but then says, 'Very well, then.' She begins to re-plait my hair. 'I'll cut it off in the braids,' she says.

'And then give Natalya nice hairdo,' says Marichka.

'Yes, and give your friend a nice hairdo,' says Mrs Marshall.

Later, we leave the hairdressers arm in arm, Marichka with her glossy black curls and me with a peculiarly light head and cool neck. Mrs Marshall tells me I have a natural wave in my hair and that she has given me what she calls a bob. I assume it's this ear-length cut which has a satisfying curl at its ends. Marichka and I turn our heads to one another to admire ourselves.

She laughs. 'Natalya, you have entered the modern age at last.'

We part at the furniture shop. Marichka has helped me get the cash for my bed but she draws the line at the banal task of actually buying it. So I go alone to make my choices and arrange for the delivery to the Burrows' house to take place the following Saturday.

But I have still to meet my husband with my new hairstyle.

Since the men came back from Suffolk, the Saturday dances at the hostel have resumed. As expected, Taras arrives late. He and Stefan have painted our room and cycled back to the camp to smarten themselves up for the evening. Taras has also had another errand to do, of which I know nothing yet, but am about to find out.

I wait for him sitting on the hostel step.

When he arrives on his bike, he dismounts, leans his bike against the lamp-post and stands before me. 'Excuse me, beautiful lady, but I'm looking for my wife, Natalya.'

'Do you like it?'

'You do look beautiful.'

I stand up and he kisses me.

'It is lovely, but why now?'

I explain that I have sold my plaits to pay for our new bed. 'Then we don't have to use the savings for the house,' I say.

'What would your Mama say?'

'She'd think I'd been sensible and I'd driven a hard bargain. My *kosi* paid for the bed, the pillows, the sheets and the blankets. We will have everything we need.'

He kisses me again and then says, 'I have a surprise for you too.'

'Have you?'

'Since I came back here, I have been working not only for the Misses but also for their neighbours. I too had a little extra money.'

He reaches into his pocket and draws out a small black box. 'You need this,' he says.

I open it to find a plain gold band. I can't help a sob escaping me as he takes the ring and puts it on my finger.

'There you are, *Pani* Sidorenko,' he says.

Chapter 19

Vera moved slowly along the hedge, her fingers stained purple by the ripe blackberries she was picking. The fruit was abundant on the south side of the hedge where Vera had pruned the dead branches the previous autumn so only the newly fruiting ones remained. She was methodical, picking each strand clean of its ripe fruit before moving on to the next one. She dropped the fruit into a saucepan, ready to be cooked with a little sugar. She could hear voices approaching along the lane and thought she recognised some of the village girls but the hedge was too high and too thick to be able to see. As the girls came nearer she could make out their words.

'It gives me the shivers going past here now,' said one.

'I know,' said another voice. 'How she can live with him I don't know.'

'Well, it's not just living,' said a third voice. 'Where do you think that baby came from? The Immaculate Conception?'

They all laughed at this, but the first voice began again. 'It would be like going to bed with the devil.'

They shuddered audibly. 'Oooh, stop it,' said another voice as they passed the spot where Vera stood immobile on her side of the hedge. She tried not to listen to their words as they moved away along the lane but simply waited for them to be gone. When she could no longer hear them, she continued to pick the blackberries. The seventeen-year-old girl could not help remembering her mother's oft-spoken warning:

'Nobody knows what they might have to do to survive in this world.'

Vera picked more quickly now, the gathering of the fruit a chore to be completed rather than a pleasant task on a sunny afternoon. When her pan was full she returned to the cottage.

Lyubka was lifting Michaylo out of his crib. 'He's just woken up,' she said smiling. She held her nephew to her and kissed his head.

Vera nodded. 'I'll just get these started and then I'll feed him,' she said, putting the pan of fruit on the stove.

'Are you alright?' asked Lyubka coming closer.

'Of course.'

'You're not. What's the matter?'

'I'll tell you later. It'll disturb his feeding,' she said, taking the baby in her arms. She had checked his body minutely in the days after his birth, trying to convince herself there was no mark on him which should not be there. More than once, Lyubka had said to her, 'What are you looking for? He's perfect.'

And he was. Vera held him close, opening her blouse to feed him. He was hers, hers and Lyubka's, not Kripak's.

Lyubka put some sugar in the pan and stirred the fruit and then she passed a cup of water to her sister. When Vera had fed the baby, she asked again. 'What's the matter?'

Vera shrugged. 'Nothing. Silly chatter from the girls in the lane. I shouldn't have been eavesdropping. Serves me right.'

'What were they saying?'

Vera shook her head.

'What?'

'That I sleep with the devil,' she whispered.

'Oh, Verochka,' said Lyubka taking her younger sister in her arms. 'You don't. He's a man who abuses his little bit of power. God will punish him.'

Vera rested her head against Lyubka's shoulder, allowing herself a moment's comfort. Then she shook herself and said, 'I knew it was the price we'd have to pay.'

'Everyone wants to survive,' said Lyubka. 'This is fine.'

'What's fine?' asked Kripak coming into the cottage.

'These blackberries,' muttered Lyubka, moving away from the stove and going out into the garden.

138

Kripak went over to peer in to the pan. He put a long finger into the bubbling contents but pulled it out quickly. 'Damn, it's hot.'

'Of course it is,' said Vera. 'You can have some when it cools.'

'When will that be?'

'Soon.'

'Good. Get on with it. I have to go out again.'

Vera stirred the fruit and took the pan off the heat. She ladled some of the purple liquid into a bowl and fetched her husband some cream she had made. 'Want this in it?'

'Yes. Put it in.'

She spooned the cream into the fruit and passed him the bowl.

'Give me a spoon.'

She handed him a spoon, not allowing herself to tap him sharply on the skull with it. 'There you are.'

He shovelled a large spoonful into his mouth and she had to turn away to hide her smile as he spluttered and hissed to try to cool the liquid. She put Michaylo on her hip and went to stand in the doorway with him.

'Look at the little birds,' she said to him.

'You'll make that baby crazy, talking to him,' said Kripak.

'Why?'

'He can't understand anything yet.'

'Well, he'll learn.'

'Not yet he won't.'

He will, she thought. He'll learn who loves him and what it is to be good or bad. But she showed her husband a bland face while he scraped the bowl clean.

'Give me some more.'

'Are you going to eat it all?'

'You can pick more fruit, can't you?'

She did not bother to reply but gave him another helping.

Just as the blackberries were making a welcome appearance, the woods too were full of mushrooms. The following morning when the sun peeped over the rim of the valley, Vera stirred herself. Michaylo was beginning to whimper so she left Kripak lying on his back and snoring through his open mouth. Vera crept into Lyubka's room where the baby slept once he had settled for the night, alongside his aunt. She lifted her son out of his crib and fed him sitting on the edge of her sister's bed while Lyubka woke up slowly.

'Are we going out for mushrooms?' she asked.

'We should. They're ready,' said Vera.

The sisters wrapped themselves in their warm shawls, then Lyubka helped to bind the baby to his mother's back with a long piece of linen. The women picked up their baskets and left Kripak to his slumbers. They also left their footprints in the dew-covered grass as they made their way across the meadow to the woods where they had gathered mushrooms in the early autumn with their mother and Natalya ever since they could walk.

They stooped to pick the little *pidpenki* growing on fallen branches and tree stumps, gradually filling their baskets. They worked alongside one another, wasting no opportunity to gather the fungi. They would eat some now but they would dry the majority over the stove for the winter. Vera worked a little more slowly with the weight of her son on her back, so she looked up startled when Lyubka cried out.

'What is it?' she asked hurrying forward.

'I think it's a body,' said Lyubka, looking down at what looked, at first glance, like a small pile of old clothes.

Vera peered at the hump of brown cloth and then lifted a corner of it. She saw a narrow face covered with waxy yellow skin drawn tightly over the skull.

'It's *Pani* Semenenko.' She lifted the fabric higher. 'She's just skin and bone.'

'What do you think she died of?'

'Hunger. Grief.' Vera laid the corner of the shawl back down.

'What should we do?' asked Lyubka.

'Tell him.'

Lyubka looked doubtful.

'Well, we can't just leave her here. The children might come across her body.' Vera paused. 'We can't move her ourselves. They could say we'd done it.'

'Alright,' said Lyubka. 'Are we going to tell him now?'

'Yes. We'll have to go back.'

As they turned their footsteps towards home, Lyubka sighed. 'The poor woman.'

'She's best out of it.'

Lyubka looked at her sister, suddenly afraid.

'Well, what did she have to live for?' asked Vera. 'She had no one. Only the memory of what they did to her boys.' She shuddered. 'No one's going to do anything like that to my boy,' she announced, picking up the pace.

When they entered the cottage, she called out, 'Wake up! Wake up!'

Kripak sat up immediately. 'What's wrong?'

'We just found *Pani* Semenenko's body.'

'Who?'

'Her whose boys were beaten to death,' said Vera, hoping he might remember only one such pair of deaths. 'You ordered her house to be burnt.'

'Where is she?'

'In the woods.'

He lay back down on the pillows.

'Aren't you going to do something?' asked Vera.

'There's no hurry. You said she's dead.'

Vera turned away from him. She understood both that he did not care about others and that, if he thought she was trying to influence his behaviour, he would do the opposite of what she wanted.

She put down her half-filled basket of mushrooms and Lyubka helped to lift the baby off her back. Vera placed him in his crib while Lyubka went to the stove to make the *kasha* for their breakfast.

'I'm going to milk the cow,' said Vera, glad of an excuse to leave the room her husband was in. She tried not to think of the old woman, somehow living in the outhouse which was all that remained of her home, wandering the woods alone. She forced herself to focus on her son's pink cheeks and his rounded limbs so her grief would not touch the cow and make her hold on to her milk.

When she returned to the house, Kripak was still dozing in bed. She clattered the bucket on the floor and then he got up. He dressed, ate and left in quick succession.

Vera and Lyubka looked at one another after he had gone.

'Those girls might have been right.'

'No. He's just a block of wood. No feelings.'

Chapter 20

I wait until Lesia and my other two roommates have gone down for breakfast before I complete my packing. I open my drawer and take out the worn and not-so-worn items of clothing, placing them on the bed. Then I remove a *rushnyk* from the bottom of my drawer, the one which I have been carrying since 1943 when I left home. I open it out carefully and look at the photograph tucked into its folds. The girl I was stares out of the picture with such a serious expression on her face, but as I look I feel the touch of Roman's hand. He too is looking serious but we posed for the photograph standing so close together we were able to hold hands without it being visible to the viewer. Roman, my partisan husband. I stroke the photograph knowing he will never look any older. He lies on a mountainside in the Carpathians where I had to leave him. Dead. Shot by the Nazis. I bow my head but the tears don't come. The death of my first husband has become part of the weft of my being. I fold the *rushnyk* I embroidered for the home we never had and place it and the photograph in the bottom of my bag. He will come with me wherever I go. Even now…to my first home with my second husband, Taras…whom I also love.

I hear footsteps along the corridor.

'Do you want to borrow my holdall?' asks Lesia, coming into the room.

'Yes please. I don't know how I've managed to double the number of things I have.'

'A year's a long time. And you've been a magpie.'

She's right. I have gathered all sorts of things, from extra towels to a jug and bowl set which Mrs Bough-Smith was going to get rid of because it had a little chip. Despite her meanness, she throws away a great many useful things.

When we have bundled up my worldly goods, I say, 'Thank you for saying you'd help me. I couldn't carry all of this on my own.'

Lesia smiles. 'It's nosiness really. I can't wait to see your room. Stefan says it's a palace.'

'Not quite, but it will look better now he and Taras have painted it.' I hug her and say, 'You'll find somewhere of your own. Taras and I will keep our ears open and tell you as soon as we hear of anything.'

'I know you will.'

We gather up my bundles and go down the stairs, past the canteen where there's not the usual workday rush for breakfast but a leisurely Saturday time for sharing plans for the day off. I wave to Maryna and Paraska, our roommates, and call, 'See you tomorrow,' which is when we will meet in the park as usual on a Sunday.

Thus begins another journey. Despite our luggage, we march along to the Burrows' house, where there is a lorry parked at the kerb. It seems a bit of a rough vehicle for transporting a bed. The front door is open but I knock and call out, 'May we come in?'

Mrs Burrows bustles out of her living room. 'Of course, my dear. This is your home now. You don't have to knock when you come in. Mr Burrows has given your husband two keys so you can both come and go as you please.'

'Thank you. That is very kind. This is my friend, Lesia.'

'How do you do, dear,' says Mrs Burrows.

'She and Stefan…' I begin.

'He's upstairs with Mr Sidorenko.'

'Stefan? What are they doing?' I ask.

She smiles. 'You'd better go up. I think it's meant to be a surprise.'

Lesia and I climb the stairs.

144

As we reach the attic, I call out, '*Dobroho dnya*,' and then peer through the doorway.

In the bright room, Taras and Stefan are opening up a metal and wooden structure underneath the window.

'What is it?' I ask, dropping my bags and going forward to look.

Taras is grinning from ear to ear. 'A treadle sewing machine.' He lifts up the hinged wooden lid and from the belly of the wooden structure, turns up a sewing machine.

'Where did you get it?'

'A second-hand shop opposite the factory.'

'Does it work?'

'Yes, but I need to overhaul it first.' He knows I'm dying to ask, so he adds, 'Five pounds.'

'A week's wages.'

'I'm going to make suits for people in the evenings and at weekends. We'll soon make it back.' He smiles at me, a tell-me-I'm-right smile.

This week we have both found new jobs. Taras went for an interview at a factory where they make women's clothing. He is to be the pattern-maker for them. When they offered him the job, he asked for a job for me too. I am to be a finisher, doing the fiddly tasks at the end of the garment-making. The wages are not much higher than we've been earning, but it will be cleaner work than we have been doing and this machine will help us to add to the deposit for a house of our own.

I kiss his cheek. 'You're right.'

Lesia says, 'Where do you want these, Natalya?'

'In the corner please, until the bed has been delivered.'

Right on cue, Mr Burrows calls from downstairs, 'There's a furniture van here.'

After the bed has been installed and made up, Stefan and Taras manhandle the Burrows's chest of drawers up the stairs. Somehow Taras got it to the camp and recovered the top during the week. It was brought back on the lorry with the sewing machine. As we position it in place, our room begins to look a little more like a home.

From the top of Lesia's holdall I take out a small icon of the Virgin and Child and my second *rushnyk*. Lesia and I smile at one another.

'I need a nail and a couple of tacks,' I say.

Taras looks at the length of white linen with its bands of red and black embroidery at either end. He shakes his head and smiles. 'So many secrets…'

We put up the icon and the new *rushnyk* and the four of us stand back. None of us can help a sigh escaping as we remember how in our homes with our families, we would kneel down together at the end of the day to say our evening prayers.

We hug one another when Lesia and Stefan leave to return the lorry to the farmer who lent it to us.

'Are you ready for a spot of lunch?' asks Mrs Burrows after we have waved them off.

'Yes. Thank you. Then we must go to the police station.'

She looks startled. 'The police station?'

'Yes. We have to report our change of address. It is because we are aliens.'

'Aliens. That's a bit harsh.'

'That is what it says on our registration certificates.'

'And at the police station too,' she says.

'It is the law. We in trouble if not.'

'Then we'll have our lunch quickly and you can get off to do it.'

There is also someone else who needs to know our new address. When we return from the police station, I sit on the side of our bed with a notepad and pen.

'*Dorohenka Olha*,' I write. '*We have a room of our very own…*' and I tell her about our domestic adventures. '*It is the first step, my dear friend, and now we plan to work and save to buy*

146

a house which will be big enough for you to come and live with us, if Dmitro does not come alone first.'

I stop writing.

'What's wrong?' asks Taras.

'Should I mention those men you've met who are here without their wives?'

'The ones with wives and children in Germany?'

'Yes. I don't want them to think I'm meddling but there are more ways than one of getting here.'

'Mention it. They'll follow it up if they want to.'

'If Dmitro wants to.' I sigh and turn back to my letter. We're not in a position to help them yet but I wish I could. I would like to share my happiness with my friend.

***

The sunlight wakes us the following morning. Our windows are in the roof so no one can see in but we have no curtains for them yet. Perhaps I'll leave them bare. It's nice to see the moon and stars at night and in the morning we have to be up early for work.

Taras stirs behind me and I luxuriate in the warmth of the touch of his skin against mine. He strokes my back and I turn to face my husband.

1949
Chapter 21

Another autumn morning and another baby, thought Vera as she followed Lyubka up the slope into the woods. Andriyko was strapped to Vera's back and despite the two months which had passed since he was born, and despite the fact that she was still breast-feeding him, she thought she had the lighter burden than Lyubka. Her older sister had fashioned a rucksack to wear on her back into which one-year-old Michaylo could be slid. He had begun to take his first steps but was still a long way from being able to accompany his mother and aunt on a mushroom picking expedition. Vera's breath came out in visible puffs as they climbed up into the woods. The mist still hung between the trees, the birds were quiet, and the cold told her it would soon be winter again.

As they reached the top of the hill, both women stopped to catch their breath. Their eyes met.

'We won't be able to manage more than two babies,' said Vera.

Lyubka flushed. She thought the price her sister was paying for their relative safety was already too high. She could make no comment on what Vera might choose to do. She could only say, 'We'll manage. Whatever happens.'

'I know you'll help me,' said Vera, 'but we're going to have to help ourselves…or I'm going to have to help myself.' She stepped toward her sister and patted her arm. 'Don't worry. I'll think of something.'

The problem would not go away though. It kept repeating itself in her mind as she bent to pick the *pidpenki*. She could not have another baby yet. Two small sons were enough work and, despite her youth, Vera was always tired. However, she dared not risk denying Kripak his side of the bargain, so there had to be some other way. She remembered the old woman in the woods, *Baba* Chara, but shuddered at the thought of what she might suggest. She would have to go to *Pani* Lazarenko to see if the midwife could, or would, help her.

When the boys were napping that afternoon, Vera left them with their beloved aunt and, armed with a gift of butter, walked to *Pani* Lazarenko's house.

The midwife opened the door to her. 'Not again, surely?'

'Not yet, no,' said Vera, as the midwife ushered her into the cottage.

'Then what?'

Vera placed the block of butter on the table. 'That's exactly the problem.'

'What? That you're young and fertile?'

'Too fertile.'

'Hmm. I could get into a lot of trouble for helping you like this.'

'I know, but who am I going to tell?'

The older woman looked at Vera. 'Are you pregnant now?'

Vera shook her head. 'No, but I might be soon.'

'If you become pregnant, then we can deal with it.' The midwife paused. 'But it can be dangerous.'

'I wouldn't tell him.'

'No, physically dangerous for you.'

Vera considered this. 'Is there any other way?'

'Without him knowing?'

'Oh yes. He would never agree to preventing more sons. He already thinks he's the most virile man in the village.'

'There is an old way,' said *Pani* Lazarenko, 'and you won't be the first to use it.'

'What is it?'

'Wild carrot seeds.'

'Wild carrot seeds?'

'Yes. You're lucky. If you collect them now you'll have enough to last you until next autumn.'

'What do I do with them?'

'Gather them, grind them into a powder, and store them on a high shelf.'

'And then?'

'After each occasion when you have intercourse, take a spoonful of the powder in water - hot or cold – preferably within eight hours, or within twenty-four hours at the latest.'

'Is that all? It seems too easy.'

'My mother told me it's the oiliness in the seeds that does the work.'

'And what will it do?'

'Stop any more babies.'

'Does it have any other effects?'

'Not that I know of.'

'Then, thank you,' said Vera.

'No need.' The midwife paused. 'He's raped fewer women since he's been married.'

Vera stared at *Pani* Lazarenko. She did not know which was worse, that she was servicing a monster, or that he still raped a woman occasionally.

'I'm sorry,' said *Pani* Lazarenko.

'I'm glad you told me.' And she was. It would put her and Lyubka on their guard. They could not become complacent that the beast had been tamed. She also knew she would have to warn her sister, just as *Pani* Lazarenko had warned her, despite the terror it would bring.

Later, as darkness fell and the wind began to whistle around the house, she turned to Kripak. 'Sounds like a storm's brewing up. Are you still going out?'

'Of course. Why?'

'You need to take care. It sounds nasty.'

'What do you know about nasty? Give me some *borshch*.'

She served him the soup and passed him some bread. 'Do you want sour cream in it?'

'*Davay*.'

She spooned a dollop of cream into his bowl, then turned away from him to fold the boys' clothes while he slurped his way through his supper. She tried not to be impatient, knowing he must not sense how much she wanted him to go…and be struck down by a falling branch or some such thing. God will punish me, she thought. I must try not to wish him dead.

When he had gone to whatever work was so urgent he had to do it in a storm, she banked up the fire in the stove and made herself ready for bed. She peeped into Lyubka's room where Andriyko had taken over the crib and Michaylo now slept in a narrow bed by the wall.

'Are they asleep?' whispered Vera.

'Yes, they're fine. Fast asleep.'

'I hope this storm doesn't wake them.'

Just then the rain began, not with a gentle pattering at the window but with the pounding of gunfire on the corrugated iron roof. When the village had been burnt out during the battles between the Germans and the Red Army in 1944, almost all of the cottages had lost their thatched rooves. These had been replaced by the ugly but practical metal sheets which now provided the perfect surface for the rain to hammer on.

Vera and Lyubka looked up at the ceiling. They could not have heard each other speak. Vera leaned over each of her sons in turn and kissed their warm cheeks, then she kissed her sister goodnight and went to wait in her own bed for Kripak.

When he finally came home, he woke her from her dozing by leaning over her, his wet hair dripping onto her face.

'Get up and help me undress.'

She did as she was told, helping him to peel off the layers of sodden clothing. When he was naked, he went to get into bed.

'Wait,' she said and, taking a towel, rubbed his torso vigorously. 'You'll have got cold. We need to get your circulation going.'

He stood watching her in the firelight, her hair a nimbus around her face still warm from sleep.

'Come on, now,' he said, snatching the towel from her and dropping it on the floor. As he pulled her into the bed, she knew the most urgent task the following morning would be to gather some wild carrot seeds.

***

When she opened the cottage door at dawn, she saw the toll the wind and rain had taken. The last of the hollyhocks and dahlias around the cottage door were battered and broken, and across the yard Vera saw the walnut tree had shed a branch which now showed itself to have been rotten. She sighed. There would be a lot of clearing up to do in the vegetable garden.

But later that morning, after Kripak had gone out, she slipped away leaving Lyubka to keep an eye on the boys. She found what she needed in the hedgerow and began to gather the seeds. She remembered there was an almost unbroken border of it beside the drainage ditches through the fields and decided she would have to make time over the next few days to gather as much as she could. But she was safe for now.

Which was more than could be said for two people who had been long forgotten.

As she returned to the cottage, Vera saw Lyubka at the front gate peering into the lane.

'What is it?'

'I'm not sure. There was a lot of shouting and then Kripak went past with a couple of his men.'

'Where were they going?'

'Towards the church.' The church, of course, was no longer

standing. It had been destroyed by the Bolsheviks after they had defeated the Nazis. Stalin was determined Ukrainians would receive no succour from God. The land now stood barren and unused although the villagers were still buried in the cemetery beyond.

'What's happening?' called Vera as Zladko, one of the witnesses of Kripak's marriage, went past.

'The rain's washed the soil away just behind the bell tower wall. There are some bones.' He grinned. 'I'm going to get spades.'

The sisters looked at one another.

'Does he mean the graves have been damaged?'

'I don't know,' said Vera.

They waited until Zladko returned with his spades.

'Have the graves been damaged?'

He laughed. 'Not the official ones.'

The sisters remained puzzled until Kripak came home to eat.

'Was there trouble in the cemetery?' asked Vera, as he swallowed whole the *varenyki* she had put in front of him.

'No trouble.'

'A mess?'

'You could say that.'

She swallowed her irritation. 'What kind of mess?'

'Two bodies.'

'That's not unusual in a graveyard.'

'No, it's not. Unless the bodies are only a couple of feet down and the garrotte is still visible around their throats.'

Vera gasped and looked round at her sons.

'They don't understand yet,' he said. 'They will though.'

'What do you mean?'

'They'll need to know who the traitors are and what to do with them.'

'Were these traitors?'

'Zladko remembered their story…and their clothes. They

had done their duty and told the NKVD about the partisans in this area. It must have been in '41. The partisans' brothers-in-arms,' he sneered, 'came for revenge and killed them.'

Syksoti, she thought. Traitors. So many traitors. She remembered her own and Lyubka's fearful cries when Natalya had told Mama that Roman's *kurin* had been betrayed and that she, and they might be in danger. Natalya had fled to Germany pretending to be a compliant slave labourer to keep them safe.

'What will happen now?'

'We'll bury them as heroes.'

1950
Chapter 22

I wake up to a mouthful of saliva and the absolute knowledge I am going to vomit. I leap out of bed and lean over the bowl on the chest of drawers beneath the attic window. A grey January light adds to my feeling of misery. It is as I thought. I am pregnant, despite our efforts to delay this consequence until we have the deposit for our house.

'Are you alright?' asks Taras, sitting up in bed.

I nod and wipe my mouth on the towel.

He looks anxious. 'Are you…'

'Yes. I've missed a period and you know how regular I am.'

He nods then smiles at me. 'Our own baby,' he says as he gets out of bed and comes over to take me in his arms. We hold one another and he rocks me gently. 'We'll be a family.'

'But can we afford it?'

'We could wait forever to afford it,' he says. 'Let's get into bed where it's warm.'

We lie entwined among the sheets and blankets and talk about our baby as we watch the sky lighten.

'What are you thinking?' he asks.

'Whether either of my sisters has had a baby yet.'

'How old are they now?'

'Lyubka's twenty and Verochka's eighteen. They might have babies. They start early in the village.' I pause. 'I wish I could write to them.'

Taras holds me tighter. 'We will, just as soon as we can.'

We turn in towards each other.

'But at least one thing will be simpler for a few months,' he says as his warm hand strokes my thigh.

***

I meet Mrs Burrows in the hall as I return from work carrying a new bucket in my hand.

'Hello,' she says. 'You haven't bought a bucket have you? I've got two. You could have had one of mine.'

I blush and hesitate to explain I would prefer to vomit into my own bucket.

She looks at me and smiles uncertainly. 'Would you like a cup of tea?'

'No, thank you. I go lie down.' The thought of my bed has been haunting me throughout the day. All I seem to want to do is sleep. I climb the stairs to our room, take off my coat and headscarf, undo my shoelaces and ease them off, then I lie back in a bliss of exhaustion. I think of Olha when she was pregnant and remember she slept a lot too. At the time I just thought she was avoiding the cold and hunger of the DP camp. I wonder now what else I had failed to notice about pregnant women.

There's a knock at my door.

'Come in.'

Mrs Burrows peers around the door. 'I brought you a cup of tea anyway,' she says. 'You need to look after yourself now.'

How does she know? I wonder as I struggle to sit up in bed. I can feel myself blushing again as I say, 'It's only early, the baby.'

'That may be, but pregnancy can be very tiring.' She puts the cup on the packing case beside the bed. 'I've put lots of sugar in it for you.'

'You are very kind.'

'Have you registered with a doctor yet?' she asks.

'No.'

'You must.'

'But I may not need the doctor.'

'You will when the baby comes.'

'But is it expensive?'

She laughs. 'No, dear, it's free.'

'To me too?'

'To everybody. It's the National Health Service. Why don't I take you down to my surgery on Saturday morning and you can sign up there and then?'

'Alright,' I say.

She smiles and pats my hand. 'Albert and I always wanted grandchildren.'

Tears fill my eyes. That seems to be another symptom. I cry easily now. 'My Mama…' I begin but can't continue as the tears choke me.

'Oh, there, there. I've upset you. I'm sorry.'

'No,' I say, shaking my head.

She passes me a clean cotton handkerchief, ironed so its embroidered rose in one corner is displayed.

I wipe my tears. 'Thank you.'

'No need, dear. Drink your tea and have a rest. I'll call you for supper when the men are back from their work.'

After we have eaten, Mrs Burrows nudges her husband. They look at us across the untidy supper table and Mr Burrows says, 'Would you like me to do a studio portrait of you both? Perhaps we could do it at the weekend when we might have a bit of spare time.'

'A studio portrait?' asks Taras.

Mr Burrows raises a finger to signal wait a moment, then he goes into the front room. He returns with several posed photographs of couples. 'This sort of thing,' he says.

'I don't suppose you had any wedding photographs taken,' says Mrs Burrows.

'No,' I say. 'We didn't.'

Taras looks at the photographs. 'Beautiful,' he says, 'but…'

He's right. They are wonderful photographs and it would be

lovely to have one of ourselves but it is a luxury we can't afford.

'It would be a late wedding present from us,' says Mr Burrows. 'A memento of this time for you both.'

I daren't look at Taras but he knows me well enough to say, 'Thank you very much. Natalya and I would like.'

I smile at my husband and hope I'm never called upon to lie to him. Then I say to the Burrows, 'Very generous. Thank you.'

We pose for the portrait on Saturday afternoon. Taras has worked overtime this morning, Mr Burrows has seen clients, and Mrs Burrows and I have visited the doctor's surgery. Taras and I tidy ourselves up and put on our best clothes. I wear the spotted silk dress he made for me with his first Petticoat Lane purchase. Taras had gone to London alone on the train to explore the bargains he'd been told were to be had in the street market. He had practised his numbers in English, ready to haggle for suit lengths and remnants and had returned triumphant, proud both of his purchases and his battle with the London Underground. The dress is already tight over the bust so I know I will soon have to put it away until after the baby has been born. Taras wears a charcoal grey suit he made for himself and his best tie. He has two: one for work and one for best. This one has slashes of black and cream across a maroon ground. Very fashionable.

Mr Burrows seats me in an armchair, while Taras perches on the arm of the chair. We look straight at the camera and smile. Mr Burrows takes several photographs and then says, 'I'll do you a framed photo and some smaller prints which you can send to your friends.'

'Thank you,' says Taras, while I think of Marichka's glamorous wedding photos taken by a US Army colleague of her Major's. She looked so elegant in her lace dress, fitted tight to her skin in the bodice and flaring out into a wide skirt. She wore white as if born to it and I smile to myself as I remember the victorious glint in her eyes.

When the photographs are developed I do send copies to Olha and Marichka. I also explain there are three of us in the shot. I know neither of them will be surprised but whereas Olha will see the baby as a blessing, Marichka will see it as a necessary evil.

Marichka's response, though, should not really have surprised me. I come home one day from work to find a very excited Mrs Burrows.

'I had to sign for a parcel for you today,' she says as I come through the front door. 'It's from America!' she says as she hands me the parcel.

'It's from my friend, Marichka,' I say as soon as I see the handwriting.

I take the parcel upstairs and snip through the string and paper to find a small pile of baby's clothing. Beautiful soft vests, minute socks and a couple of romper suits. As I separate them, I find the letter I was looking for. However, it is wrapped around another rectangular parcel. I open the letter.

Dorohenka Natalya,

I suppose I should say congratulations to you and Taras. I knew you would have your first baby sooner rather than later and I am very happy for you. I have sent you some little garments but do let me know, once you have had the baby, what you need. The clothes here are much better quality than in England and there is no rationing so I will be able to get whatever you want. Please don't be polite, Natalya, just let me know what you need.

I have enclosed another gift for the baby. It is a contribution to your house deposit fund. You need your own home now more than ever so I give this money to you and Taras for your baby. He, or she, deserves it.

All is well here. We are settling into our new house and I will send you some pictures when I have had them taken. I am learning to drive because John wants to buy me a car. The cars here are beautiful, like ships, and petrol is not scarce as in England. It is also cheap. Natalya, why not re-consider? Come and live near us, then I will be able to keep an eye on you and you can have an easy American life. Talk to Taras about it. I'm sure we could help him find work.

Take care of yourself, my dear friend, and try not to work too hard. I send you my love and best wishes,

Marichka

As I pick up the smaller parcel, Taras comes in from work.

'I hear we have presents from America,' he says.

'Yes. Marichka, of course. Look at these lovely baby clothes.'

'Good fabric,' he says fingering the cloth. Then he sees me holding the small packet. 'What's that?'

I show him Marichka's letter and he grunts when he reads her comment about our baby deserving its own home.

'What is it?' he asks, although we have both already guessed. I open the package to find a pile of dollar bills. I count them and say, 'One hundred dollars.'

Taras shakes his head. 'We can't accept it.'

'She knew you'd say that. That's why it's a gift for our baby.'

'Clever.'

One hundred dollars. I don't know exactly what it's worth but know it will give a significant boost to the precious pot of money which has been growing so slowly despite our best efforts.

Taras reads the rest of Marichka's letter and then sits on the side of the bed. 'Do you think she's right?' he asks.

'About what?'

'About going to live in America.'

My stomach clamps with fear. 'No,' I shake my head. 'We don't know when things might change.'

'And we could go home,' he finishes for me.

I nod. 'It's too far to go home from America.'

'Yes,' he says. 'She has no family so it makes sense for Marichka to be over there. It's different for you.'

I look at him relieved he has understood.

He stands and takes me in his arms. 'We will use her money,' he says. 'You can have your own house here and then one day…'

'Soon…'

'Soon, we will go home.'

'And I will see Mama and my sisters.'

'And you will see your Mama and your sisters.'

1952
Chapter 23

Vera pushed the spade into the soil with her boot and then heaved gently to reveal the treasure of her potato crop. She scrabbled about with her fingers, not wanting to damage any with the sharp edge of her blade. She picked them out and dropped each one into a shallow box to dry out before storing them in sacks for the winter. As she moved forward to begin the next row, she could hear men shouting and laughter coming from her garden. She straightened up to listen but could not distinguish the words. Her boys had run up to the house as soon as they had heard their father return. She drove her spade into the soil and set off to investigate, but she stopped after a couple of steps and went back for the spade.

Gripping the spade, Vera strode into the yard. The shouting and laughter was coming from several men in black Militia uniforms. The cottage door stood open but there was no sign of her sons. She ignored the men and entered her home. Kripak and his henchman, Zladko, were standing with their backs to her. They were leaning over the table which held half a dozen ancient rifles and several revolvers. Michaylo and Andriy were kneeling up on the bench, their eyes wide as their little fingers caressed the dark weapons.

'What's this?' asked Vera.

Kripak turned to her. 'Our latest haul.'

'Who on earth would have so many weapons?'

'Traitors.'

Zladko turned to her with a grin. 'We had a good tip-off.'

I'll bet you did, she thought. There were always those who wanted to benefit from the misery of others.

162

'Where were they?' she asked, wondering who would pay for this secret.

'Beneath a pig-sty,' laughed Zladko.

'Ugh!' said Michaylo, drawing his hands back from the pistol he had been attempting to hold.

'They were wrapped in sacking, little man,' said Zladko scooping up the pistol in his large hand.

'Never mind that,' said Vera. 'Michaylo, Andriy, have you finished helping me by bringing in the logs?'

Michaylo hung his head. 'No, Mama.'

'Can't we just look at these?' whined Andriy.

'Go and help your mother,' said Kripak.

The boys slid down from the bench and as they went towards the door, Michaylo said, 'Sorry, Mama.'

'That's alright,' Vera replied. 'Now go and finish your work as I asked you.'

As the boys went out into the sunlight, Zladko muttered, 'I'll wait outside too,' and he left the cottage.

Kripak looked at his wife. 'What are you doing with that?'

She realised she was still holding the spade. 'Digging up potatoes,' she said. She looked towards the table. 'You're not leaving those there?'

'Why not?'

'The boys,' she said. 'I'd rather they didn't handle them.'

'The sooner they get used to handling weapons the better.'

'It's dangerous, letting them handle guns.'

'It's more dangerous if they don't know what they're doing with a gun.'

'They're only boys. Michaylo's not even five yet.'

'They're my boys,' he said. 'They need to be able to show people who's boss or they'll get trampled.'

She lowered her head. He would know all about trampling over people. 'Leave them a little longer,' she said.

'Not much longer. Michaylo could come with me now

when I go to work.'

'No. He's too young. You can't have him yet.'

'And you can't keep him tied to your apron strings.'

'I know I can't, but let me have him for a little longer.'

'For a little longer,' he said as he scooped up the loose bullets on the table and dropped them into his jacket pocket. Then he picked up the long metal ramrod which usually leaned in the corner by the door and left the cottage.

Vera followed him out into the yard.

He gestured to Zladko who was talking to the Militia men. 'Get the guns and take them to the office.'

Vera despised the tools of Kripak's trade. His pistol was not only for show. He was known to use it. He also had the steel rod. It was a couple of metres long and had a pointed end, the better to poke into walls and thatch, stockpiles of beets and manure heaps, to discover hidden partisans. It did not matter there were fewer and fewer of them. He was prepared to travel far and wide to flush out the last survivors who opposed the state. He poked them out with the rod and if the gun wasn't enough to warn them, then he'd wound them. A dead partisan was less use to him than a live one who could be encouraged to talk. Vera was grateful Kripak's instruments of torture were stored in the prison at Buchach and not in her kitchen.

The boys appeared from around the corner of the house.

'Where are you going, *Tatu*?' asked the younger child.

'Work.'

'Can I come?'

'No. Stay here and help your mother.'

'When can I come?'

'Another time.' He glanced at Vera. 'When you're bigger.'

'When will I be big?'

'When I say so.'

Zladko passed the weapons out of the house to the waiting Militia men, then they marched off up the lane, making enough

164

noise to bring the neighbours to their doors.

But at least they were gone, thought Vera. She kept the boys beside her until she was certain the men would be back at headquarters with their cache. Then they helped her to gather the potatoes and put them in the wooden bin in the barn. As the afternoon wore on, she said, 'Go up the lane to see if *Teta* Lyubka is on her way. Help her carry her basket.'

The boys left, eager to see what treats their aunt had found for them. She always managed something. It was Lyubka who now walked to the market regularly to do their trading. Despite the fact that she lived in the same house as Kripak, she did not share his bed, so people were more willing to trade with her than with Vera.

The boys returned a little later, flanking their aunt who still walked unevenly. The limp was no longer as obvious as it had been but it was still there. Andriy carried a small heavy-looking sack while Michaylo carried a large sack which looked much lighter.

'How did you do?' asked Vera from the cottage door.

'Pretty well. Sold everything and bought some salt and sugar.' Lyubka winked at her sister as they entered the kitchen. 'Come, boys,' she said. 'Put the sacks here.'

They placed the sacks on the table and stood waiting for their aunt to reveal whatever treasure she had found at the market.

Lyubka passed the heavy sack to Vera who poured the sugar into a large crock. She took a jar of honey from her basket and a brown paper packet.

'What's that?' asked Andriy.

'Seeds,' said his aunt.

The boys did not take their eyes off her as she removed other small packages from her basket. When it was empty, she bustled over to the stove. 'Shall we have a cup of tea, Vera?' she asked, opening the canister of dried linden flowers.

'Yes. You must be thirsty,' replied Vera, hiding a smile.

The boys waited as Lyubka boiled water and then steeped the linden flowers. They tried not to fidget but finally Andriy could not hold out any longer.

'Did you bring anything for us?'

'Oh, I forgot,' said Lyubka. 'Just have a look in the other sack. There might be something for you in there.'

The boys were already opening the sack. Michaylo tipped it over and a large leather ball rolled out onto the floor.

'Where on earth did you find that?' asked Vera.

Lyubka laughed. 'It's amazing what people have tucked away. I've seen all sorts of weird and wonderful things on the market. I bought it from an old woman and when I asked her where it came from, she said, 'What do you care? Are you buying it or not?' So I did. They can take it outside, can't they, Mama?'

'Yes,' said Vera, 'but don't break anything with it.'

The boys hurried out of the door, Andriy attempting to help Michaylo carry the ball.

When they'd gone, Vera turned to her sister. 'You spoil them.'

'Of course I do. What else are aunts for?'

'You should have been here earlier,' said Vera, and she related the story of the guns.

Lyubka was less concerned about the find than about Kripak's words. 'Do you think he means it?'

'To let Michaylo see the work he does? Yes, I do.'

'But he's just a child.'

'I know. I think I might have managed to hold him off for a bit longer. Andriy would go now if he could but I think Michaylo might be less keen. But if Kripak said he had to go, there'd be little choice.'

'What are we going to do?'

'Keep an eye on the boys for now, but I'll have to think of

something,' she said, not for the first time. 'I don't want them to have any part in what their father does.'

1952-53
Chapter 24

I am picking the peas for dinner when I hear a call from the house.

'Cooee, Natalya. Are you there?'

Holding the full colander of peas in one hand, I take two-year-old Lyuba's hand in the other and say, as we go up the long narrow garden, 'That sounds like Aunty Rose. Let's go and see, shall we?'

Lyuba nods and sets off on her sturdy legs. Halfway up the garden, we meet Mrs Burrows, or Aunty Rose, as she has become, looking pink from the heat.

'There you are,' she says and bends down to my Lyuba. 'How are you little one? Wait till you see what I've brought you.'

'Tea?' I ask, knowing the answer.

'Yes, please,' she says.

We walk slowly back up to the house. Our first precious house. It is at the end of a terrace and has two rooms downstairs and two rooms upstairs. It was derelict when we bought it but I really wanted its garden. It is a long narrow strip at right angles to the more usual tiny plots, so I have made a series of vegetable beds after the little lawn by the house. It is not nearly as big as our *horod* at home but it is better than anything I have had for the last ten years. We have even made room for hens in the last section of the garden.

'It's all growing well, Natalya,' says Mrs Burrows, looking at the beds in a riot of green.

'Yes. Taras got me some good manure over the winter.'

'The way to a girl's heart,' laughs Mrs Burrows.

'It is to mine.'

She leans down and takes Lyuba's hand in hers and the old and young heads are bent together as my baby girl tries to explain the pea pod she has in her other hand. Mrs Burrows' Ukrainian is not good, and neither is Lyuba's English yet, so they compromise by speaking their own languages to each other.

When we reach the yard, they sit on the bench together. Taras has proved himself able to make or find much of what we need and this rustic bench is exactly like the ones we would have had in the village by the cottage door.

'You should sit down too,' says Mrs Burrows.

'I will in a minute. I'll make our tea first.'

'You need to rest,' she insists.

I place my hand on my round belly and feel the new baby kicking. 'I'm fine,' I say, and I am. My babies will be close enough in age to play together. But she's right. When the tea is made I am glad to sit down with my girl and her aunty on this sunny day.

Mrs Burrows is peeling a banana for Lyuba. 'Do you remember the first time you had one of these?'

I smile at the memory of Mr Burrows bringing a bunch of bananas home from the market in a high state of excitement.

'Rose! Rose! Look what I found,' he had cried, holding up the yellow fruit.

'Bananas! I haven't seen any of those since before the war.'

He had bought four, one for each of us, although Taras and I had had to be taught how to open and eat them, just as Mrs Burrows is showing Lyuba now.

'There you are, sweetie,' she says, breaking off a chunk and holding it out for Lyuba to bite. 'You tuck into that. It'll help you grow up into a big girl.'

Lyuba chews on the soft fruit while we sip our tea.

Mrs Burrows smiles. 'She is a love. I wonder what your next one will be.'

'Another good one, I hope.'

'Have you chosen names yet?'

'Yes. If it's a girl, I'll call her Vera after my youngest sister. But if it's a boy, perhaps Ivan, for my father.' I look away at the hollyhocks and dahlias I have planted near the house and I wonder about the grown-up Lyubka and Verochka. 'I wish I knew how they are.'

'Of course you do.' She pats my knee. 'How's Taras? Busy as usual?' she asks, nodding to the shed where he has created his own sewing room.

'Oh yes. There have been a couple of weddings so he has had lots of suits to make.'

'Those men are very lucky to get such good quality suits.'

'And at good prices, although Taras makes some money too.'

'I should think so.'

'His boss, Mr Kapstein, has helped him a bit. He lets Taras buy fabric from the factory much cheaper than in the shop.'

'That's good of him. I suppose you finishing off the garments for Taras saves money as well.'

'Yes, and it's another thing I can do at home.'

'You must be careful not to overdo it, Natalya.'

'I am but we need the money.'

She sips her tea. 'There must be a lot of weddings with youngsters like yourselves getting married.'

'Yes, most of the girls are married now, but some of the men haven't been able to find Ukrainian girls.'

'Not enough of them, were there?'

'No, but they're finding English or Italian girls.'

'Well, it's only natural,' she says, breaking off another piece of banana for Lyuba. 'There you are, my pet.'

After we have drunk our tea, Mrs Burrows says, 'Shall we pod these peas, Lyuba?'

I go indoors to fetch a saucepan. When I return, Lyuba is

170

chuckling at the pop of the pods and discovering the sweetness of baby peas.

'Are you still cooking for everyone?'

'Yes,' I say. 'It's my job.' And it is. When they knew we were planning to buy a house, Lesia and Stefan begged us to let them have a room. Since their rent would enable us to borrow more to buy a slightly better house, we were happy to include them in our plans. Stefan has also helped Taras make our almost derelict house into a home. 'They go out to work,' I say to Mrs Burrows, 'and since I can't at the moment, I must work here.'

'But I hope you're going to have a rest this afternoon.'

'I will. I've only got to prepare tonight's dinner which isn't like hard work,' I say and I smile in case she thinks I'm being critical of when we lodged at her house. But she nods and I know she understands the joy of having my own kitchen.

She sips her tea and then says, 'You haven't got long to go now, have you?'

'A couple of weeks.'

'Let me know as soon as you need me and I'll come and look after little miss here.' She strokes Lyuba's fine baby hair. My child leans against her Aunty Rose and my heart constricts. She does not know her own *Baba* but this kind English woman has been a good substitute. When she stands up to leave, she kisses Lyuba's round cheek and gets a sticky banana kiss in return.

'Bye bye, Lyuba,' says Mrs Burrows.

'*Pa pa,*' says my baby.

They're not demonstrative, these English, but Mrs Burrows pats my arm as she goes. 'Call me as soon as you need me,' she says, and I can't help myself. I lean forward to kiss her soft pink cheek. 'I will,' I say.

Lyuba and I both have a nap before making the supper. When it is almost time for Taras to come home, we go out of the front door and stand on the pavement. I hold my baby up so she can call out when she sees her *Tato* coming up the street.

***

It is only a few days later when my waters break and my second baby announces her arrival to the world. A week later we take Vera to the Ukrainian Church to be baptised and this time it is Maryna, my roommate from the hostel, who stands as godmother. I wish it could be Olha, but Dmitro insists it is nearer to go home from Germany and so they are still there, in an unsettled existence. Taras and I have both written to them, urging them to join us but Dmitro won't budge.

There is little time to miss my dear friend though, as Vera demands a feed and Lyuba wants to play. I give Lyuba the doll Taras brought home for her from one of his trips to Petticoat Lane and she sings to it while I feed my newer baby. I was afraid I would not be able to love this one as much as her sister who has taken so much of my heart. But when Vera was born, I found a secret store of love especially for her. As I relax against the back of the secondhand armchair, I think of my own sisters again and wonder if they ever think of me. Lyubka will be twenty-two now so she must be married. Even Verochka at twenty would be a confirmed spinster if she's not already married. But were there any men left in the village? I sigh. So many questions but no answers. None of us here in exile have yet heard from home. We only know the fates of some of those who left. The rest is a mystery. Even the English press does not know what is happening behind the Iron Curtain.

***

But there is a momentous event which they can and do report the following March. I am at the window with Vera in my arms and Lyuba standing on a chair beside me looking out

172

for Taras. He comes hurrying down the street from work. When he sees me at the window, he waves a newspaper frantically at me. I help Lyuba down off the chair.

'Let's open the door for *Tato*.'

As I open the door, Taras almost knocks me over as he rushes in.

'Stalin's dead!' he shouts.

Vera begins to cry and Lyuba looks startled.

'What do you mean?' I ask.

'He's dead. He's dead at last.'

Lyuba now joins Vera in wailing loudly.

'You're frightening the children.'

'No, no, my little flowers. There's no need to cry.' He thrusts the newspaper at me and bends down to pick Lyuba up. He dances her around the small room. 'He's dead, he's dead,' he chants and Lyuba tries to join in with her father's excitement through her tears.

I put the newspaper on the table and read the headline: 'Stalin Dead' in big dark letters. I look at Taras who is still jigging about with Lyuba but I can't take it in. 'Is he truly dead?'

'Yes. The English papers wouldn't lie.'

I look back at the newspaper. There is a photograph of Stalin, smiling into the camera, his right hand raised. 'He won't be smiling anymore,' I say.

'No, but we will.'

I sit at the table and put Vera in my lap while I read that it took Moscow six hours to announce the dictator's death. 'Why do you think they waited so long?'

'To make sure the devil was really dead.'

'What do you think it will mean?' I ask Taras. But I dare not voice my next question… Can we go home now?

The front door rattles and Stefan and Lesia rush in, Stefan holding a bottle of vodka in his fist.

'He's dead, he's dead!' They are as delirious as Taras while I can't speak for shock.

'It was on the radio at work,' says Lesia. 'It's been on all day. The dictator of twenty-nine years…'

'The tyrant more like.'

'The English are too polite to say that.'

Stefan fetches glasses from the kitchen and pours us each a slug of vodka. He raises his own glass. 'May he burn in Hell.'

I hesitate and then think of my father shot dead in our yard and of the years without Mama and my sisters and I swallow the vodka in one eye-watering gulp.

The men sit at the table and Stefan pours a second glass.

'Not for me,' I say. 'I'll get the dinner.'

Lesia takes off her coat and headscarf and takes Vera from me while I go and boil water for our *varenyki*.

When I serve them, Stefan says, 'Good choice, Natalya. A perfect Ukrainian meal to celebrate.'

'Should we celebrate?'

'Aren't you glad he's dead?' asks Lesia.

'Of course, but what comes next?'

Taras looks at me. 'What do you mean?'

'Well, will Ukraine suddenly be free? Someone will take over. Beria, for example.'

'That bastard,' says Stefan.

'Stefan, the girls,' I murmur.

'Sorry.'

Taras helps Lyuba load her fork. 'Natalya's right. We don't know who will take over but whoever it is, they won't want to give Ukraine away.'

'The British and the Americans might help us now,' says Lesia.

'I doubt it,' says Taras. 'They've done nothing to help Ukraine in the last eight years.'

'They might have been afraid of Stalin.'

'With good cause,' I say.

174

'Come on,' says Stefan, 'let's not get gloomy about this. We've been living out of suitcases for more than ten years and now it's over. Today we celebrate, tomorrow we'll find out how we can go home.'

1953
Chapter 25

She hummed as she picked, leaning over the bank of the bramble's whippy stems and prickly leaves. The thorns plucked at her skirt but Vera was not concerned. The cotton was heavy and could withstand snags and tears. She cleared the area in front of her of its ripe fruit and moved on to the next mound of plants on the south side of the wood. She continued to pick the delicate berries, squashing the occasional overripe one between her fingers but licking them clean of their sweet dark juice. When she had stripped the bushes, she glanced around to see if anyone else was taking advantage of the wood's bounty. There was no one. She was alone. Alone on a late summer's day.

She stepped off the path and went deeper into the wood until she came to the other plant she was seeking. It was a tall bush, almost two metres high whose bell-shaped flowers had given way to shiny black berries. She withdrew a small cotton square from her sleeve and opened it out. She picked five of the smooth round berries being careful not to puncture their skin, and then wrapped them in the fabric which she tucked into her blouse where it was looped over the waistband of her skirt. She stepped back onto the path and followed it out of the wood.

At home, Vera cooked the blackberries so when the boys came in, breathless from their race up the lane, she could give them some of the fruit with a slice of bread.

'Can I have another piece, Mama?' asked four-year-old Andriy.

'You can have some more bread but leave the fruit for your father. You know how much he likes it.'

'He'll give me his share,' said Andriy, confident of his

176

father's patronage.

'Only if he's home before you go to bed.'

Vera's sons knew better than to ask where their father had gone and the hours passed until their bedtime without Kripak reappearing. Michaylo and Andriy now shared the bed their mother and aunt had shared as girls, while Lyubka slept on a settle in the room with her nephews.

As soon as she heard Kripak lift the latch, Lyubka nodded goodnight to Vera and went into the bedroom, leaving her sister alone with her husband. Vera went to the stove to stir the soup she had ready for Kripak but, as he stumped over to the table, he said, 'Don't bother. I've already eaten.'

'I have some blackberries. Will you eat them cold?'

'No. Warm them up for me.'

She placed the pot on the stove and stirred the fruit with her back to him. She slid her hand into her blouse and carefully extracted the five berries she had picked. She dropped them into the pan and stirred again with the metal spoon.

'Don't make it too hot.'

'I won't.'

She poured the fruit into a bowl and took it over to him.

He took the bowl and, leaning over the table, shovelled the sweet fruit into his mouth. When he had finished, he grunted. 'Anymore?'

'There's a little bit but I was saving it for Andriy.'

'Give it here.'

She spooned the last of the fruit from the pan into his bowl. He didn't wait for her to finish, but ate as she served him.

Vera washed the pot and spoon, pouring the waste water into the empty slop bucket. No one would touch it even if she did not get up before everyone else to dispose of it well away from any other living creature.

However, Vera was woken while it was still dark. Kripak was thrashing about in the bed and shouting loud curses. She tried to wake him by shaking his shoulder.

'Wake up. You're dreaming.'

She was not able to rouse him from his nightmare. He continued to cry out for some time before falling silent. Vera listened to his breathing. As soon as it became even again, she fell asleep.

Vera woke early and rose to take the slop bucket outside before either her sister or her sons were awake. She opened the cottage door to a sky streaked with red and black clouds. She walked down the garden to the far corner where the weeds were heaped and emptied the bucket onto the pile. When she returned to the house, she made sure her hands were clean before milking the cow and feeding the hens.

Kripak woke later than usual that morning. 'I have a terrible headache,' he groaned.

'Did you have a drink wherever it was that you ate your supper?'

He looked at her blankly. 'I'm not sure. I can't remember.' He sat immobile in the bed, searching through the events of the previous evening.

'Do you want some *kasha* now?'

'Maybe.'

There was a knock at the door. Vera went over to open it.

'Morning Missis. Is he ready?' asked Zladko.

'Not yet. He'll be out shortly,' she said, closing the door on him. 'Zladko seems to think you should be ready. Have you got an appointment?'

He climbed out of bed and poked his skinny legs into the trousers he had dropped on the floor the previous night.

She watched him struggling with his fly buttons and asked, '*Kasha*?'

'No. Give me some water.'

She passed him a cup of water and watched while he tried to drink it. She could see he was thirsty but he dribbled most of it down his chin. He thrust the cup back at her, wiped his face on his shirtsleeve, and stumbled across the room, dropping onto the bench to put his boots on at the door. He heaved on his leather jacket, picked up his two-metre ramrod for rattling out traitors, and left.

As soon as he had gone, Lyubka came out of the second room. 'Is he alright?' she asked.

'Yes, why?'

'He seems worse than usual.'

'I think he's hungover.'

'Did I hear him shouting in the night?'

'Yes. He had a nightmare.'

'Conscience hurting him?' asked Lyubka.

'I doubt it.'

'Grief for Comrade Stalin?'

Vera looked at her sister, putting her finger over her lips but she could not help her eyes sparkling.

'The whole country's in mourning,' continued Lyubka in the same dry tone.

'Of course. How will we manage without our dear Father?'

'Better than before...if we're lucky.'

Vera looked towards the door. 'I don't know,' she said, returning to the subject of Kripak. 'You know how hard he's been working in the last few months. Maybe he wants to make sure of his own position.'

'Especially after the bonfire.'

There had been a flurry of activity in the NKVD offices shortly after the announcement of Stalin's death, followed by a bonfire which had consumed much of the paperwork of recent years.

'Whoever takes over, they'll still be Bolsheviks,' said Lyubka.

'They will indeed since they've killed all the opposition.' Vera turned away so her sister could not see her face. 'I'm going out to pick some more fruit later. Will you keep an eye on the boys?'

'Of course, but I can go and pick the fruit if you'd like me to.'

'No, I'll go.'

'Alright,' said Lyubka.

Later, Vera set off towards the hedgerows beyond the wood, returning by the damp, shady spot she had visited on the previous day. This time as she picked, she counted under her breath until she had twenty smooth black berries. She wrapped them in the same piece of cotton cloth and stowed them carefully in her blouse. As she stepped over the undergrowth to the path, she checked her fingertips. They were clean.

Her heart turned over at the sudden thought of *Baba* Chara. 'Be very careful when you handle the black berries.' Had the old witch known even then what Vera would be driven to?

As she walked towards home, Vera stopped to pick more blackberries, filling her basket to the top and not letting herself dwell on the memory of the old woman in the stinking hovel. When she reached her garden, Andriy saw her first.

'Oh, good, you've got lots.'

'Yes, my son. There should be enough this time.'

In a quiet moment when the house was empty, Vera took the parcel of berries from her blouse. She placed it in a drawer among her menstrual cloths, certain that no one, not even Lyubka, would look there.

The boys had finished their supper and gone to bed by the time Kripak came home accompanied by Zladko.

'I've brought him home for you,' said the henchman.

'Why? Is he drunk again?'

Kripak sat down heavily on the bench. 'Boots.'

'No, but he's not been himself today.'

'Was he ill?' asked Vera, bending to pull off Kripak's boots.

'Not really…but he was complaining of chest pains.'

'Chest pains?' Vera looked up at her husband.

'Indigestion,' he mumbled.

'Maybe you just need a good night's sleep.'

'I'll leave him to you, Missis. See you tomorrow, comrade,' said Zladko and left.

'You've missed the boys,' said Vera.

Kripak grunted.

'Would you like some supper?'

'What have you got?'

'*Borshch*. Blackberries.'

'Blackberries. And some water. I've been thirsty all day.'

Watching him from the corner of her eye, Vera bustled about, reaching for the cotton parcel she had placed above the stove after the boys had gone to bed. She dropped the smooth black berries into the pot of wholesome fruit, bursting them open with the back of the metal spoon as she stirred.

When she handed him the bowl, he asked, 'Any cream?'

She shook her head. 'No, the boys ate the last of it.'

'You spoil them.'

'They're growing. They need to eat.'

'Make some more.'

'I will,' she said, but not yet, she thought. The cream would line his stomach and weaken the berries' effect.

Vera watched him eating the warm fruit while she tidied the kitchen. He was swallowing more easily than he had in the morning, but he was eating more slowly than usual. Nevertheless, he finished all the fruit.

Once again, Kripak woke Vera in the night.

'Get away!' he was bellowing.

She reached for the lamp and lit it to see him sitting bolt upright. 'What is it?'

'No! No!' he yelled.

She tried to touch him but he flinched from her, screaming.

'What's wrong?' she asked again, trying to feel his chest. Before he could thrust her hand away, she felt his heart pounding against his ribs.

The door to the second room creaked open. Vera turned at the noise. Lyubka was peering out with the boys clinging to her night shirt. Andriy pushed the door open wider and he and Michaylo approached the bed, Kripak bawling all the while.

'What's wrong with *Tato*?' asked Michaylo.

'I don't know.' Vera touched Kripak's arm. 'Do you want some water?'

But her question was met by a long shriek. It seemed as if Kripak would hold the note forever but he suddenly fell silent.

'*Tatu*,' sobbed Andriy. He too reached out to his father but Kripak yelled, 'Get back! Stand back now!' He began to rummage among the bed clothes.

'He wants his gun,' said Michaylo.

'God help us,' whispered Lyubka. 'He'll kill us all.'

She hurried across the room to where Kripak's jacket hung on the nail behind the door. She took the gun from the pocket, then glanced at Vera.

'The rod,' Vera mouthed to her sister.

Lyubka nodded and, taking the fierce metal ramrod, she slipped out into the darkness clutching both of the mad man's weapons to her breast.

Vera remained beside the bed, holding her sons to her while Kripak continued to search the bedding.

When Lyubka returned, she closed the door securely and came to stand beside the little family. 'What can we do?'

'Fetch Zladko?'

'What can he do?'

'I don't know. Go for a doctor?'

'But it's still dark,' said Michaylo.

Vera stroked his head. 'The curfew doesn't apply to everybody.'

Kripak seemed to have given up searching the bed. He stared at the group in front of him. 'Who's there? Who are you?'

The little boys began to cry again.

'It's only us,' said Vera. 'I'm here…and Michaylo and Andriy…'

'Who's she?' demanded Kripak.

'Lyubka. You know Lyubka.'

He peered at them from the bed.

'Can I get you some water?' asked Vera.

'Yes, water.'

Vera unwound herself from the boys, handing them over to their aunt while she fetched Kripak a cup of water. When she drew near the bed, she offered him the cup. He smashed it out of her hand and shrieked as the water struck his skin. He fell back onto the bed screaming in agony.

'Mama,' cried Andriy, 'what did you give him?'

'Just water,' said Vera. 'Look.' She picked up the cup.

Andriy touched the few remaining drops. 'Why is he doing that?'

'I don't know, my son.'

The women stared at the man screaming in the bed and wondered how long he might keep this up. They held the children close to them, wishing the boys did not have to witness the scene before them but knowing it would be worse for them if they could only hear their father raving. They stood holding one another until Kripak fell back on to the bed exhausted. He lay breathing stertorously for some time before beginning to thrash about. Then he began to work himself up into a frenzy again.

'I'll fetch Zladko,' said Lyubka and she hurried into the bedroom to fling on some clothes. She returned within moments and said, 'I'll be as quick as I can.'

When Lyubka had left the cottage, Vera spoke to her sons. 'You'll get cold standing here. Fetch your *pyryna* and sit on the bench.'

While the boys went into their room to pull the eiderdown

off their bed, Vera went to stoke up the fire in the stove. She opened the fire door and riddled the warm embers back into flame. She placed small sticks over the remains of the fire and, as they caught, she dropped the cloth in which she had gathered the berries, into the stove. She placed bigger pieces of wood over the cloth and then closed the door as the boys returned, pulling their quilt between them.

'Jump up on the bench,' she said and then she draped them with their warm duvet, making a nest for them.

It was not long before Lyubka returned with Zladko, who slept on a cot in a storeroom above the NKVD office. He wiped his feet as he entered the cottage but glanced at Vera as he tiptoed across the room in his boots. Kripak was lying on his back mumbling to himself as Zladko leaned over him.

'Now then, comrade,' he said loudly. 'What's the matter?'

Kripak turned his head towards the voice but appeared unable to make sense of what he was hearing. He stared at Zladko and began to mumble again.

'What? Don't you know me?'

Kripak continued to stare at the man with whom he had sought, tortured and killed.

'His eyes look strange,' said Zladko.

Vera looked more closely. Kripak's pupils were dilated despite the dim light cast by the lamp.

'I don't know why,' said Vera.

Zladko shook Kripak's shoulder. 'What's wrong, comrade?'

At his touch Kripak began to shout, 'Get off me!' He reared up in the bed, bellowing at the top of his voice. The watchers waited until he had bawled himself out.

'How long's he been like this?' asked Zladko.

'About an hour,' said Vera.

'He's very hot.'

'Yes. I tried to give him some water but he wouldn't take it.'

'He's not sweating though.'

184

'No,' said Vera. 'I don't know what to do.'

'I think I'll fetch the doctor,' said Zladko. 'It won't take me long to drive to Buchach.'

'Don't leave us,' cried Andriy.

Zladko looked at Vera.

'They're frightened,' she said. 'We all are.'

Zladko continued to ponder the problem.

'Could you send someone else?' asked Vera.

The big man looked relieved. 'Yes, that's what I'll do. I'll go and wake Postyuk now. I'll be back soon,' he told the boys as he hurried from the cottage.

Vera and Lyubka slumped on the bench beside the boys and leaned against one another. Everyone dozed until a knock on the door told them Zladko had returned. Lyubka got up to open the door and, as she let in Kripak's henchman, she noticed the darkness of the sky cracking open to let in a sliver of light in the cold dawn.

'I've sent Postyuk for the doctor,' said Zladko. 'I told him to hurry so he should be back in less than an hour.' He walked over to the bed. 'He seems quieter,' he said, standing over the man who had ordered him about for the last six years.

Vera stood on the other side of the bed and they both watched Kripak lying on his back, his mouth wide open, snoring loudly. They stood for some time then Vera fetched a stool for Zladko.

'Sit. We don't know how long the doctor will be.'

'I told Postyuk not to take no for an answer.'

Vera felt a moment's sympathy for the doctor, opening the door in the dark with the NKVD car parked outside his house.

Before Zladko sat down, he took off his coat. He turned to put it on the corner of the bed but as he swung it round it caught the stool which fell over with a loud clatter.

The noise startled them, but it woke Kripak. He sat up straight in the bed and shouted, 'Who's there?' When he received no reply, he shouted again. 'Speak up. Who's there? I'll find you,' and he looked to either side for the long metal rod. 'You can't hide from me,' he roared.

'It's alright, comrade, no one's hiding from you,' said Zladko, as he tried to make Kripak lie down again. But Kripak struggled like a wild thing. Zladko tightened his hold. 'Now stop this foolishness…' but Kripak would not be held. He managed to wriggle out of Zladko's grasp and leapt from the bed.

As Vera and Zladko moved closer to Kripak, he ran towards them, his face bright red, his mouth wide open, roaring incoherently before faltering. He clutched his chest and groaned, 'The pain…'

Vera tried to get close to him as he continued to grasp at his chest.

'I can't breathe…' he gasped.

Again they moved towards him, one on each side, but before either of them could reach him, he stopped, still groaning, stood erect for a second, then fell to the floor in a heap.

There was a moment's silence. Vera hurried towards Kripak's inert figure. She touched his back and, looking up at Zladko, said, 'Help me turn him over.'

As they rolled him over, the big man asked, 'Is he dead?'

Vera put her hand on Kripak's chest but all was still. She looked up at Zladko. 'I don't know. I can't feel his heart,' she whispered.

Zladko felt for Kripak's pulse in his neck and shook his head.

'Mama,' cried Michaylo.

Vera turned towards her sons. She rose and went across the room to them, taking them in her arms.

'Is *Tato* dead?'

'I think so, my loves.'

The boys set up a howling, releasing the terror they had

186

been feeling since their father had woken them in his delirium. Lyubka moved towards them and put her arms around mother and sons.

This was the sight which met the doctor when he entered the cottage.

'Now then, what's going on here?' he asked.

He stepped forward to where Kripak lay on the floor and knelt beside him. He tried to find a pulse in Kripak's neck but found nothing. He turned to Vera. 'Could the boys go with their aunt?'

Vera nodded and Lyubka shepherded the boys to their room.

'What's he going to do?' asked Andriy.

'He's just going to examine *Tato*, that's all,' Lyubka replied as she closed the bedroom door.

The doctor turned back to his patient. 'Did he fall on his back like this?' he asked.

'No,' said Zladko. 'We turned him over.'

'How long ago was that?'

'Not long.'

The doctor took his stethoscope from his bag and, holding the man's shirt open, he listened for a heartbeat. Then he held his hand in front of Kripak's mouth and nose but felt no breath. He took a small torch from his bag and, lifting each eyelid in turn, he shone the light in Kripak's eyes. The pupils did not change. He tried to find a pulse once more, but failing to do so, said, 'I'm sorry. He is dead.' He looked up at Vera and Zladko. 'Had he been unwell recently?'

'He said he had had some chest pain yesterday,' said Vera, 'but he thought it was just indigestion.'

'Did you see him yesterday?' asked the doctor, looking at Zladko.

'Yes. He was odd all day. Not quite with it. He kept grumbling about the pain in his chest until I brought him home last night.'

'And then what?'

'He had a bit of supper and went to bed,' said Vera. 'He woke us though a couple of hours ago. He was yelling as if in a nightmare.'

The doctor looked at her. 'Yelling?'

'Yes. We couldn't make any sense of what he was saying and the boys were frightened so Lyubka went for Zladko.'

'What did you do?'

'I couldn't get any sense out of him either. He was roaring and making himself really hot.' He paused and then added, 'He was clutching his chest before he collapsed.'

The doctor looked at Vera.

She swallowed and said, 'He was crying out that he was in pain.'

'And then?'

'He collapsed.'

'That's when we turned him over,' said Zladko, 'but we couldn't hear his heartbeat.'

'Hmm,' said the doctor. 'It sounds like a heart attack to me.' He paused. 'We should move the body. Where do you want him?'

'On the bed,' said Vera.

Vera hurried over to remove the bedding and straighten the bottom sheet while the men lifted Kripak.

When the body had been laid on the mattress, the doctor turned to Vera. 'Do you know what to do or do I need to call *Pani* Lazarenko to help you?'

'We did it for our Mama,' she murmured.

'Ah. Well, in that case, I'll leave you to your work and presumably you,' he turned to Zladko, 'will organise the digging of the grave.'

'Yes, comrade.'

'Then I must get back to Buchach. I'll fill out the death

188

certificate when I get back. Someone can come and collect it later…But now, I have patients who will be waiting for me. My condolences,' said the doctor with a final glance at Vera as he left the cottage.

'As he says, I'll get on with the grave,' said Zladko. 'I'll be back later.'

Vera nodded. 'Thank you.'

As the outer door closed, Lyubka came out of the bedroom alone.

'What did the doctor say?'

'Heart attack.'

Lyubka went to embrace her sister but Vera shook her head. 'The boys.'

'Shall I take them to *Pani* Lazarenko's?'

'Yes, please.'

Lyubka went over to pick up the boys' *pyryna* and returned to the bedroom, saying, 'Come now, we need to get you dressed.'

When they came out of the bedroom, Michaylo and Andriy looked towards their father lying on the bed. Before they could begin to cry again, Vera went towards them and embraced them, standing between them and the body of their dead father. '*Teta* Lyubka will take you to *Pani* Lazarenko's while we look after *Tato*.'

'What do you have to do?' asked Michaylo.

'We have to wash him and get him ready for the funeral.'

'Will it be today?'

'Yes, probably,' said Vera. 'It will depend on Zladko's men.'

'Come on, boys,' said Lyubka.

When they had gone, Vera fetched water from the well and set it to boil in a pan on the stove. They would wash Kripak's body and prepare him for the burial which would take place quickly before the body could begin to decompose.

As soon as Lyubka returned, she asked Vera again, 'Are you

alright?'

'Yes, I am. Let's get this done.' She went to the stove and poured the hot water into a bowl which she took over to the bed.

'Shall I help you take his shirt off?' asked Lyubka.

Vera shook her head. 'I'm going to cut it off.'

Lyubka looked surprised.

'Well, who would wear it? I'll wash it and we'll use it for rags.'

Lyubka watched while Vera took the scissors and cut along the centre of the shirt up to the placket. Then Lyubka helped Vera draw the corpse's arms out of the sleeves. Vera threw the shirt on the floor and passed Lyubka a piece of fabric. They moistened their cloths and began to wash Kripak from the head down. Although Lyubka followed Vera's lead in laying out the man who had both terrorised and protected them, she was glad he was dead.

The sisters worked dry-eyed to prepare the body for burial, not blinded by the tears which had accompanied the laying out of their mother. Vera took a thin piece of cotton and cut it into small segments to block Kripak's orifices. She looked up to see Lyubka watching her.

'I'm alright.'

'I know. I just can't help being worried about you.'

'I'm alright,' she said again. She looked down at the body on the bed. 'He can't hurt anyone now.'

'No.' Lyubka sighed.

'He deserved the agony he was in.'

Something in Vera's tone made Lyubka look up. 'Verochka?'

Vera returned her gaze and then lowered her chin in a slow nod.

Lyubka drew in her breath and went to her sister's side. She put her arms around her and held her close, neither of them saying a word. Lyubka could feel Vera trying to hold herself in check. She stroked her sister's back. 'It's alright, my love,' she said.

Vera broke then and the tension of the last few days flooded out in her tears. She sobbed with relief in Lyubka's arms.

There was a knock at the door. Zladko opened it and poked his head into the cottage. He took in the sight of Vera's distress. 'Oh, I'm sorry. I just wanted to tell you, the coffin and the grave will be ready soon. But we can wait if you want us to.'

'No, let's go ahead,' said Lyubka. 'We've almost finished dressing him.'

'I'll come back with the men to carry him to the cemetery,' he said.

Lyubka thanked him while Vera blew her nose and mopped up her face.

Zladko slipped back out of the cottage closing the door gently behind him.

'Can you manage this?' whispered Lyubka.

'Yes,' said Vera taking a deep breath. She went to the drawer to pull out fresh clothing for Kripak. They dressed him in a clean white shirt and his black trousers.

'What about his jacket?' asked Lyubka.

'We'll put it on him. I don't ever want to see that again.'

It was a struggle to get him into the creaking leather jacket but in the end he lay as he had lived, wearing the wretched garment.

'What did you do with his gun?'

'It's under the manure heap. With the rod,' said Lyubka.

'They can stay there for now.'

'He wouldn't want any prayers, would he?' asked Lyubka.

'They won't help him where he's going,' said Vera. Nor me, she thought.

Lyubka stroked Vera's back. 'You did the right thing, Verochka. He would have wanted to start showing Michaylo the devil's work,' she whispered.

'I know but we must never talk about these things again,' Vera whispered back.

'We won't need to. I will always be with you.'

'And I with you.'

They stood in silence for a moment, then Vera shook herself. 'The boys.'

'Yes. I'll go and fetch them.'

While Lyubka collected the boys from *Pani* Lazarenko's, Vera washed her face and re-plaited her hair. She put on the black headscarf she had worn for her mother's funeral, murmuring, 'I'm sorry, Mama.' By the time her sister returned, Vera was ready to face the village.

But first, she drew the boys to the bedside. 'Let's say goodbye.'

The boys leaned over their father in turn to kiss his forehead. They began to cry again but Lyubka hugged them and washed their faces as she had done since they were born.

'What about Mama?' asked Michaylo, through his tears.

'What about her?'

'Will she die too?'

'Not yet.'

'How do you know?'

'Because she isn't ill.' Lyubka wiped Michaylo's face. 'There's no need to worry. You have both of us to look after you,' and she hugged the boys to her.

There was a loud knock at the door and Vera went to open it. Zladko stood in the yard with a dozen of Kripak's cronies and men from the Militia. Two of them held a pine coffin on its end while others held the lid.

'Wait a moment,' she said. 'I'll bring the children outside.' She turned back into the cottage. 'Let's wait in the garden.'

Lyubka led the boys out and Vera turned with her to take her sons into the vegetable garden. They stood and waited with their backs to the lane where some of the villagers had gathered. Zladko led the men back out of the cottage. They struggled with the coffin through the low doorway but then rested it in the yard on two blocks of wood. The lid had not yet been placed on it. The sisters came to stand beside the coffin with the children between them so the men of the Militia and anyone else could pay their respects to the man who had torn lives apart.

When those who wanted to had filed past, the lid was placed on the coffin and hammered down. As each blow was struck, the women held the boys to them, then they turned to follow the men carrying the coffin down the lane to the cemetery.

Since God was dead, Kripak was merely placed in a hole in the ground. His henchman mumbled a few words which he hoped were appropriate and the earth was shovelled over the coffin.

Chapter 26

I sit at our table with the thin blue paper in front of me. The house is completely quiet. My girls are having their afternoon nap and Taras and our lodgers are at work. I look at the airmail paper and think about what I want to write. What is it safe to write? Yesterday, at church, one of our community had received a letter from home. We were so excited. As if the letter was for each one of us. We crowded around the man with the letter and listened to him reading out snippets from it.

What shall I tell my family? Where shall I start?

I look out of the kitchen window and see the sunflowers my baby Lyuba and I planted, and I think of my mother and my sisters. Even though Stalin is dead, am I putting them in danger by writing? But I want to write to them so much. I pick up my pen.

My dearest Mama, and my dear little sisters, Lyubka and Verochka…

I know my sisters are now grown women but I can't help seeing them as the girls they were, disappearing behind the dust the wagon threw up as I left the village eleven years ago.

I hope you are in good health, my dearest ones. I have thought of you every day since I left home and have longed to know how you are. I am well and so much has happened to me since I last saw you. As you can see from the address I am now living in England. I am married to a good man who comes from Tishiv in Lvivska Oblast. We met in Germany where Taras had also been sent to work. We have two little daughters whom I named Lyuba and Vera after you, my dearest sisters. Lyuba is three and Vera is almost a year old.

Mamochko, you would love them and they would love you, I am sure.

We have our own little house and you can write to me here if it is possible for you to do so.

I cross the last bit out. I don't want to give anyone who might read the letter any ideas.

We have a garden, although it is not as big as the one we have at home. But, Mama, you would be proud of me if you could see it. Apart from some flowers near the house it is full of vegetables. We keep our own chickens. I think of you every day but I think of you especially when I am in the garden. I am always asking myself, how would Mama do this?

I kiss your hands, dearest Mama, and I live with the hope that we will meet again soon. England is not so very far away. Take care of each other and please write to me to tell me how you are.

Your loving daughter and sister,
Natalya.

I seal up the letter. I'll send them a photograph of our little family if I get a reply. My heart thumps at that thought…when I get a reply.

Just as soon as my little girls wake up, we walk down the street to the Post Office. I place my blue letter under the grille and the postmistress weighs it.

'That's going a long way,' she says, looking at the initials USSR.

'To my Mama and sisters,' I say. I swallow sudden tears. 'It is the first time.'

She looks at me through the wire. 'The first time you're writing to them?'

'It was not possible before.'

She smiles. 'Won't they be excited to hear from you?'

I smile back. 'I hope.'

But I don't find out whether they were excited for some

time. The weeks pass, and autumn arrives before a letter.

The reply comes in the middle of an afternoon, by the second post. I am giving my girls a drink after their naps when I hear the letter box rattle and an envelope falls onto the mat. I put Vera in the baby chair and go to pick up the blue envelope. It is not the blue of my airmail envelope but a plain soft blue paper with four red stamps carrying the letters CCCP. It is addressed to me, with my name, my old name, Natalya Ivanovna Palmarenko, in the middle of the envelope. It's in the middle because the writer has set out the address beginning with the country, England, and then the town and the street, all written first in Cyrillic letters and then in English. After my name, a line has been ruled and then begins the sender's address starting with YPCP and ending with the name Lyubka Ivanovna Palmarenko.

This gives me pause. Why is Lyubka writing the letter and not Mama? I realise as I look at the envelope that it is not Mama's small tight handwriting but Lyubka's more open script. My heart thumps in my chest as I pull at the kitchen drawer to get a knife to slit open the letter. The envelope contains a sheet of lined paper taken from a child's exercise book. The writing covers every bit of space, from edge to edge, on both sides. I try to grasp its message but realise I'm not reading it, it's all a blur. I make myself start from the beginning. I read it in a whisper to make myself focus on its meaning.

V pershe, Slava Isusu Christu…To begin with, Praise Jesus Christ…

I find myself replying to this greeting, 'Praise Him forever…' before making my eyes read the next words:

Natalya, our dear sister, it is Lyubka who is writing to you. Verochka is here beside me as I write.

I stop to look out of the window. It is beginning to rain and the wind is picking up. I force my eyes back to the paper.

We are so sorry to tell you our beloved Mama is not with us.

She left this world forever in 1947 when there was an outbreak of typhus in the village. We did all we could for her, dearest Natalya, but we could not save her. We buried her with Tato…

Somewhere, I can hear somebody howling and I look down at my own little Lyuba who is staring at me with her mouth wide open. I realise the noise must be coming from me so I put my hand over my mouth to push it back in. My baby Vera has also realised something new is happening because she too is staring at me. I look back at them and say, 'Your *Baba* is…' but I can't say the word. It is too big for them. I don't know how to contain the feelings which are threatening to burst out of me so I look at the clock. Taras won't be home for another two hours. I can't wait that long. I lift Vera into the pram and say to Lyuba, 'We're going to see *Tato*.'

As I open the front door, I see the rain has got heavier so I squeeze Lyuba into the pram beside her baby sister, under the hood. I try to clip the cover over their legs but I can't do the last clip up. I just leave it and manoeuvre the pram out of the house. I slam the door and walk as fast as I can down the street. When I reach the corner I hurry across the road, tipping the pram over the kerb and turn towards the town and Taras's factory. The pram wheels hiss against the wet pavement as we bowl along. Both babies are crying now as they bump against one another. We reach the factory and I turn to pull the pram up the three steps onto the concrete platform by the door. I pull at the heavy door and hold it open with my hip while I pull the pram into the factory after me.

I can no longer hear my babies crying over the noise of the sewing machines and the radio which is on full blast. I leave the pram inside the door and run along the long room, past the rows of machinists to the far end where Taras's room is. I pull open the door into an oasis of calm. There are no machines here, only long tables where Taras makes the patterns and cuts out the cloth for the garments which are made in their hundreds. He looks up at me from across the room.

'Natalya?'

I run to him.

He doesn't move but continues to stare at me. I have to get to him. When I reach him, I throw myself against him and cling to him.

'Natalya, what's happened?' He holds me tight, but then he says, 'You're wet. Is it raining? Where's your coat?'

I can't speak but grip his shirt sleeves in my fists.

'Taras, Taras,' I hear someone calling.

'Where are the girls?' asks Taras. 'Has something happened to the girls?' He moves me with him back to the open doorway where his boss has appeared.

'What's going on, Taras? Your children are out here crying...' He stares at me. 'Is everything alright?'

I can't find the words to explain to him. There is too much to explain so I turn to Taras. 'It's Mama,' I say to him. 'She's dead.'

'Oh, Natalya,' he says and holds me to him.

Now I can cry. I howl against his chest and let my grief pour out of me. I don't care who can hear me. I howl on and on while Taras holds me tight.

Eventually I am able to pause for breath and Taras gives me his large white handkerchief to wipe myself up.

'Have you had a letter?' he asks.

I nod.

He holds me again and rocks me as I swallow and try to recover from the storm. Then he says, 'Natalya, where are the children?'

'Here,' I say and we go out onto the factory floor where I see Lesia and another woman holding my little girls. They have found a bit of chocolate and are breaking it into small pieces for the girls to suck. It is too far to walk to them. I sink down onto a chair by the wall while Taras walks the length of the room to gather up our daughters who are no longer crying but whose faces are covered in chocolate. He takes the baby from Lesia and, holding Lyuba's hand, he walks towards me. Lyuba is smiling at the women as she goes past the rows of machinists and is nodding and waving as they greet her.

'Hello, darling…'

'Hello, sweetie. Come to see your Daddy, have you?'

They reach me and I try to take Lyuba onto my lap but she's too interested in the attention from these smiling ladies to need me now.

Taras's boss reappears and I sense, rather than hear their conversation. Taras leans over me and says, 'Come, I'll take you home. He says I can make the time up later.' Taras takes the girls with him into his room to fetch his coat and I sit and wait. Lesia approaches me and, as Taras emerges from his room, she takes the baby again while Taras gives me his coat to put on. I look up and see Taras mouthing to Lesia, 'Her Mama.'

When he has put on his coat around me, he takes Vera in one arm and leads Lyuba with his other hand back to their pram. As I stand up, Lesia takes me in her arms and holds me tight for a moment before we walk towards the factory door where my husband is arranging our daughters in their pram. I follow Taras out of the factory. He lowers the pram down the steps and we return to our little home.

He waits until we are in the house before asking me anything more. He picks up the letter which is lying on the floor where I dropped it and sits on a chair with the little girls.

'Have you read all of it?' he asks.

I shake my head.

'Want me to read it to you?'

I nod and continue to stand.

He begins again with the greeting, '*Slava Isusu Christu…*' and I have to hear him say aloud the words which told me Mama had been dead for the last seven years. I pay a different kind of attention when he reaches the words I have not yet read.

This must be a shock for you, dearest Natalya, but despite our loss, Verochka and I are alive and well. We were very happy to hear about our namesakes, your little daughters, and about your good husband. I am not married but Verochka was and she has two young boys. Michaylo is five and Andriy is four. Verochka's husband was very ill and died quite suddenly so we are just two women in the house with our lovely boys.

We still have the garden you will remember and it keeps us well supplied, as do the hens and the cow. So you see, Natalya, we are lucky to have had God's blessings so far and although winter is almost here we have enough wood. We have not had the first snow yet. There is no need to worry about us. We are looking after one another as we hope you and your husband are looking after each other. If you can, please send us a photograph of your family.

That's all for now, dearest sister, brother-in-law and dear little nieces.

Lyubka and Verochka

Taras puts down the letter and takes me in his arms. He speaks low in my ear. 'I am very sorry, my dearest, about your Mama.' He rocks me a little and rubs my back, then he says, 'There is much to be happy about though, Natalya. Your sisters are alive and it sounds as if they are managing well together.'

He's right but I can't take in the rest of their news yet. I can only hear the words about Mama. I cannot believe she is no longer in this world and that I will never see her again. I cannot believe I didn't know she'd gone. How have I lived all this time without knowing? The tears come again and Taras sits me down and makes me a cup of tea.

Time passes while I sit and stare. Taras feeds our little girls and when Lesia comes home from work, she helps him to bathe them and put them to bed. There is much whispering when

Stefan comes home and then he goes out again almost straight away. The routines of our home have been broken but everything which needs to be done is done. By the time Stefan returns, Lesia and Taras have cooked a meal too. They serve the food and the four of us sit around our table. I stare at my plate. I have no need to eat.

Taras takes my hand and says, 'You must eat. Our children need their Mama just as much as you have needed yours. In fact, they need you more. They are only babies.'

'I know,' I manage to whisper but I want to say, Not yet. I'll do it tomorrow, but not yet.

He continues. 'Stefan has been to see Mrs Burrows and she's going to come and help you with the girls tomorrow and he's been to see Father Yaroslav. He will say Mass for your Mama on Sunday.'

I look at Stefan who is staring at me across the table, his brown eyes anxious that I should approve of his arrangements. 'Thank you,' I say.

He nods. 'Nothing can replace your Mama but we are your family too.' He gets up and comes around the table to kiss the top of my head.

He's right. This is my little family, these strangers I met coming across Europe into exile…but I also have my flesh and blood family in my home thousands of miles away.

Chapter 27

Vera came across the snow-filled yard carrying the empty slop bucket. She was surprised to see the postman walking towards her.

'*Dobroho dnya*,' he called.

'Good day,' she replied.

He pushed her gate open. 'You have a parcel,' he said, handing her a small rectangular package.

She put the bucket down and wiped her hands on her skirt before taking the brown paper parcel from him. 'Thank you,' she said.

'It's come all the way from England,' he said, watching her face.

'My sister,' said Vera. 'It must be from my sister.' She turned the package over in her hands and saw the clumsy re-sealing. She touched the creased tape.

'They have to open all parcels,' said the postman.

'Yes. Of course they do.' She looked up at him. 'Thank you again.'

'Well, good day to you and I hope it's good news,' he said, turning towards her gate.

Vera stood a moment longer, touching the stiff brown paper which she knew Natalya must have folded with her own hands. Then with a thump of the heart she remembered the blue envelope of Natalya's first letter. Baba Chara could not see what had happened to Natalya when Vera had visited the wise woman. She could only see the colour blue. Vera stroked the paper as she entered the house.

Lyubka was cleaning the boys' bedroom which they had had to themselves since their father's death. She and Vera now shared the bed behind the stove again.

'Lyubka.'

Lyubka appeared in the bedroom doorway. 'What is it?'

Vera held up the parcel.

Lyubka drew in her breath then hurried forward. 'Is it from Natalya?'

Vera nodded and turned the parcel over.

'It's been opened.'

Vera nodded again.

They continued to look at the parcel.

'Shall we open it?' asked Lyubka.

Vera laid the parcel on the table and prised off the tape. She unfolded the stiff brown paper and lifted out two rectangular headscarves. Between them lay an envelope addressed to them both. She placed the scarves on one side and picked up the envelope. Turning it over, the sisters saw that it too had been opened. Vera removed the letter from the envelope and took a photograph from its folds.

The sisters gazed at the photograph. Natalya was seated in an armchair with a baby on her lap while Taras was perched on the arm of the same chair with a little girl standing beside his knees.

'Is that our Natalya?' said Lyubka at last, tracing her sister's short hair with her thumb. She turned to Vera whose cheeks were wet with tears. 'Oh, Verochka,' she said taking her younger sister in her arms.

They stood for some moments, holding on to one another, then Lyubka stepped back. 'She looks well and so do her children.' She peered into the photograph again. 'And Taras has a kind face.' She picked up the letter and began to read aloud:

My dearest little sisters, Lyubka and Verochka,

'We'll have to send her a photo of us. She doesn't seem to realise we have aged ten years too.'

I thank you with all my heart for your letter but that heart is broken because our beloved Mama is no longer with us.

'Of course it is.'

Ever since I left our village, I had thought of the three of you at home together so it has been a terrible shock for me to find out that she died so long ago. But you, my dearest sisters, how hard it must have been to see our mother ill and then to have to bury her with Tato. I am so sorry I was not there to help you. I think the grief I am feeling now must be a little like it was for you when Mama passed into eternity. Although I am also sure you are still grieving.

Verochka, I send you my deepest sympathy on the death of your husband…

Lyubka glanced up.

I thank God you have Lyubka to help you. Your boys must be a blessing in your lives.

I have sent you two headscarves as a small gift. Please let me know how big your boys are then I can send some things for them. I am glad you still have the garden and wood for the winter but let me know what else you need.

I have also sent you a photograph of my little family. These are our lovely daughters, named for their aunties, and my dear Taras who is good and kind. He sends his love and condolences to you both, and my little girls would if they understood.

I kiss you both, my dearest sisters, and I wish I could be there with you to take you in my arms. I kiss your boys, Michaylo and Andriy and hope they are being good for their Mama and Teta. Please write to me again as soon as you can. I have missed your voices so much.

Your loving sister,
Natalya

Vera peered at the date on the envelope. 'This took longer than her first letter to get here.'

'Did it?' Lyubka looked over her sister's shoulder. 'Oh, yes. That one took four weeks. This has been nearly two months.'

'It might have been because they were checking its contents.'

Lyubka picked up one of the headscarves. It had brightly coloured roses on a maroon background. 'These are really good quality,' she said. 'People go mad for these on the market, especially with the flowers.'

Vera picked up the second scarf which had the same design of flowers but on a black ground. 'Do they?'

'Shall we keep them? Or shall we sell them?'

'What would they sell for?'

'Between two hundred and fifty and three hundred roubles each.'

'Michaylo desperately needs new boots,' said Vera.

'Then let's sell them,' said Lyubka. 'I'll take them to market the next time I go.'

'It was good of Natalya to send them.'

'Yes, it was but I'm sure she wouldn't mind how we used them.' Lyubka looked at her younger sister. 'What's wrong?'

'What will she think of me marrying Kripak?' whispered Vera.

'Natalya is still alive so she must have made some hard choices too.'

'Yes, but Taras looks like a good man.'

'Her second husband.'

'I know. I just don't want her to be ashamed of me.'

'Stop that,' said Lyubka. 'There is no shame here. You and I have survived and we have two beautiful boys. There is no shame,' she said again. 'Think how excited the boys will be when they find out they have two little cousins.'

Lyubka was only partly right in her prediction. When the boys returned red-cheeked from their sledging, it was Michaylo who peered eagerly into the photograph to look at *Teta* Natalya and his cousins.

'They look too small to play with,' said Andriy.

'We might be able to play with them when they're bigger,'

said Michaylo. 'Will they come here, Mama, or will we visit them?'

'I don't know, my son. We can't see them at all yet.'

'Why not?'

'Because we're not allowed to travel out of Ukraine and they can't come here.'

'But you'll be able to see them one day,' said Lyubka.

'I don't want to see them, anyway,' said Andriy. 'They're just babies.'

That night, Vera tried to lie still but could not. She turned over again, trying to disturb Lyubka as little as possible but sleep would not come. She lay with her eyes wide open in the pitch dark, replaying the scenes of what she saw as her descent into hell. It began with the image of Kripak on top of Lyubka not many metres away from where they lay now. Should she have tried to kill him then, instead of cowering in the corner while her sister absorbed his onslaught? How had she thought they would be safer if she married him? She saw again the crowds of silent men and women climbing aboard the trucks to go east, but she could have refused him and they could have taken their chances in Siberia.

'Verochka, let it go,' whispered Lyubka out of the darkness.

'Maybe we should have risked Siberia…'

'Maybe. But we didn't.'

They lay in silence for a few moments and then Lyubka said, 'We can't change the past. We did what we thought was necessary.'

'Mostly what I thought was necessary.'

'You wouldn't have had to if I'd taken more responsibility for myself,' said Lyubka.

'None of this is your fault.'

'Nor yours neither.'

'But I married him.' Vera lowered her voice to a murmur, 'And I killed him.'

'You were protecting our boys.'

'But I committed a terrible crime.'

'Think of the crimes he committed.'

'Do you think anyone suspects me?'

'No. Why should they? He died suddenly when his heart gave out.'

There was another pause and then Lyubka said, 'Would it help you to visit Father Antin?'

'To hear my confession?'

'Well, to talk to him, at any rate.'

'Perhaps.'

The sisters lay in the dark and eventually Lyubka slept but Vera could not sleep. The following morning, she told her sister she would go to see the priest that day.

'Would it be better to wait until the weather's warmer?'

'Till spring?'

'It might not look so odd,' said Lyubka.

Vera thought for a moment. 'You're right. What could be so urgent as to make a journey in the snow?' She paused. 'I'll go tonight.'

'In the dark?'

'It's light enough with the snow.'

'And if you're seen?'

'People will be sleeping…and I'll be careful.'

After the boys were in bed, Vera left the house. She let down the latch as gently as she could to dull its usual clack, then she turned to face the snow-filled garden. However light she tried to make her footsteps, they still crunched and thrumped as she walked towards the end of their plot, through the gap in the winter hedge and around the neighbouring field. She felt sure someone was bound to hear the snow's cries, 'She's here. She's here.' She tried to think of herself as invisible but her dark clothing would give her away against the white landscape. Only her white headscarf was in sympathy with the snow and from a distance, if she had been observed, she might have resembled a headless figure grinding her way through the winter woods.

The snow under the trees was less deep and more forgiving. It muffled the sound of cracking twigs and rustling leaves. Vera tried to control her breathing as she climbed uphill but the tingling cold in her nostrils made her breathe through her mouth. She stopped to catch her breath and leaned against the snow-free side of a pine tree. She peered around its gnarled darkness wondering if she was truly hidden in this white world or whether someone observed her as they usually did. Sighing, she heaved herself away from the tree's shelter and plodded upwards towards the priest's house. There was no baby for whom to request a sacrament this time, but Vera hoped Father Antin would take pity on her and hear her confession. When she reached the priest's home, she stood under cover of the trees at the edge of the clearing for a few moments to check there was no one observing her. The only sound she could hear was the wind sighing through the trees and she watched as it blew a fine powder of snow across the priest's garden. She made herself stride across the thick snow of the open ground to the cottage door. She knocked, hoping the priest had not left his house this night on a mission of mercy. No sound came so she knocked again and risked speaking.

'*Pane* Antin,' she said in a low voice, remembering not to give him his priest's title.

After a few moments she heard a man ask, 'Who is it?'

'Vera Ivanovna.'

There was another pause. 'What do you want? It's late.'

'I need to speak to you.'

The door opened a little and the priest peered around it.

'I'm alone,' she whispered.

He opened the door further. 'Come in quickly.'

She entered the cottage and stood beside the door in her snow-covered boots.

'Were you followed?'

'I don't think so. I kept stopping to check.'

'What is it you want?'

She lowered her eyes and said, 'Would you hear my confession?'

He sighed.

'I know you don't do this anymore but my need is great.'

There was a noise from the neighbouring room. 'It's alright, Yurko. Go back to sleep.' He turned to Vera. 'Take off your boots and wait here,' he said pointing at the hearth while he disappeared into the second room. He returned with his priest's stole, a long narrow piece of cloth embroidered with a cross, which he kissed before placing it around his neck. He seated himself in a chair and Vera knelt beside him.

'*Bless me, Father, for I have sinned…*' she began.

'It's alright, my child, just confess your sins,' he said, waving away the ritual words.

Vera swallowed and then said, 'I killed Kripak.'

There was a moment's silence and then the priest said, 'Have you come to seek God's forgiveness?'

'Yes, Father.'

'Vera, you have to be truly sorry for your sin to receive God's forgiveness.'

'I know, Father.'

'Do you repent?'

'I feel ashamed…'

'That's not the same thing.'

'I know. I regret what I did.'

'That you killed him? Or that you married him?'

Vera bowed her head. 'Both.'

'What about your marriage vows?'

Vera's eyes filled with tears. 'There were no vows. We signed a paper in the *Silrada*.'

He sighed. 'Then say the Act of Contrition.'

The words from her childhood came tumbling back. '*O my God, I am heartily sorry for having offended Thee…*' She chanted the words but knew God could see into her heart. She had done what she felt she must do to protect her family and she could not regret saving Michaylo and Andriy from their father. Her only regret was in seeking God's forgiveness while knowing what she had done was unforgivable.

When he had finished his blessing, the priest turned to her. 'Vera, I know you think you cannot be forgiven, but one day I will bring you a penance which will help you to earn God's forgiveness.'

'Thank you, Father.'

'Now dry your eyes and we'll see if it is safe for you to leave.'

As Vera slipped and slid down through the trees, she made herself pause and listen from time to time. The snow flashed white in the moonlight and despite her desire to be home with her boys, she made herself be patient and advance cautiously. She could not go back. She could only go forward and deal with what was yet to come.

1954
Chapter 28

In the spring, Olha writes to me from Germany. She has been waiting for Dmitro to accept that he cannot go home yet, but he must come to England like the rest of us. He has been willing to move his little family from camp to camp as they have been closed by UNRRA, one after another, but he has not been willing to move to England where they must become more independent. Now, where Olha's powers of persuasion over the last six years have failed, Khrushchev's have succeeded.

My dearest Natalya,

I hope this letter finds you well. Please excuse me if I jump to the most important thing. Dmitro is trying to get our papers completed so we can travel to England but he needs to give an address where we can live. Can we come to you temporarily, please? We will not be allowed to come unless we have a place to stay.

You may wonder why the sudden rush after all this time. Have you heard what Khrushchev has done in East Germany? Has it been in your newspapers? Well, that is what has made Dmitro anxious to leave…

When Taras gets home from work, we discuss Olha's letter.

'They must come to us, mustn't they?' I say to Taras.

He looks at me for a moment before he says, 'Will you be able to manage having them here?'

'Of course.'

'There's no "of course" about it. You've been very tired since you had the letter from your sisters.'

He's right, although I had thought I had kept my sorrow

inside me. But he knows.

'It has been hard,' I say, 'but it might help me to deal with the grief. To have Olha here.'

'Hmm.'

'If Olha were here, she might help me to look after our girls and then I could start earning some money again.'

'To send to your sisters.'

My eyes fill with tears and I can only nod.

Taras takes me in his arms and rocks me as he says, 'We'll help them as much as we can.'

I hold on to him and try not to cry. I tell myself there is much to be thankful for, but the tears keep betraying me, despite the passing months since I found out Mama was dead.

Taras knows I can be rescued by being practical. 'Perhaps they'll be able to manage in the attic.'

But it is not an attic like the one we had at the Burrows house. This one is not really habitable. There is no window, no floor and only a ladder to reach it. When Taras climbs up to inspect the space he sees there is no ceiling either, just the underside of the roof tiles. 'Maybe not,' he says as he comes back down the ladder.

Neither is there a spare bedroom. We share one room with our girls, and Stefan and Lesia have the other one. We can't ask them to move out because our old friends want to join us from Germany. That leaves downstairs. We eat in the little room next to the kitchen and there is the front room. But that opens onto the street and everyone has to come through it to enter or leave the house. We go to assess its possibilities.

'We could let them have our room temporarily and we could sleep in here with the girls,' I say.

'It would be easier for us to have this room, but are you sure you want to give up your own bedroom?'

'I don't mind…if it's not for too long. Besides, it might be easier with the girls down here.'

'We'll need another bed,' says Taras.

I think of our sparse savings and wonder where the money might come from. 'Could we manage with just a mattress on the floor?'

'We could but you're making it very hard for yourself.'

'It will be hard for you too.'

'That doesn't matter but you need your rest. You've got the girls to look after and then there's your Mama…' He tails off. He knows I haven't been sleeping well since I had the news of her death.

'I know but I don't feel I can put Olha in here with Dmitro and Levko.'

'Alright. We'll try it out.'

Taras is measuring the front room when Stefan comes home from work.

'What are you doing?'

'Natalya and I are making this into a bedroom.'

'Who for?'

'Us. Me and Natalya.'

'Why?'

'We're expecting visitors.'

'Our *kumi* from Germany,' I say. 'I'm godmother to their son.'

Taras tells Stefan the story of Dmitro and Olha staying on in Germany with their baby, Levko, when we left in 1947.

'So Levko will be about seven now,' says Stefan.

'Yes, he will.'

'He must have somewhere to sleep too,' says Stefan.

'There is nowhere else. He'll have to share with his parents,' says Taras.

'Do you want us to go?' asks Stefan.

'Of course not,' Taras and I say together.

'We'll manage,' I say.

'It's only temporary,' says Taras.

'Everything's temporary,' says Stefan. 'We're still living out of suitcases.'

When we have eaten supper, Stefan asks, 'What's the big hurry if your friends have been living in Germany all this time?'

'They're frightened,' says Taras.

'Dmitro is,' I say.

'What of?' asks Lesia.

'Khrushchev.'

'Why? What's he done?'

Stefan turns to Lesia and says, 'You know the East Germans rose up after Stalin's death.'

'Yes, but they still want to be Communists.'

'But not Stalinists.'

'What's that got to do with Khrushchev? He's not Stalinist either.'

'No, but he's not going to lose any bit of power the Bolsheviks have managed to get.'

'What's that got to do with the East Germans?'

'Khrushchev had the uprising crushed and he's aligned himself with Ulbricht's regime in East Germany. So the East Germans are worse off than before.'

'But I thought your friends were in Bavaria?'

'They are.' Taras sighs. 'Presumably, Dmitro thinks Khrushchev is capable of anything.'

'Even re-unifying Germany?'

'Why not? The West won't stop him.'

Lesia rests her head on her hand. 'I keep hoping the British or the Americans might stand up to Russia. I thought we had a chance after Stalin died.'

'So did I,' I say and start to clear the dishes from the table. Instead of moving forward towards an independent country, we seem to be moving backwards.

'They're not going to help us,' says Stefan.

'No, they're not,' Taras agrees.

'But we must help our friends,' I say. 'We promised we would.'

On Saturday, Taras works overtime in the morning so we do our shopping in the afternoon. I had hoped to ask Lesia to look after the girls while we priced up mattresses but she and Stefan have gone out. We gather up the babies and try to spend as little as possible on this unforeseen expense. We buy the cheapest possible mattresses for ourselves and Levko and arrange to have them delivered.

Over the next few weeks, Olha and Dmitro complete the required red tape and begin their journey to England. Their boat will arrive at Harwich so Taras goes down to meet them and bring them back to us. Meanwhile, Lesia and I engage in a frenzy of cleaning and cooking to welcome them into our little home.

As I bake the bread to welcome our guests, Lesia peels the potatoes to accompany the roast chicken.

'How long is it since you've seen them?' she asks.

'Almost seven years.'

'Is Olha from your village?'

'No, we met in Germany.' Then I shake my head. 'Actually, we met on the train to Germany. She and her friend had tried to run away from the Nazis but they were caught and put on the train at gunpoint.'

'She was lucky they didn't shoot her.'

'She was. Then she worked in a munitions factory and I became a maid for the Kuhns so I didn't see her for about a year. I met her again in '44. When the Kuhns were bombed out, they went to the children's grandmother in the country and I went back to the *Ostarbeiter* camp. Olha and I worked in the same factory till the Liberation and then we stuck together till Taras and I left for England.'

'Where did she meet Dmitro?'

I laugh. 'In a barn.'

'A barn?'

'It was when the Germans knew it was over and we escaped into the countryside. Olha and I were with some other girls, including Marichka, and we were searching a barn for food. Taras and Dmitro turned up with a couple of other Ukrainian men and we hid out on the farm until the fighting was over.'

'It seems like a dream now, doesn't it?' says Lesia. 'All that we went through.'

'Yes, it does. And it's going to be crowded here but I can't not help my friend.'

'No. I understand that. But Stefan and I, we don't want to be in the way.'

'You're not in the way.' I put my arm around her shoulders. 'Stefan is Taras's *odnoselchan* and you are my friend.'

As the afternoon draws on, I wait outside our house in the sunshine, Vera in my arms and Lyuba hanging onto my skirt, looking down the street for Taras and our visitors. We are festive in our embroidered blouses, even little Vera with a touch of embroidery on her baby dress. Lesia has put on her *vyshyvanka* too and we try to contain our excitement as someone turns the corner. But it is only Stefan who has been to buy a bottle of vodka.

As he reaches us, Lesia says, 'Quick, go and put your best shirt on.'

'Why?'

'Stefan,' she says.

He tuts and goes indoors.

We smile at one another.

Not many minutes later, I see Taras and our friends approaching. I hand the girls over to Lesia and hurry into the kitchen to fetch the bread and salt. I place the round loaf with its plaited top on a *rushnyk* making sure the little pot of salt is sitting firmly in the centre of the bread. Then I take these symbols of welcome out into the street to await our friends.

Taras and Dmitro are struggling with heavy suitcases and even Levko has a rucksack on his back. Olha hurries towards me, her arms outstretched, tears on her cheeks.

'Natalya, Natalya,' she calls out.

I smile and hold out the bread and salt to them.

'With this bread and salt we greet you and welcome you into our home.'

She can barely speak but she and Dmitro break off a piece of bread, dip it into the salt and taste it. Olha shows Levko what to do and then we crowd into the home we will be sharing.

Olha and I hug one another and I swallow my tears for my beloved friend…and for the loss of Mama and the absence of my sisters. At least Olha has been found.

Taras introduces our two sets of friends to one another while Levko hangs back behind his parents. I bend down to him.

'Hello, Levko. You won't remember me. You were just a baby when I last saw you.' I smile at him.

He hangs his head.

'There's no need to be shy with *Chresna*,' says Olha.

'He's had a long journey,' I say. 'You'll soon get used to us, won't you, Levko?'

'He will,' says Taras. 'Let me show you where the three of you will be sleeping.'

As they leave the room, Lyuba grasps her father's trouser leg. 'Alright, you too. You can show them where they'll sleep.' He picks her up and having got her own way, Lyuba now buries her face in her father's shoulder.

They mount the narrow stairs and I hear Taras say, 'It's not a palace but at least we have a roof over our heads.'

Later, while the men take the heavy luggage up to the bedroom, I say to Olha, 'I'm sorry the three of you will have to share a room.'

'Don't worry. We'll manage. But what about you? Where are you going to sleep?'

'In the front room.'

She peers into the room she passed through earlier. It is crowded with our double mattress, Lyuba's baby bed, Vera's cot and the pram. 'Natalya…' she begins.

'It's alright,' I say. 'As Taras says, it's not a palace but it's our home and we are glad to share it with you.'

Lesia busies herself at the stove with the vegetables. I know it will make a difference to their comfort too but it is our house after all and we have a promise to keep.

Olha shakes her head. 'It can't be for long. Will Taras help us to find work?'

'Of course,' says Taras coming down the stairs, 'but that's for Monday.'

'First a toast,' says Stefan. He breaks the seal on the bottle and pours six small glasses of vodka. Then he pours the tiniest drop into a glass for Levko. 'Here, young man, you can have a little taste too.'

We raise our glasses.

'Welcome to England,' says Taras.

'*Nazdorovya*!'

Chapter 29

'Eat your soup, Michaylo,' said Vera.

'Mama…' Michaylo laid down his spoon and looked across the table at his mother.

'Yes.'

'Is Siberia in Ukraine?'

'No, my son.'

'Then why can people travel to Siberia but not to England?'

Vera and Lyubka glanced at each other.

'Because it's the law.'

'They can come back from Siberia too,' said Michaylo.

'In theory, yes.'

'What does that mean?'

'The law says they can come back but it doesn't happen very often.'

'It's happened now,' said the child.

'When?' asked Vera and Lyubka together.

'Now. Ihor told me his aunty had come back.'

'When did he tell you that?' asked Lyubka.

'This morning, when we were playing.'

'What's her name?' asked Vera.

'I don't know. He just called her *Teta*.'

'He was boasting,' said Andriy.

Vera looked at her younger son. 'It's a funny thing to be boasting about.'

'He wanted to be as good as us,' said Andriy.

'As good as us?'

'Yes, all the boys think we're going to be rich now because we've got an aunty in England.'

'*Teta* Natalya can't make us rich,' said Vera.

'No, but she will send us things.'

Vera and Lyubka exchanged another glance over the boys' heads.

'She might send us a gift from time to time but she has her own family to look after. We're still going to have to work as we did before,' said Lyubka.

'And you mustn't boast if she does send us anything,' said Vera. 'It might make other people jealous.'

'It's better not to tell anyone what happens inside our house,' said Lyubka.

'That's what *Tato* used to say,' said Michaylo.

The following day, the sisters stripped the linen off the beds and took it to the laundry. They stood beneath the trees in the dappled sunlight and washed and wrung the cloth while listening closely to the chatter around them. Sure enough, Ihor's aunt from Siberia was discussed.

'They say many have been pardoned since his death last year,' said one woman, failing to say Stalin's name.

'But I thought she only had a ten year sentence anyway,' said another.

'Lidia Romanivna did but her husband got twenty-five years.'

'What for?' asked Lyubka.

There was a pause as the speaker decided whether to explain. 'It was in '41 when the Bolsheviks were clamping down on suspected partisans.'

'And was she?'

'Was she what?'

'A partisan.'

'I don't know but she was a nurse so the NKVD claimed she'd been helping the partisans.'

Vera shivered despite the sunshine and the woman fell silent.

'But she's back,' said Lyubka.

The woman nodded.

220

'That's good then,' said Lyubka.

'It is and it isn't.'

'How?'

'She can't walk properly.'

'Why not?'

The woman shrugged and turned back to her washing.

On the way home, Vera said, 'We could ask *Pani* Lazarenko. She's sure to know the story.'

'And she'll tell us,' said Lyubka.

So the sisters called in to see the midwife.

'What can I do for you, girls?' she asked.

'We're being nosy,' said Lyubka.

'You won't be the only ones. What might I be able to tell you?'

'Lidia Romanivna,' said Vera.

'Ah,' said *Pani* Lazarenko, nodding at Vera, who wondered if the midwife could read hearts as well as deliver babies. 'She was sentenced to hard labour as an Enemy of the People, Article 58.'

'Hard labour?'

'Yes. The poor woman was sent to a logging camp near the Urals. She told me she would have died of hunger or overwork, or both, but she was lucky.' The midwife gave them a wry smile. 'She was working as a logger, cutting down trees, when one fell on her and broke both her legs. She spent a year in the camp hospital where she was able to rest and they fed her so she survived.'

'Which is why she can't walk properly,' said Lyubka.

The midwife nodded.

'Poor woman.'

'Where does she live?' asked Vera.

'The little house down by the stream, below the laundry.'

'But it's derelict,' said Vera.

'It's what she wants,' said *Pani* Lazarenko. 'She wants to be alone.'

'But she has a family,' said Lyubka. 'Our Michaylo said his friend Ihor called her his aunty.'

'Oh, yes, she does have a family. But they're ashamed of her.' She looked at Vera. 'Don't be upset, Verochka. You know better than most how cruel the world is.'

'It is. Everybody knows how hard it is and nobody knows what they might have to do in this life and yet still they judge us. Come on, Lyubka. I have another errand to do.'

Vera marched down the lane from *Pani* Lazarenko's with Lyubka hurrying behind her.

'What are you going to do?' asked Lyubka.

'I'm going to take her some food and I'm going to see if she's got any wood.'

'She might think you're interfering.'

'I don't care. That could have been us.'

Lyubka took her sister's arm and they hurried home. Once inside the house, Lyubka said, 'I have no objection to helping Lidia Romanivna but she may not want our help.'

'You mean mine.'

'She may know who you married and if she doesn't, someone will be sure to tell her.'

'I'm still going,' said Vera, picking up her basket. She went out to the barn and took some potatoes from the sack, then she returned to the kitchen. She cut the loaf of bread in half and put some salt in a screw of paper. Lyubka passed her a jar of the jam they had made and a piece of butter she had wrapped.

'Want me to come with you?'

'No,' said Vera. 'Thank you though.' She kissed her sister, picked up the basket, and left the house.

She strode back to the laundry and took the path downhill on the wooded side of the stream, ignoring the last few women who were finishing their washing. She had to slow her pace as she descended where the ground was bare and slick with mud.

She wondered how a crippled woman was going to manage to get into the village.

The house stood in a small clearing with the woods on three sides and the stream in front. Vera approached the door and knocked on the slatted wood. As she waited for a reply she wondered if *Pani* Lazarenko had been right. The house looked more like a shack and the one window was boarded up. She knocked again and called out, 'Lidia Romanivna, it's me, Vera Ivanovna.'

There was still no reply but Vera thought she heard a shuffling movement. She waited.

'What do you want?' a voice asked.

'I wanted to see if you were alright. May I come in?'

There was a pause. 'If you must.'

Vera lifted the latch and pushed the door open. The hut was dark inside but she could see the packed earth floor and a flickering light from a small fire. She took a step into the woman's home.

Lidia Romanivna sat hunched on a wooden bed wearing a blanket around her shoulders. 'I'm not sure I remember you. Ten years, well, twelve, is a long time.'

'I have two older sisters,' said Vera. 'Lyubka and Natalya.'

'Ah, Natalya,' said the woman, 'I remember her. Is she still in the village?'

Vera shook her head. 'No. She had to go to Germany to work. She lives in England now.'

'Didn't she have a boyfriend?' The woman paused.

'Roman.'

'Yes, I remember him. What happened to him?'

'He was killed by the Nazis.'

Lidia Romanivna gazed out of the doorway. 'So many dead…and lost.'

'I brought you a few things,' said Vera after a few moments.

'Did you? Why?'

'I wasn't sure what you might have…' she tailed off, placing the basket on the table. 'May I leave these things for you?'

Lidia Romanivna looked at her. 'You haven't answered my question.'

'Because I lost one sister and I've tried very hard not to lose the other,' said Vera. She took the groceries from the basket. 'Is there anything else I can bring you?'

The woman shook her head. 'No, *donechko*, but I thank you for what you have brought.'

'There's nothing to thank me for,' said Vera, thinking the other woman was probably not old enough to be her mother. 'May I come again?'

'If you want to.'

'Then I will.' She moved towards the door. 'Where's your woodpile?'

The woman shrugged. 'I live in the woods. I can gather enough wood for a fire.'

'Perhaps you can now but it won't be so easy in winter.'

'*Donechko*, I have seen winter.'

'Yes, I'm sure. But I will come back.'

'As you wish.' The woman lay back down on her wooden bunk. 'Leave the door open,' she said as Vera stepped outside.

When Vera returned the following day, she took an axe and a saw with her. And her two sons.

'Where are we going, Mama?' asked Michaylo.

'To see a lady who needs our help.'

'Why?' asked Andriy.

'Because she has difficulty walking.'

'No, I mean, why are we helping her?'

'Because we can. We're able to walk and gather wood for her so that's what we're going to do.'

As they reached the cottage, Andriy said, 'Does she live here?'

'Yes,' said Vera.

224

'But it's falling down.'

'Yes, it is.'

'Why doesn't she live in a proper house?'

'Because she chooses to live here.'

Vera knocked on the door.

'Who is it?'

'It's me, Vera Ivanovna.'

'Go away.'

'I've come to get you some wood.'

'I don't want it.'

'Why doesn't she want it, Mama?' asked Michaylo.

'Who's with you?'

'My sons, Michaylo and Andriy. They came with me to help gather wood.'

'Open the door.'

Vera pushed the door open.

'Stand where I can see all of you.'

Vera placed her sons in front of her.

Lidia Romanivna looked them over. 'They look like good boys.'

'They are,' said Vera. 'Can they collect some kindling for you?'

'Yes.'

Vera touched her sons' shoulders. 'Take the basket,' she began but they had already stepped back from the threshold. They walked along the side of the house and disappeared around the corner.

'Have they gone?'

Vera nodded.

'Are they his?'

Vera nodded again. 'But they're good boys,' she repeated. 'They're not to blame for what their father was.'

'No, they aren't.'

'So, may I gather some wood for you?'

'I would have sent you away if you'd not brought them with you.'

'I know.'

'What do you want from me? You married him.'

Vera hung her head for a moment and then said, 'Kripak raped my sister and threatened us with deportation. Lyubka would not have survived...and I might not have either. I had to do something to save us.'

Lidia Romanivna looked at Vera. 'We have all survived one way or another.'

Chapter 30

On Monday morning Taras and I are up early as usual. He shaves at the kitchen sink, leaving the bathroom for Stefan and Lesia and our newer guests. However, there is no sign yet of Dmitro and Olha. I make the *kasha* and then feed the little ones while Taras, Stefan and Lesia gulp theirs before setting off for work.

Taras lingers for a moment. 'Bring Dmitro down to the factory for ten o'clock. Mr Kapstein said he'd see him then.'

'What about Olha?'

'Bring her too. They might as well both get set up as quickly as possible.'

'Alright,' I say and give him a quick kiss. 'See you later.'

He kisses the girls and leaves for work.

I glance at the clock. It is only seven thirty so I think I can leave our guests for half an hour longer. I clear the breakfast dishes away and fill a bowl with warm water. I wash Lyuba's face and hands and take the girls into the front room. I put Vera on our bed while I take Lyuba's pyjamas off and dress her for the day. Then I brush her hair and part it down the middle. Her fine blonde hair will now make two short plaits about the thickness of my little finger. She helps me to undress Vera.

'This one,' she says, as she chooses a blue dress for her baby sister.

'Let's go and feed the chickens,' I say when they're both dressed. I take Vera on my hip and hand Lyuba her little plastic bucket with some of yesterday's potato peelings in it while I carry the rest. We go out into the garden, past the green rows where the seedlings are beginning to flaunt themselves and down to the chicken pen. Lyuba scatters the peelings and I fill up the water trough, then Lyuba and I pull the cord to open the door to the chickens' coop. I hook the loop over the nail while Lyuba points out today's delicacies to the hens.

'*Barabolya,*' she says, pointing to the peelings.

The hens cluck their appreciation and grab scraps to eat, away from the rest of the flock. Lyuba clucks back at them, then turns to me with a grin.

'Shall we see if there are any eggs?'

We lift the laying box lid and find two eggs. Lyuba lifts them out one by one and lays them in the bottom of her bucket. We lower the lid and return to the house. As we go up the path, she hands the bucket to me and bends to pick a cowslip.

'Who's that for?' I ask.

'*Teta* Olha,' she says.

In the kitchen, she puts the flower on the table as I re-set it for the sleepers. I check the time again and listen but can hear no movement so I mount the stairs and knock on the bedroom door.

'Olha, Dmitro, it's gone eight o'clock.'

There's a groan on the other side of the door, then I hear Olha's voice.

'Coming, Natalya.'

I go back downstairs and warm up the *kasha*.

Olha and Levko come down looking neat and tidy.

'Good morning,' I say. 'Did you sleep well?'

'Yes, thank you,' says Olha.

'What about you, Levko?'

He nods once.

I begin to put out the *kasha* but there is still no sign of Dmitro. I pause over his empty bowl. 'Is Dmitro up?'

'I think so,' says Olha. 'Levko, go and tell *Tato* breakfast is ready.'

Levko goes up the stairs but returns quickly. 'He's still in bed.'

I glance at the clock. 'Olha, he must get up. Taras's boss is

228

expecting to see him at ten o'clock.'

Olha goes upstairs and I hear her remonstrating with her husband. She returns alone. 'Perhaps we could go without him,' she says.

'How is Taras supposed to ask for work for a man who is still in bed?'

Olha ducks her head.

'I'm sorry, Olha, but Taras is well thought of at the factory and the boss has agreed to see Dmitro as a favour.'

'I know.'

'Taras can't afford to lose his job.'

She mouths at me so Levko can't see. 'He's stubborn.'

'So am I.'

I go upstairs to my bedroom and open the door without knocking. Dmitro is lying in the bed I bought with my plaits.

'Dmitro,' I say.

He groans and pulls the blankets over his head.

I walk over to the bed and pull the blankets off him. 'Get up,' I hiss at him. 'If not for yourself, then for your family and your friend. Get up now!'

I go downstairs, put his *kasha* in a bowl and leave them to eat their breakfast, taking my girls into the garden.

'Let's see how the vegetables are doing,' I say to Lyuba.

I try to focus on my babies and not on the spectre of Taras losing his job and of us losing our home as we potter about the garden until it is time to go to the factory.

'Is it far to walk?' asks Dmitro.

'About fifteen minutes. It's lucky it's so near. Taras doesn't have to waste money on bus fare.'

'And does he walk home?'

'Of course.' I look at Dmitro. 'This house isn't ours. Every month we have to pay our mortgage. It takes a large part of his earnings.'

'I realise that,' he says.

'And I'm not earning much at the moment. I do outwork for the factory but I don't earn as much as I did before we had the girls.'

'What's outwork?' asks Olha.

'Taras brings garments home for me to finish by hand. I get paid for each piece I do.'

'When do you do that?' she asks, glancing at the pram.

'When the girls are having a nap, or in the evenings.'

Olha looks at Dmitro but he appears not to notice.

When we arrive at the factory, I show them into the main room. 'I'll wait for you outside with the children,' I say over the din of the machines.

After about half an hour, Olha emerges alone.

'Everything alright?'

'Yes. They said Dmitro might as well start straight away. I'm going to start next Monday after we've got Levko into school.'

'Sounds sensible,' I say. 'It'll give you time to settle in.'

'And to catch up,' she says, taking my arm.

When we get home, we take the children into the garden and sit in the sunshine. Levko sits beside his mother who puts her arm around his shoulders and says, 'We're going to look at a school for you this afternoon.'

He looks away from her.

'Did you go to school in Germany?' I ask him.

He nods.

'There was a school but it got smaller as people left the camps,' explains Olha. 'But Levko was learning to read and write, weren't you?'

He nods again.

'In German?' I ask.

'And in English,' says Olha.

'Well, I'm sure you'll soon settle in here,' I say to him. 'Besides, you'll be cleverer than the others since you speak three languages.'

230

'Not much English,' he says in Ukrainian.

'I can help you a bit,' I say. 'My English is quite fluent. Do you want to practice what they might ask you this afternoon?'

He looks at me doubtfully.

'Let's try.' I switch to English. 'Good afternoon.'

Levko is silent. I dip my head to him and smile.

'Good afternoon,' he says.

'Good afternoon,' chimes Lyuba, who is watching the big boy with something like awe.

'What is your name?'

Levko looks at me.

'Levko,' shouts Lyuba.

'Yes, thank you, *donechko*,' I say to Lyuba. 'I want Levko to answer.'

'Levko, Levko, Levko,' she chants.

Because Olha and I laugh, Lyuba shouts even louder and then marches off down the garden path, chanting to herself and any neighbours who are not at work.

'She's just a baby,' I say to Levko. 'Don't worry about school. The English have been very kind to us.'

We meet the headmistress that afternoon. She is a tall, middle-aged nun, although she might be older than her smooth complexion suggests. She sits ramrod straight at her desk as she listens to me recounting Levko's history, the light glinting off her spectacles.

'Leo,' she says, giving him his formal name, 'tell me how you travelled to England.'

He stares at her but she waits, hands clasped on the desk in front of her.

'On boat,' he says at last.

'On a boat. And then how did you reach Lincoln?'

'Train,' says Levko.

'Good. Where do you live?'

'With *Chresna*,' he says, pointing to me.

Sister Augustine raises an eyebrow.

'I'm his godmother,' I say.

'Does he know your address?'

'Not yet.'

'He needs to learn it.'

'Of course,' I say.

'Can you read, Leo?'

'Yes. Little.'

'And write?'

He nods.

'I think he was beginning both those things in the school in the camp.'

'Bring him tomorrow at nine thirty. I will arrange for him to be assessed,' she says. 'He may have to go into a class of younger pupils if he hasn't made the required progress.'

I translate quickly for Olha.

Sister Augustine passes a page of instructions over the desk. 'This is how we expect pupils to dress.'

I look at the list and begin to explain to Olha.

'You can look at that later,' says the nun. 'Will Leo be having school dinners? They cost 10d per day and we expect pupils to pay for the week on a Monday morning. The children are given meat and vegetables and a pudding.'

'Yes, I think he will stay in school for lunch,' I say. 'His mother will be at work.'

'Very well. Bring him tomorrow morning and collect him at midday. He can begin with us properly next Monday.'

'Thank you, Sister,' I say.

'Thank you,' says Olha and we troop out of the school.

'That's enough business for one day,' I say to Olha. 'Let's take the children to the park.'

That evening, after supper, I say to Taras, 'Come and help me with the watering.'

He follows me down the garden, 'What is it?'

'I'm worried,' I say.

He puts his arm around my waist. 'What about?'

'Dmitro.'

He raises his eyebrows.

'He wouldn't get out of bed this morning. I had to make him get up.'

'I'll call him tomorrow.'

'We shouldn't have to. He's not a child.'

'No, but he needs to get used to the idea of working.'

'And being responsible for his family,' I say.

'So what are you worried about?'

'He might make things bad for you at work.'

'He won't. The boss has already said he won't keep him if he's not up to it.'

I stare at him in horror.

'He doesn't mean me. He already knows we're different kinds of men.'

'Didn't he work hard today?'

'You know Dmitro. In his own time.'

'Oh God.'

'Natalya, we're not responsible for him. If he gives up this job…'

'Or loses it…'

'Or loses it, then he'll have to find another one.'

'Have you talked to him about rent?'

'Not yet. They've only just got here.'

'And groceries?'

'Natalya, my love, you're worrying too much.'

I'm trying not to cry so I can't explain how disappointed I am, in Dmitro and in myself. I was looking forward to seeing our friends again, but the sight of Dmitro in our bed this morning when everyone else was up to face a working day has filled me with dread and anger. I'm also disappointed I can't find it in myself to be more generous.

Taras hugs me again. 'I'll talk to him. It'll be alright.'

'Maybe you should show him the letter.'

'Which letter?'

'The one from the police.'

When we had first moved into our own home, we had been so busy we had forgotten to register the change of address with the police. Taras had received a letter from the Chief Constable which had reminded us both of our status.

Dear Sir,

It has been reported to me that you and your wife changed your address about a month ago which neither of you reported to the police, in accordance with the conditions of your aliens' registration certificate.

Solely out of special consideration for the peculiar position of persons of your nationality which exists at the present time, no action is being taken in connection with this matter, but if you are reported again, it may be necessary to take proceedings. I would, therefore, strongly advise you to familiarise yourself with the very reasonable regulations under which aliens are permitted to live in this country, as clearly set out in your certificate, and see that you comply with them in the future.

Yours faithfully

'Why would I show him that?'

'So he knows it's not all milk and honey.'

Chapter 31

As the anniversary of Kripak's death approached, Lyubka asked her sister, 'Are you going to mark it in any way?'

'No.'

'Not for the boys?'

'Why would I want to remind them of him? Or honour him? Let him lie.'

Vera left the cottage and went into the vegetable garden. She would dig up some potatoes. The smell of the earth, as it was broken up by the spade, always calmed her and she could give herself up to a physical task which required no thought. As she lifted the earth and spilled the potatoes onto its surface, relief came creeping in. He'd been dead for a year and no one had come for her. She put her weight onto the lug of the spade and tilted it again. More smooth cool potatoes spilled from the soil.

Lyubka came down the garden carrying an old basket. She stood close to Vera and said in a low voice, 'I'm sorry. Did I upset you?'

'No.'

'Are you sure?'

'Yes.' Vera straightened up. 'I'd like us to be ordinary. With nothing remarkable about us. So nobody notices us.'

'I know. I just wanted you to feel free to mark the anniversary if you wanted to.' Lyubka bent to gather the potatoes.

'Thank you. I don't want to.' She drove her spade into the ground again and tipped it up. 'There. That's enough for now.' She turned to look around the garden. 'Shall I help you pick the beans for market?'

'Yes, please,' said Lyubka.

They stood on either side of the tall canes, picking the long green pods and dropping them into their baskets.

'Mama would be proud of us, growing as much as we do,' said Vera.

'I've arranged a lift for tomorrow,' said Lyubka. 'I want to take some squashes to market and they're too heavy to carry.'

'Good. Do you want to pick them now?'

'We might as well and then I'll be ready in the morning.'

Lyubka set off early in the cool light while the boys slept on in their frowsty bed. Vera let the chickens out and milked the cow, then she went to wake Michaylo.

'Come on. It's your turn to take the cows.'

He rose quickly, excited to have the responsibility for the beasts on their part of the lane.

Andriy climbed out of bed too. 'Can I go with him, Mama?'

'Yes, but make sure you do the job properly. No playing about.'

When the house was finally quiet, Vera took her basket into the garden to harvest the cucumbers. She would pickle them for winter. She picked swiftly and returned to the kitchen to prepare the brine. As she trimmed the cucumbers, there was a knock at the door. Before she could answer it, Zladko had opened the door.

'Can I come in?'

'Of course,' said Vera. 'What can I do for you?'

'Well, it's been a long time since I saw you, Vera Ivanovna,' said Zladko.

Vera looked at the man who had assisted her husband in the Communists' pursuit of any traitors, real or imagined. He was right, they had not really conversed since the spring. He had called several times over the winter to see if they had everything they needed but since then, they had only exchanged greetings when they happened to meet in the village. He stood now, turning his cap in his hands just inside her door.

'No boys?' he asked.

236

'They've taken the cows to pasture.'

'Oh, they're growing up then. Becoming young men.'

'They're certainly growing up but they're a long way off being young men.'

'And your sister?'

'Gone to market.'

'She's a good trader,' said Zladko.

Vera glanced at him. He knew Lyubka went to market every week and he might have seen the boys taking the cows…so why did he want to speak to her alone? She waited.

He shuffled his feet. 'And you're keeping busy?'

'As you see,' she said, pointing at the cucumbers with her knife.

He stepped towards the table. 'I've been thinking…'

Vera remained silent, trimming the stalk ends of the cucumbers.

'It's a year now,' he began again, looking at her for help.

'Yes, it is.'

'You could marry again.'

'I'll never marry again.'

'No, no,' he waved his big hands at her. 'Don't say that. You could. You're still young.'

'I don't want another husband.'

'I know it was terrible for you to lose him. I was hoping…' He looked at her but Vera simply returned his look. 'You and me,' he said. 'Together.'

'I have my family,' said Vera. 'As you said, my boys are growing up. I would not ask them to replace their father.'

'No, no. I wouldn't want to replace him. I could help you.'

'Thank you but we're managing well enough.'

He looked at her from beneath his brows. 'Problems can always arise,' he said, deepening his voice. 'There are those who say he died very quickly.'

'He did. You were here.'

'That's not what I mean.'

Vera reached across the table and picked up the head of garlic. She broke off the cloves and began to peel them.

'They say it was odd how he died,' he tried again.

'You didn't think it was odd. Nor did the doctor.' She watched him flush. He must have been the one who delivered the blows, she thought, when he and Kripak questioned prisoners. 'You saw the death certificate, didn't you?'

His flush deepened. At length he said, 'Yes, I did.'

'Was there a problem with it?' she asked, remembering his inability to sign his own name on her marriage certificate.

'No.'

'Well, there you are then,' said Vera, lifting two large jars onto the table. She placed some of the garlic and some fresh dill in the bottom of the jars before packing the cucumbers into them.

He watched her for a few moments.

'Was there anything else?' asked Vera.

'No,' he said, but he seemed unable to turn his feet to leave the cottage. 'If you change your mind…'

'I won't but thank you for asking.'

Still he stood watching her as she poured water into a saucepan and sprinkled salt into it.

'I'd better go,' he said at last.

'Goodbye,' she said.

'Goodbye.' Zladko stumbled from the cottage, leaving the door open behind him.

Vera stirred the water in the pan before going over to close the cottage door. She leaned against it and let out her breath. She did not know whether to laugh or cry. Some people thought Kripak's death was odd, did they? Well, let them gossip. No one in authority had come to her door. After Kripak's death, no one had replaced him as the senior NKVD figure in the village. Zladko and the others now answered to an officer in Buchach who had not been near Vera since they had buried Kripak. The doctor had issued the death certificate with no discussion as far as she knew, so the rest was rumour. Zladko had been waiting to propose to her but he was not the man his master had been.

Meanwhile, Lyubka was setting out her wares in her usual spot at the market. Her regular customers came knowing the quality of her vegetables to be good and hoping she had brought eggs or butter with her. Although she stood on a side street, it was as busy as the main market.

'Good morning, *Pani*,' said a stout matron. 'What have you got today?' She peered at the beans and handled the squashes. 'You've brought a lot with you.'

Before Lyubka could answer, another female voice piped up. 'Perhaps she's selling up to go to England.'

Lyubka's heart thumped in her chest, but before she could reply, the first woman asked, 'How can she go to England?'

'Ask her. She and her sister get parcels from there.'

'That doesn't mean she can travel there,' said the first woman, looking at Lyubka. 'Does it?'

'Of course not,' said Lyubka.

'Well, they say you sleep on pound notes and dollars now in your house,' continued the second woman, loudly enough to draw the attention of those walking past.

'That's nonsense,' said Lyubka, angry with the woman, and with herself for blushing. She pointed at her wares. 'We're still growing vegetables and I'm still bringing them to market so my family can survive.'

'Oh, survive,' said the second woman. 'Some do that better than others.'

'Yes, and some have nothing better to do than to criticise,' said a new customer shouldering the woman aside. 'I'll have six of your eggs,' she said to Lyubka. As she gave over her money, she said, loudly enough for the passers-by to hear, 'Take no notice of these harpies.'

Lyubka continued to serve those who had come to buy, not raising her eyes to the curious as they walked past. She dealt with each new customer politely despite the pricking waves of embarrassment which kept flooding her. By lunchtime, she had cleared her stock. She gathered up her empty baskets and hurried to complete her own errands, still meeting no one's eye but determined not to be driven away. However, she breathed a sigh of relief when she climbed onto Balanchuk's cart for the journey home.

'You're quiet,' he said, after they had travelled several kilometres.

'I'm tired,' she said. 'Market day can be hard work.'

'So can the people,' he said.

She looked across at him.

'You should know by now it doesn't matter how you live, someone will always find something to criticise.'

She nodded but could not speak.

As they rolled past the wheatfields, Balanchuk glanced at the crop. 'It's almost ready and then people will be too busy to talk.'

When they reached Lyubka's house, she climbed down stiffly from the cart. Balanchuk passed her her baskets.

'See you next week,' he said.

'I'm not sure…'

'Yes, you are. Don't let them drive you away. They'll only think they're right.'

She nodded and before she could thank him, he had clicked his tongue to his horse and the cart had pulled away. As she walked into the cottage, Vera was putting the kettle on the stove. She turned to Lyubka to say, 'You'll never believe…' but asked instead, 'What's happened?'

They told each other their stories.

'Jealousy and an unwanted proposal,' said Vera. 'What next?'

'I don't know what we should do,' said Lyubka.

240

'Brazen it out. What other choice do we have?'

'Perhaps if we explained how little Natalya is able to send…'

'We should explain nothing. Whatever we say will only be misinterpreted.'

The decision to continue as usual carried the sisters into the harvest. Like every other able-bodied person in the *kolhoz*, they worked to get in the wheat and received a small wage for their labours. They toiled from dawn till dusk in the heat, their work unsweetened by songs or romance but soured by sideways looks and muttered conversations.

As they trudged home in the pink of the evening, Vera tried to let her heart lift with the skirling of the swallows swooping over the stubble but it was only as she spied her two boys in the distance that she was able to raise a smile.

Chapter 32

Olha and I peer at the faces in the photograph which I received this morning. My sisters stare into the camera with stern faces framed by the scarves we sent them most recently. In front of them stand two solemn boys with cropped hair. All seem unwilling to let the photographer take their image.

'They've aged so much,' I say.

'How old are they now?' asks Olha.

'Lyubka is twenty-four and Verochka is twenty-two.'

'And you still call them by their baby names,' she smiles.

'I do.' She's right. Their childlike diminutives no longer suit them. 'That's how I remember them though.'

'Of course you do. They'll always be your little sisters.' She looks again. 'So the boys are Verochka's?'

'Yes.' I look at the sisters' hands resting on the boys' shoulders in front of them. They look like a family.

'She's young to be a mother of two such big boys,' says Olha.

'Yes. She married at sixteen…but then they often marry early at home, don't they?'

'Yes, they do. What happened to her husband?'

'All I know is he became very ill and died suddenly.'

'That's hard.'

'Yes, it is.'

Olha looks at me. 'You sound doubtful.'

'Only because I know very little about him.'

'Wasn't he from your village?'

I shake my head. 'He came to the village after I left.'

We look at one another, both knowing but not wanting to say, who it was who came to Western Ukrainian villages after 1943. The NKVD. Sent by Stalin to root out anyone hoping for an independent Ukraine.

'I don't know…' I begin.

'Don't go looking for trouble. Your sisters look well and your nephews look healthy.'

'You're right. That has to be enough. I just don't want to think they've had troubles and I wasn't there to help them.'

'We've all had troubles,' says Olha.

'Have you been in touch with your family yet?' I ask.

'No, but I think I'll write to them from here. It might be less dangerous for them to get a letter from England rather than from Germany.'

'Yes, you're right. Lesia has written to her parents but she hasn't heard anything yet.'

Verochka has sent the boys' measurements, so Taras sets about making long trousers for them from offcuts and remnants. I buy some yarn on the market and begin knitting sweaters, hoping to have them finished in time for winter. There are two colours: one dark green, the other navy blue. I begin the back of the navy one in the evening when the girls have gone to bed.

'Oh,' says Lesia, 'let me. I know how to knit. I used to do it with Mama.'

When I finish the rib, I hand her the larger needles and she continues to knit the back, while I start on the rib for the front.

When Olha comes down from settling Levko for the night, she begins the sleeves.

'We'll soon have these done,' says Lesia. 'Did you buy any wool for your sisters?'

'No, but I will if you're both going to help me.'

'We could have our own little factory,' says Olha.

My heart is full as I look at my friends who have not heard from their own homes yet. We sit looping the yarn around the needles, making garments of our love and hopes.

After weeks of waiting, Lesia is the first to receive a reply from Ukraine. When she comes in from work, I am feeding the girls so I point to the envelope on the mantelpiece. She snatches it up and runs upstairs to her room. When Stefan comes in a little later, he says, 'No Lesia?'

'She's upstairs. She's had a letter from home.'

He hurries up the stairs to his silent wife.

Olha and Dmitro return from work, then finally Taras and I prepare to put out our supper.

'Do you think I should call them?' I ask Taras.

'Yes,' he says. 'I'll do it,' and he goes to the bottom of the stairs. '*Vechera hotova*,' he calls.

Stefan comes down the stairs and stills us with a look.

'Stefan…' I begin.

He shakes his head. 'The letter was from the *starosta*.'

We wait. The head of the village council can only be sending bad news.

'Her parents were deported to Siberia in 1945 and no one has seen her brother.'

'Oh Stefan,' I say, 'may I go to her?'

He nods.

I climb the stairs to the woman who took me under her wing on a bus in a foreign land. I open the door to her bedroom. She is lying on her side, looking out of the window. I lie beside her, spooning her and I hold her till the sky begins to darken.

'Come down and have a little soup,' I say.

She shakes her head.

'Then I'll bring you some up.'

I fetch a bowl of soup and feed her the first spoonful. She eats a few spoons herself and then pushes the bowl away.

'My brother was in the UPA,' she says.

So, because their son was in the Ukrainian Insurgent Army, the parents were punished.

'Do you think he might still be alive?'

She shakes her head. Eventually she says, 'It was all for

nothing.'

'No, it wasn't. We did what we had to do.' I wonder whether I should tell her about Roman, my young husband who died in my arms on a mountain path so long ago. Eleven years ago. But it won't help Lesia.

'Come down and have a cup of tea. You'll feel better.'

She shakes her head.

'Lesia, there are five other people in this house and three children and we all love you. We are your family now, just as you are mine.'

The tears course down her face.

I let her cry and then pass her a handkerchief. 'You don't know they're dead,' I say. 'We can ask Father Yaroslav to say Mass for them, wherever they are.'

'It won't help.'

'It might.'

She wipes her face again.

'Come downstairs.'

'In a minute. I'll just wash my face.'

I go down ahead of her wondering if she's right. Was it all for nothing? Did I have to lose Roman and leave my home? My family in exile is seated around the kitchen table and I see by their faces that each one is thinking about their own absent family and wondering what has happened to them.

The news spurs Stefan and Lesia on though. They come into the kitchen on a Friday after work.

'Are you busy tomorrow, *kum*?' Stefan asks.

'I'm working in the morning. What did you want?'

Stefan ducks his head and smiles, first at me, then at Taras. 'We'd like you to come and look at a house with us.'

'Of course,' says Taras. 'Where is it?'

'Around the corner,' says Stefan. 'The board's just gone up.'

'It will be lovely for you to have your own house,' I say to Lesia.

She shrugs. 'There's nothing to go home for. We might as well have our own house here.'

I go over to her and put my arm around her waist. 'And we'll be neighbours.'

She nods and looks at the floor.

The following afternoon, we leave the girls with Olha while Taras and I walk around the corner with Lesia and Stefan, who is clutching a small bunch of keys. It is a house in the same style as ours and it shows a similar level of neglect.

'An old lady had it,' says Stefan. 'We'll need to decorate everywhere.'

'I'll give you a hand,' says Taras and I remember the evenings these two *odnoselchani* spent hanging wallpaper in our house.

'Is there a garden?' I ask.

We go through the kitchen and Stefan unlocks the back door. There are a couple of steps down to the yard and then a screen of knee-high grass.

Lesia and I go outside while the men examine the meters in the pantry.

'Oh dear,' says Lesia.

'We'll soon have this sorted out,' I say. 'It's a manageable size and big enough so you can have your own vegetables.'

'Mama was such a good gardener.' Lesia's eyes fill with tears.

I put my arms around her. 'The only thing you know for certain is that she's not at home.'

'But I don't know where she and *Tato* are,' she sobs.

I rock her a little. 'I'm sorry you can't find out where they are but in the meantime you can live as they would want you to.' I give her my handkerchief. 'This will be a nice house when the boys have decorated it.'

She wipes her face. 'I know…it's just hard.'

'I know it is.'

She looks at me. 'Oh, Natalya, I'm sorry. I was only

thinking of myself.'

I shake my head. 'I miss Mama and my sisters every day, but every day I have Taras and my little girls. And you are like a sister to me.'

She kisses my cheek. 'And you are mine.'

As Stefan comes out into the yard, he glances our way and then comes across to us looking worried. 'Don't you like it?' he asks Lesia.

She nods and over her shoulder I mouth, 'Mama,' to him.

'Come and look upstairs,' he says. 'We can choose our bedroom.'

We go back into the house and mount the echoing carpetless stairs. There are two bedrooms and a tiny bathroom.

Stefan grimaces at the bath. 'We'll have to see if there's anything left from the savings to replace that,' he says to Lesia.

'Kostiuk could fit it for you,' says Taras. 'He probably won't charge you much.'

'Who's he?' I ask.

'He was in the camp with us here. He helped the English plumber so he learned how to do this kind of work.'

I think of our own ugly bath.

'One thing at a time,' says my mind reader of a husband.

As the weeks pass, Stefan and Lesia go through the paperwork of buying a house. I snatch moments here and there among my days with the babies and the garden to embroider a cushion cover as a housewarming gift. I choose a design of roses and put in as many cheerful pinks and greens as I can.

When the sale is finally completed and Stefan has the keys, the work on the house begins in earnest. Stefan and Dmitro strip the walls of the faded paper while Taras burns off the old paint, scraping the pungent brown curls away from the doors and window frames. Olha helps Lesia to scrub out the kitchen while I dig over the little patch of ground for a vegetable garden. It's too late to plant much but we'll be able to make a start with winter cabbages. Levko plays with Lyuba and Vera in the yard. He's very patient with them and I hide my anxiety that he hasn't yet made friends at school. He feels himself to be different from the other children, even those with Ukrainian parents, because he was born in Germany.

After his first day at school, I asked him how he had got on.

'Alright.'

'Only alright?'

He shrugged and then he said, 'The teacher hit a girl.'

'Hit her? Why?'

'She left her dinner money at home.'

I thought of Olha checking the unwieldy coins with me. Two florins and two pennies for Levko to clutch all the way to school.

'Maybe her parents didn't have it,' I said.

'Maybe. But she hit her legs with a ruler.'

'That's terrible.'

'She stinks.'

'The teacher?'

'No, the girl. The teacher made me sit beside her.'

'Oh, Levko. It might not be for long. Pupils get moved around.'

'I hate her.'

'It's not the girl's fault…'

'No, Mrs Lawson. She's stupid and cruel.'

'Levko, I'm sorry.'

'She calls me Leo. Not Levko or even Lev. Leo.'

'This year will pass quickly.'

'I will learn anyway,' he had said, his jaw set, 'and one day I will go to America to live.'

Now my gentle godson sits on a wooden box, Vera in his lap, Lyuba behind him, clinging to his shirt as they pretend to be galloping away on a cart. He bounces Vera on his knees and Lyuba pumps her legs as they shout, '*Yidem, yidem!*' to their imaginary horses.

Olha comes out of the kitchen and we smile at one another that this part of our dream came true, that our children would play together in a free country.

'They're almost ready for a break,' she says, nodding her head towards the house.

'Then I'll go home and warm the *borshch*.'

I take the children and we go around the corner to our house to prepare lunch for the workers. Levko holds Lyuba's hand as they trot behind their horses and Vera sets up such a howling that she and I have to trot too behind the clatter of hooves only we can hear.

1956
Chapter 33

Michaylo picked up the canvas bag which held his exercise book and his pencils. *Teta* Lyubka had bought them for him at the market along with his *Bukvar,* his alphabet book. He did not mind that the illustration on the front was of a girl with neat plaits and large bows just like the girls in his class, but after a week of learning he wondered if he would ever be able to master the delicate shapes his fingers were supposed to make between the pink and blue lines of his exercise book. He looked at his hands and especially his nails to make sure they were as clean as he could manage. His friend, Ihor, had had his hands slapped with a ruler because they were not clean enough in *Pani* Tetiana's opinion. She strode up and down the aisles between the single desks, carrying out, as she told them more than once a day, the wishes of their great leaders, Lenin and Stalin. Those great men did not deign to look down on the pupils from their portraits on the walls, but rather looked towards their more important goals in the distance. Michaylo was relieved though that for this first year of learning, the eight-year-olds were taught in Ukrainian. But *Pani* Tetiana had warned them, her mouth a thin line, that next year they would be learning in Russian. A sigh escaped him and Vera ruffled his hair.

'Never mind, my son. You'll get used to it.'

He looked up, his eyes serious. 'There's so much to learn, Mama.'

'Yes, there is. Just concentrate on today and next week you'll look back and realise how far you've come.' She dropped a kiss on his forehead. 'Off you go. Don't be late.'

'I won't.' He shouldered his bag and left the cottage.

As he walked down the garden path, Ihor shouted from the lane, 'Come on, I'll race you!'

Vera stood in the doorway and turned to look at Andriy watching the children hurrying towards the schoolhouse.

'Why can't I go?'

'Because you're not old enough yet.'

'I'm six.'

'I know but you have to be eight.'

'That's stupid.' He poked a stone with his foot. 'I want to go now.'

'Never mind. Come and help me gather some mushrooms.'

'Huh, girls' work.'

'Don't you like to eat them?'

'Yes.'

'Well, then. First they have to be gathered,' said Vera, reaching into the cottage for the foraging basket.

'I'm not carrying that,' said Andriy.

Vera smiled. 'No need. I've got it. Come on, my little son.'

'I'm not little,' he said, stomping off down the path between the vegetables towards the meadow below. As they crossed the open ground, Vera could see he wished he had a stick to swish against the seed heads which scratched his legs. She knew he would find a good one in the woods for their return journey.

Despite his grumbling, Andriy worked almost as hard as his mother. They began to race one another, stooping to strip one patch of *pidpenki* before moving on to the next, Vera occasionally overtaking her younger son. However, more often, she lingered behind him, making sure they had cleared the ground of mushrooms.

As they walked back to the cottage with a full basket, Vera paused in the meadow to look across the river Dniester which was beginning to run a little faster now autumn was on its way. Across its wide water, the dark trees cloaked the hills and she wondered about the hidden village of Rashkiv which had been closed off for weeks. Vera and her neighbours had been warned against going across the river because Rashkiv was said to be suffering a typhus epidemic. The dreaded word 'typhus' had done its work and no one had visited the stricken village. It was shunned as if the plague had come. The inhabitants of Krasivka remembered their own disaster of a decade before when typhus had taken so many of them, including Vera's mother.

Vera turned when she heard a swish followed by a crack to see Andriy cutting a swathe across the meadow. She shook her head and followed his frustration, wondering how they would wait out the two years before he could go to school.

But the weeks passed with autumn's work and Andriy was kept busy collecting and storing kindling and helping his mother to harvest the vegetables. The task he enjoyed most was going to market with *Teta* Lyubka since he found other young boys to swoop around the stalls with like a flock of mischievous starlings.

As the weather began to turn colder, a meeting was called. People stood and waited in the village hall until the sound of a motor car announced the arrival of the doctor. He entered the hall, his trilby hat in his hand, wearing a dark woollen coat. He strode to the front of the crowd and announced that the epidemic in Rashkiv appeared to have run its course. The villagers could now go about their business as usual.

Despite some anxious questions about contagion, the doctor's swift replies convinced the inhabitants of Krasivka that all was well. As they began to disperse to their homes, the doctor made his way through the crowd towards Vera and Lyubka.

'I need to call at your house in a moment,' he said in a low voice.

'Oh,' said Vera, 'very well.'

'I wonder what he wants,' said Lyubka, as the sisters walked back to their cottage.

Vera shrugged but her stomach had roiled with fear as soon

as the doctor had spoken to her. Had he been speaking to Zladko, she wondered?

The car drew up beside them as they entered their garden.

'I have a request for you,' said the doctor leaning out of the window.

'Would you like to come in?' asked Lyubka.

'Yes. I'll be in in a moment.'

The sisters went indoors. Vera busied herself putting a kettle on the stove to boil for tea.

There was a tap on the open door and the sisters turned to see the doctor standing in the doorway holding a small child in his arms.

'Oh,' said Lyubka, 'Come in.'

Vera stared at the dark haired child.

'What can we do for you, doctor?' asked Lyubka, also looking at the child in the doctor's arms.

'It's not what you can do for me. It's what you can do for this child,' he said, looking at Vera.

'This child?' asked Lyubka. 'What does she have to do with us?'

He spoke directly to Vera. '*Pan* Antin asked me to bring her to you.'

Vera swallowed but did not take her eyes from his face.

'To Vera?' asked Lyubka.

'Yes. It was his express wish.'

'But I don't understand…'

Vera put her hand on her sister's arm. 'It's alright, Lyubka. I think I do.'

Lyubka looked from her sister to the doctor and the silent child.

'She was the only survivor of a family across the river,' said the doctor.

'Which family?' asked Lyubka.

'The Kovalenkos.'

'But their children are all grown up.'

'They have a daughter,' said Vera, looking at Lyubka, 'in her late teens.'

'She was,' said the doctor. 'She died too.'

'She was this child's mother,' said Lyubka, understanding now.

The doctor nodded.

The sisters stared at the child.

'What's her name?' asked Vera at last.

'Zoya.'

'Zoya.' Vera blinked back sudden tears. 'How did *Pan* Antin get involved?'

'He found her and took her home when the rest of her neighbours were dealing with disasters of their own. We think she might be about eighteen months old.'

'Is she clear of typhus?' asked Vera.

'Yes, she is. She's been at *Pan* Antin's for a couple of weeks and has shown no signs of the disease.'

'Why didn't *Pan* Antin keep her?' asked Lyubka.

The doctor looked at her pityingly. 'A man and a boy in the house. How would a baby girl manage?'

'But why us?' Lyubka asked.

'You know why, Lyubka,' said Vera.

'*Pan* Antin said you would want to look after her,' said the doctor, again directing his words at Vera.

'I will,' she said. Vera took Kripak's child from the doctor.

'Will you be able to manage?' he asked.

'Yes,' said Vera. 'Besides, who else would take her in?'

'Exactly. Well, I must be going. I'll leave her with you but contact me if you have any worries about her health. I think she's well at the moment…apart from the shock she has suffered.' And with a 'Good morning to you,' he left the cottage.

Lyubka turned to look at Vera who now went to the stove to warm a little *kasha*, holding Zoya against her hip. 'Do you think he raped her mother?'

'Yes.'

'So why bring her here?'

Vera turned to Lyubka and lowered her voice to a murmur. 'When I went to confess to Father Antin…' She paused. 'He said he could grant me forgiveness but he would set me a penance one day.' She looked at the child. 'This is my penance.'

'I still don't understand.'

'I took a life so now I must give one back,' said Vera.

Lyubka put her arm around her sister. 'Oh, Vera, he can't have meant to give you such a hard penance.'

'I knew what Kripak was and what he probably did. But this child is not responsible for any of that.'

'No, she isn't.' Lyubka stroked the child's hair with her forefinger. 'I don't know what I'd have done if I'd been…' She stopped and swallowed.

'No,' said Vera and she leaned over to kiss her sister's cheek. 'But no looking back. We'll have our own little girl,' she said, looking at the child. 'We'll have a little *kasha*, won't we, Zoya?'

A short time later, the boys returned to the house together, Andriy unable to resist waiting outside the school for his older brother.

'Who's this?' asked Andriy as he entered the house and saw the child sitting in his mother's lap at the table.

'This is Zoya,' said Vera.

'Zoya?'

'Yes. Her name means life.'

'But where's she from?' asked Andriy.

'She's an orphan. Her family are dead so she's come to live with us.'

'Why us?'

'Because we have room in our hearts for a little girl,' said Lyubka.

'She'll be your baby sister,' said Vera.

Michaylo sat down next to his mother. 'Hello, Zoya,' he said. 'I'm Michaylo.'

The child looked at him with wide eyes.

Lyubka looked from one dark haired child to the other and then at her sister. Vera made the slightest of nods.

Michaylo smiled at Zoya and then, putting his forefinger into his cheek, he popped it loudly. She looked at him gravely as he repeated the action. When he laughed, she began to smile. She looked up at Vera and back at Michaylo, then she tapped his hand.

'I think she wants you to do it again,' said Vera.

'Look, Zoya,' said Michaylo and he popped his cheek again.

Chapter 34

There is great excitement as we return from the shops armed with several rolls of wallpaper. Six-year-old Lyuba and four-year-old Vera have chosen a pink candy-stripe for their very first bedroom.

'What if it's a boy?' asks Taras with a smile.

I pat my abdomen. Our third baby, unplanned but welcome, will have to share with his or her sisters. 'He'll have to put up with it.'

'He'll have a lot to put up with, with those two.' Taras jerks his head at the two girls skipping down the street in front of us.

'It'll be character building,' I say and we both laugh, feeling the luxury of having our house to ourselves at long last, now Olha and Dmitro have moved into a house only a couple of streets away despite the fact that, in the two years they have been in England, Dmitro has had three different jobs.

He first took offence at Taras's factory because he didn't like the nickname the English workers had given him.

'They call me Dim,' he had said furiously after walking out of the job.

'That's just the English way,' said Taras. 'They give us all English names. You've heard them call me Terry, haven't you?'

'And they call me Lesley,' said Lesia. 'He's Steve and even she's Olga,' she said, pointing at Olha.

'They probably find Dmitro hard to pronounce,' I said.

'I don't care. I'm not standing for it.' He looked around the table at us. 'It also means stupid.'

We had tried not to laugh but Dmitro caught us. 'You can laugh. They just think we're stupid foreigners.'

'No, no,' said Taras. 'We have met with a lot of kindness. But more to the point, what are you going to do now?'

'I've got a job on the market.'

'Doing what?'

'Moving stuff. Labouring.'

'And will you be able to earn enough doing that?' asked Stefan.

Dmitro had shrugged. He hadn't, of course, earned much and, soon enough, he had gone to join a group of Ukrainians working in a power station. It was dirty work but it paid well. So Olha and Dmitro had been able to save for a deposit on a house and they were no longer our responsibility.

Now, when we reach home, the girls want to start decorating their room immediately, so we get changed into our old clothes. Taras begins to wet the wallpaper in what was Stefan and Lesia's, and then Olha and Dmitro's room. I take a scraper and draw it across the paper to make a fresh rip and then show Lyuba and Vera how to push the moistened paper into curls and creases with the extra scrapers we have borrowed from Stefan. The bare wall beneath begins to appear, accompanied by the smell of wet paper. My little girls' marks on the wall are scattered but I follow them and scoop up the bits they leave behind on the plaster. It's not long before Vera sits on the floor to play with the torn scraps.

'Vera, stop playing,' says Lyuba.

'She's gathering up the paper, aren't you, Vera? Put it in the bucket, then we can take it and throw it out.'

Lyuba decides this is less strenuous on the arms so she starts to scoop up the damp debris too.

'Like this, Vera,' she says.

'I know,' says Vera. 'I'm doing it.'

They carry on scooping while Taras and I make some headway with the wallpaper.

There's a knock at the door and the girls scramble to run down the stairs to see who has come. Their excitement about their own room has been tempered by the loss of company in

258

the household. They especially miss their hero, Levko.

'It's *Vuyko* Stefan,' calls Lyuba, giving our friend the honorary title of uncle.

'Can I come up?' he asks.

'Of course,' I say.

He chases the shrieking girls back up the stairs with a mock bear's growl. They arrive panting and hurl themselves behind my legs, quivering with delight. Stefan lunges for them and takes Vera into his arms. 'This is how a bear hugs…'

'Me too, me too,' cries Lyuba and he picks her up and hugs both little girls before putting them down.

They hop up and down with glee and Lyuba shouts, 'We're decorating!'

'I can see that,' says Stefan. 'So maybe you won't need my help at all.' He winks at Taras.

'Are you sure you've got time?'

'Of course. There's always time for my little bear cubs,' he says lunging for the girls and setting up their shrieking again.

By evening the room is stripped of paper and the house has the scorched smell of the paint burner.

'We're going to the *zabava* tonight,' says Stefan, 'but I can help you again tomorrow.' The Saturday night dances have continued since we left the hostels and camps. Now the community hires a hall each week and a Ukrainian band plays for the dancers. Taras and I go when we can get a babysitter but tonight he will begin painting the bedroom.

'I'll have to carry on tomorrow afternoon,' says Taras, 'but don't tell Father Yaroslav we're working on a Sunday.'

'Alright, I'll come and help you. Lesia will probably come with me. She's been at the hairdresser's this afternoon.'

I smile. 'She wants to look nice for the dance.'

At bedtime, Lyuba insists on seeing her new bedroom once more.

'But it's not ready yet,' I say.

'Oh, let them see it,' says Taras. 'It might help to get them off to sleep,' he adds in an undertone.

We go up the stairs, Taras carrying Vera, Lyuba's hot, plump hand in mine. Taras opens the door to the bedroom and turns on the light. Lyuba looks bitterly disappointed as she takes in the pale plaster and bare lightbulb. Taras hands Vera to me and says, 'Look who's come to visit…'

He stands where the bare lightbulb casts the strongest shadow and entwining his fingers and thumbs says, 'Look who it is.'

The girls stare enchanted at the bare wall as a rabbit sits up and begins to wash its face. Then it flicks forward its ears and washes each ear in turn.

'There you are,' says Taras, as the rabbit disappears.

'Again,' says Vera.

'Alright, but only once more. Then it's time for bed.'

Taras weaves his magic again with his clasped hands, the actions of his fingers and thumbs bearing no resemblance to the shadow creature on the wall.

'Say *dobranich* to the rabbit,' I tell them.

'*Dobranich*, *zaychyku*,' says Lyuba.

'*Dobranich*,' repeats Vera as the shadow rabbit disappears.

'To bed then,' says Taras flicking off the light.

After Sunday Mass and lunch, Taras and Stefan set to work hanging the wallpaper. They have taken the radio upstairs to keep them company while Lesia and I hem the new curtains with the girls' help downstairs. There is a sudden roar from the men and, as we look up, Taras comes to the top of the stairs and shouts, 'Natalya, Lesia, come quick.'

We run up the stairs, fearing what we might find and the girls scramble after us. Both men are standing stock still pointing at the radio.

'They're fighting in Budapest!' shouts Taras.

Lyuba and Vera begin to cry so I bend down to hug them to

me. 'What do you mean? You're frightening the girls,' I say.

'Listen!'

We listen to the announcer on Radio Free Europe telling us the Hungarian people have risen up against the Soviets. They are demanding the right to free speech, free elections, and the immediate withdrawal of Soviet troops from Hungarian soil.

'They've been fighting the Red Army in the streets,' says Taras when the report finishes.

'What with?' I ask, wondering how ordinary civilians can tackle Soviet tanks.

'Molotov cocktails.'

'They also raided the armaments factories,' laughs Stefan. 'Oh, I hope they beat them.'

We stare at one another while trying to absorb the impossible idea of the Russians being overthrown. No one voices the hope that if the Hungarians succeed, then perhaps the Ukrainians could too.

As October ends and November begins, we listen to the radio at every opportunity, willing the citizens of Hungary on to the success of a free country. The students and workers manage to drive the Red Army out of their capital city and then they tear down the hated symbols of Soviet control: Stalin's statue and the hammer and sickle squatting in the centre of the red, white and green flag of Hungary. Taras and I listen to reports of street lynchings and of men being beaten to death as the people attack the hated secret police, the AVH. But as the week passes there are reports of other Communist countries, especially China, putting pressure on Moscow to clamp down on the rebels.

As Saturday comes around again, we sit in the kitchen with Olha and Dmitro listening to the news that President Eisenhower will not support the revolutionaries.

'The coward!' says Taras.

'What did you expect?' says Dmitro. 'He'll say it could start a Third World War so they can't intervene.'

'But the Hungarians will be crushed by the Bolsheviks unless he speaks up,' says Olha. 'Thousands will die.'

'Olha,' says Dmitro, 'what have we seen time and time again since the war ended? For the last eleven years the West has refused to help any country fight the Russians. The Hungarians were crazy to expect any help from an American President.'

'Those poor people,' says Olha.

Our fears are confirmed the following morning at Sunday Mass. Father Yaroslav announces the news from Hungary just before he begins his sermon. The Red Army has retaken Budapest. The Hungarian Revolution is over. There is the sound of quiet weeping in the church as our priest goes on to talk of peace and patience. The congregation has followed the obvious logic: if there is to be no hope for the brave Hungarians, there is certainly no hope for us.

Chapter 35

Vera woke early with the hot little body of Zoya tucked in as close as the child could get. Vera edged away from her and slid out of bed. She pulled a shawl around her shoulders and went out of the cottage into the misty morning. She walked past the walnut tree to the edge of the garden and looked out over the whiteness of the valley. She knew the river was below, but for now it was completely hidden. There was nothing to be seen. She stood alone in the blind white world.

She turned as she heard the latch of the cottage door. Lyubka came across the yard.

'Are you alright?'

'Yes. Just thinking.'

'About what?'

'What to do next.'

Lyubka looked at her sister. 'Do you think you're going to be able to love her?'

Vera nodded slowly. 'I'm going to try. None of this is her fault.' She paused. 'Besides, I killed her father.'

'Vera…' Lyubka rubbed her sister's back. 'You said I should let the past go. So should you.'

'I think I'll take her to see Pani Lazarenko today.'

'Why? The doctor said she was clear of typhus.'

'Yes, he did, but it can't hurt to have her checked over.'

At a wail from the cottage, both sisters turned and hurried indoors. Zoya was kneeling up in bed, wide-eyed and sobbing.

'It's alright,' said Vera picking her up. 'I was just outside.'

'She'll be afraid of being alone after losing everyone she knew.'

'Yes, she will. Come, Zoya, let's warm some water for those big boys to get washed.' Vera put the large kettle on the stove.

She smoothed back the child's hair which was plastered to her forehead with sweat. 'I'd like to bath her but I think it might frighten her so we'll take it step by step, won't we, Zoya?'

'She'll need more clothes too,' said Lyubka. 'I'll see what I can find next time I go to market.'

Vera called to the boys as the water came to the boil. They emerged from their bedroom.

'It's not our turn for the cows, is it?' asked Andriy.

'No. I want you to help me with Zoya.'

'How, Mama?' asked Michaylo, coming forward. He stroked the child's back as she clung to Vera with both fists, her legs tight around Vera's waist. 'She likes you, Mama.'

'Yes, I think she does. I want to wash her a little but I don't want to frighten her.'

Lyubka filled a large basin with hot water and added some cold. 'Come and wash your faces,' she said, handing the wash cloths to her nephews.

Andriy washed his face cursorily but Michaylo drooped his cloth into the water and then lifted it and let it dribble above the bowl. 'Look, Zoya,' he said, as he draped the cloth over his face. The child stared at him and then looked at Vera for an explanation.

'Where's Michaylo gone?' asked Vera.

'Peepo!' called the boy, whipping the cloth off his face.

Zoya looked startled.

Michaylo repeated the action and this time as he re-appeared both women and the boy burst into laughter. Zoya began to smile.

'Zoya do it,' said Michaylo and he washed out the cloth, then hung it in front of her face. 'Mama, where's Zoya gone?' he said before whipping the cloth away. 'Here she is!'

Zoya reached for Michaylo with one hand, still clinging to Vera with the other.

'Let's wash that little hand,' said Michaylo and Zoya allowed him to spread her fingers and wipe them with the damp cloth. He rinsed the cloth again and when he asked for her second hand, she gave it to him. 'Shall I wipe her face, Mama?'

'I'll do it,' said Vera. 'She needs to get used to me doing these things too.'

'Yes,' said Andriy to his brother. 'You're acting like a girl.'

'No, he isn't,' said Lyubka. 'He's helping us to look after a baby who's had enough frights, thank you very much. Now help me by getting out the bowls for the *kasha*.'

Meanwhile, Vera had wiped Zoya's face gently with the damp cloth and as she finished, she surprised herself by dropping a kiss on the child's forehead.

'What is she going to do today, Mama?' asked Michaylo.

'Sit on my hip all day, I should imagine.'

Zoya was still on Vera's hip as they walked down the lane to *Pani* Lazarenko's house.

'Who have we here?' asked the midwife as she answered Vera's knock.

'Zoya Kovalenko. An orphan from Rashkiv.'

'Well, come in and let's take a look at her.'

Vera entered the midwife's cottage and closed the door behind her.

Pani Lazarenko pointed to a chair and Vera sat down, sliding Zoya into her lap. The child leaned against Vera, half hiding her face from the midwife's sharp-eyed scrutiny. 'So…'

'So,' said Vera. 'Do you think he has many more bastards out there?'

'I don't know,' said Pani Lazarenko. 'I didn't know about this one.'

'Neither did I.'

'Have you committed yourself?'

'If you mean, have I said I'll raise her, then yes, I have. The doctor brought her to me because she had no one else.'

Pani Lazarenko raised her eyes to Vera's. 'You don't have to take her in.'

'I know I don't. But her mother probably wasn't to blame, just as Lyubka wouldn't have been.'

'No. What do you want me to do?'

'Take a look at her and see if she's healthy.'

Pani Lazarenko stood up and went to cut a finger of cake. She handed it to the child. 'Here you are, Zoya.'

The child stared at her and turned to Vera.

'It's alright, Zoya,' said Vera. 'It's cake.'

'You taste it for her,' said the midwife.

Vera took the cake and nibbled the end of it. 'Oooh, that's good. You try it, Zoya,' she said, placing the cake near the child's mouth. Zoya leaned forward to smell it and then opened her mouth to nibble at it. 'You hold it,' said Vera.

Zoya took the cake in her fist and continued to nibble at it.

Pani Lazarenko watched the child eating. 'Has she spoken yet?'

'No. She cried this morning when she woke up alone but she hasn't said anything yet.'

'Has she walked?'

'No. She hasn't really let go of me since the doctor handed her over yesterday.'

'Well,' said the midwife, 'her hair and skin look healthy. She's got some teeth and she looks about eighteen months old.'

'The doctor said that's how old he thought she was.'

'Did all of the Kovalenko family die?'

'Apparently.'

'And we don't know how they cared for her before that.'

'No.'

'You could be taking on a big problem, Vera. She's not behaving like a child of her age and she's decided you're her best bet. She's going to cling to you, at least in the short term. You'll just have to see how she progresses as she gets used to your family.'

266

'She's begun to react well to Michaylo, but Andriy is less interested.'

The midwife looked at Vera. 'He's a boy. Don't worry about him.'

'Michaylo's a boy too.'

'He's older.'

Vera ducked her head. Please God, don't let any of these children be like Kripak.

Pani Lazarenko patted Vera's arm. 'Try not to worry. Love and kindness can do wonders and this one's still very young.' She fetched a damp cloth and handed it to Vera who wiped up the baby's hands and face.

'That was good cake, wasn't it, Zoya?' The midwife smiled at the child. 'You'll have to come and see me again for some more, won't you?' She looked at Vera. 'Bring her over from time to time and we'll keep an eye on her.'

'Thank you,' said Vera.

'No need to thank me. Have you thought about how you're going to explain her?'

Vera knew *Pani* Lazarenko was referring to the village gossips. 'I shall say what I said to you. She's Zoya Kovalenko. An orphan from Rashkiv.'

1956-7
Chapter 36

My dearest sister, Natalya, it is just me, Verochka, writing to you today but do not worry. Lyubka is well as are our boys, Michaylo and Andriy.

I have some news I must tell you. Our little family has grown by one person. I have been asked by our village doctor to adopt an orphan. Her name is Zoya Kovalenko and she is from Rashkiv. You might remember we mentioned there has been a typhus epidemic there. All of her family died but she survived.

Natalya, she is a little child of eighteen months who needs a home. I know you will be asking why she was brought to us. This is hard for me to write because I don't want you to think badly of us. Her mother was unmarried and we think her father may have been my dead husband. I cannot tell you how much it grieves me to write this. I am telling you this, not to worry you, but because you are my sister and deserve to be told the truth. I do not think many hereabouts know the truth about her. As far as I know, only Lyubka and I suspect who her father was. As did the doctor, which is why he brought her to us. I have told Michaylo and Andriy that she is an orphan who is to be treated as a sister. I do not need to tell them the truth until they are old enough to understand.

Do not feel sad for me, Natalya. She is just a small child who needs to be loved.

I send my love to you and your family and hope you are all in good health. Kiss your little girls for me, dear Lyuba and Vera. Give my best wishes to Taras who I am sure is helping you and I hope that you will soon be delivered of another healthy baby.

Your loving sister, Verochka.

I put down the letter as my baby kicks me. I stroke my

abdomen, hoping to calm the little creature. But he or she is right. This is a shock.

My heart aches for my little sister whose husband has been unfaithful to her. I want to go to her and take her in my arms to soothe away her pain. An unfaithful husband who cannot heal the damage he has done…but my thoughts are interrupted by shouts from the garden. I get up from the chair and walk towards the back door to see what my own girls are doing.

'It's my turn,' Vera is yelling at Lyuba who is sitting on the swing with a determined look on her face. Vera pulls on the seat and, despite being only five years old, she is strong enough to try to rattle Lyuba off it.

'No, no,' I call out to them. 'Vera, stop that. Come in here now, both of you.'

They come but both of them are howling at me, though no tears appear.

'Stop that noise,' I say, wishing it weren't Saturday and that they were at school. God help me but this third pregnancy has made me tired. I glance at the clock. Taras won't be home for a couple of hours yet. I decide to give in and use bribery. 'Let's take a walk down to Woolworths.'

'Oooh, sweets!'

'Can we choose?'

'Yes. You can have threepence each for the Pick and Mix,' I tell them, thinking a bit of peace is worth it.

Later, when Taras gets home from work, I hand him Verochka's letter while I warm the soup for lunch.

'Good God,' he says.

'Read it all,' I say.

He finishes reading the letter. 'What do you make of it?'

'I'm certain she's not telling me the whole story, but what can I say to her? She obviously thinks she should take the child in.'

He looks at the letter again. 'I think you're right. There's more to this. But what can you do about it?'

'I don't want to tell her not to take the child although there's no doubt she'll be an added burden. It's her husband's adultery that upsets me. And it must upset her.'

'I wonder how they found out.'

'There's so much we don't know.' I pause and say what has been troubling me. 'There's so much Verochka is choosing not to tell me.'

Taras comes to stand beside me. He puts his arm around my waist. 'Try not to let it worry you. You can only act on what she tells you in her letters. It would be different if you could talk to her face to face.'

'I don't know what I'm going to write back.'

'Don't rush to do it.'

'I won't. I need to give it some thought first.'

And in the end, I write the only thing I can write.

Dearest Verochka, I kiss you for the goodness of your heart…

***

The winter passes slowly with a little snow and cold winds but on a warm spring day I take the girls down the street to telephone Mrs Burrows. I heave open the door of the red telephone box and we all squeeze in.

'Let me do the numbers, Mama,' says Vera, but I can't lift her.

'You can press the button in a minute,' I say. 'Lyuba put the pennies in.'

Lyuba stands on tiptoe to feed the coins into the box, then I dial our friend, the only one who is not at work. She answers my call so I tell Vear, 'Press button A,' and then I tell my friend, 'It's Natalya.'

'Has it started?' she asks.

'Yes.'

270

'Have you rung the midwife yet?'

'No, but I'm not sure it's that urgent,' I say.

'You never know with your third. I'll phone her and then I'll come straight over. You go home and put your feet up.'

We walk back to the house slowly, only stopping once for the pain to ripple through my abdomen. I hold onto a wall until the contraction passes and my head stops swimming, then we walk on. When we get home I want to slump on the sofa but am afraid to damage it if my waters should break so we wait in the kitchen.

A little later there's a knock at the door.

'Come in,' I call. 'It's open.'

Rose Burrows comes into the house saying, 'I'll leave it on the latch for the midwife,' and then she is greeted with hugs and cries of, 'Aunty Rose, Mama's having a baby.'

'Thank you for coming,' I say.

'I'm glad to, you know that.' She gives me her lovely smile and I think how aptly named she is. 'Now what needs doing?' she asks.

'We could see if the hens have got any eggs for our lunch,' says Lyuba.

'Well, let's do that then.'

She takes the girls into the garden and I know I can concentrate now on the wave of pain which washes over me. I grip the kitchen table until it passes and wait through subsequent waves until the midwife arrives and takes charge of me. She installs me in bed and the hours pass in a fume of lost moments when I'm far out to sea in agony and washed up on shore in the exhausted moments between. When my daughter arrives, my heart bursts with love for this third baby.

The midwife is all kind efficiency as she tidies us up before calling down to Mrs Burrows.

I hear the girls coming up the stairs whispering, 'Is Mama alright?'

'Your mum's fine,' says the midwife. 'Come in and see your baby sister.'

They come into the bedroom holding hands and wearing anxious expressions.

'Here,' I say, 'come and say hello to your baby sister.'

They approach the bed almost on tiptoe and I pat it and say, 'Climb up here and then you'll be able to see her properly.'

Lyuba climbs up onto the bed and Vera sits next to her. I hold out the swaddled bundle to them.

'She's all red,' says Lyuba.

'That's because she's just been born.'

'Where's the rest of her?' asks Vera.

'Here,' I say, undoing the flannelette sheet the baby is wrapped in.

A hand protrudes and Lyuba says, 'She's so small.'

'She is but maybe she wants to hold your hand.'

Despite her seven years, Lyuba looks at me with wide eyes.

'Put your finger in her hand and see what she does.'

Lyuba places her forefinger against the wrinkled palm and the baby's fingers close around her like a sea anemone.

Lyuba looks astonished and says, 'She's holding me!'

'Of course she is. You're her big sister.'

'Let me,' says Vera. 'I'm her big sister as well.' She pokes her finger into the baby's other hand and when she feels the little creature's grip, I see her torn between wonder and pride that she is now someone's big sister. Lyuba will never have it all her way again, I think.

When Taras comes in from work, the girls call out to him, '*Tatu, Tatu*, we've got a baby.'

He hurries up the stairs and into the bedroom. 'Are you alright?' he asks me.

'I'm fine,' I say. 'Say hello to your daughter.'

He takes the baby from me and as he peers at her I say, 'I don't think she'll mind pink wallpaper.'

272

He nods and smiles but he can't take his eyes off her. 'Have you decided?' he asks.

'Yes,' I say. 'Nadiya.'

'Nadiya,' he says. 'Perfect.' He turns to Mrs Burrows. 'It means hope.'

'That's lovely,' says Mrs Burrows.

'It is. There's hope for us that one day we will go back to Ukraine.'

1992
Chapter 37

Nadiya turned the key in the lock and, as she pushed the door open, she called out to Taras. 'Hi, *Tatu*, it's me.'

There was no reply. She dropped her bag in the hall and walked towards the kitchen, checking that he was not in the sitting room first. She peered around the door, her heart thumping in case he was lying on the floor. But the room was empty. So was the dining room. Before looking upstairs, she decided to check the garden. If he were still alive, that's where he would be. Each time she had come home from London to visit him since her mother's death fifteen months earlier, she had expected to find him dead too. But he was bending over his spade in the garden, digging up some horseradish. She opened the kitchen door and went out to him.

'Hi, *Tatu*.'

He straightened up and she noticed he had not bothered to shave that morning.

'Nadiya! When did you get here?'

'Just now.'

He stepped over the clods of earth towards her and leaned over. They kissed one another's cheeks.

'Bristly,' she said with a laugh. 'What would Mama say if she knew you weren't bothering to shave?'

He smiled and shrugged.

They walked up the path to the kitchen and Taras slipped off his cracked shoes at the door.

'I wish you'd wear those wellies I bought you,' said Nadiya.

'These are easier to get off.'

Nadiya filled the kettle and began to make coffee for them

both.

'How long are you staying?' asked Taras.

'Till tomorrow. Work on Monday.'

'How is work?'

It was Nadiya's turn to shrug. 'Alright.'

'And Kotyk?'

'Still my best friend,' said Nadiya, thinking of her handsome grey cat who would probably be making himself comfortable across the middle of her duvet at that very moment.

'Still no boyfriend?'

She shook her head. 'We can't all be like you and Mama.'

He sighed.

'I'll find myself a good Ukrainian when we go to stay with the aunties. Has there been a letter yet?'

Her father nodded and took a blue airmail envelope from the mantelpiece. 'Want to read it now?'

'No. I'll wait till Lyuba and Vera get here. What time are they coming?'

'I don't know. Soon maybe.'

'Are they bringing the things for the *koshyk*?' asked Nadiya. She and her sisters would prepare the Easter basket of food which they would take to the church to be blessed that evening.

'I should think so.'

'Then I'll just take my bag up to my room.'

'I've made your bed.'

'Thank you, *Tatu*, but I could have done it myself.'

Nadiya went up the stairs with her overnight bag to the smallest bedroom. They had moved into this house when she was six. Her teenage sisters had not wanted to be bothered with a little girl, so they had shared a room and she had been persuaded to have this little space. She had made a fuss which had resulted in new bedroom furniture but secretly she had loved having the room to herself. She put her bag on the floor and then went to peep around the door of her parents' room.

Her mother's things had been cleared away and the room smelt of her father's liniment. She lifted the receiver of the phone the sisters had insisted their father keep by his bedside and heard a comforting dialling tone.

The doorbell rang and a key turned in the lock.

'Hello, *Tatu,* it's only us,' called Lyuba.

'Hello, *Tatu,*' said Vera and then looked up as Nadiya came down the stairs.

'Oh, you're already here,' said Lyuba, bustling into the kitchen with her shopping bags.

'Yes, I'm here,' said Nadiya hugging Vera.

Lyuba returned and embraced her youngest sister. 'How was your train?'

'On time, for once, and speaking of trains, *Tato*'s had a letter.'

'From the aunties?' asked Vera, looking at her father.

'Yes.'

'What does it say?' asked Lyuba. 'Can we go?'

Taras opened the letter and began to read it aloud.

Slava Isusu Christu. May the blessings of Christ be upon you in this holy season.

Yes, yes, girls, please come. Please come and see us. Bring your husbands, your children and your dear father…

Taras paused.

'Will you come with us, *Tatu*?' asked Nadiya.

'No, *donechko*. It is not safe for me.'

'It is, *Tatu,*' said Lyuba. 'You have a British passport.'

'Some people have long memories.'

'But they don't know you in Mama's village,' persisted Lyuba.

'They would know I left under the Germans so I am still a traitor.'

'You've waited nearly fifty years to go home,' said Lyuba.

'Yes, but it was your Mama who really wanted to go. She

missed her sisters so much.'

Nadiya looked at her father's white thinning hair. 'Are you sure you don't want to go this year?'

'I'm sure. You can go for me. Your Mama would like that. She always wanted to take you home.'

The sisters looked at the bowed figure of their father. They all knew he had aged since Natalya's death. He raised his eyes to them. 'You go,' he said again.

'If *Tato* doesn't want to go this year, he could always go next year,' said Vera.

'Yes, maybe next year,' said Taras. 'I don't want you to worry though. You will be safe because you were born here.'

'We'll be fine,' said Vera. 'We'll look after each other.'

'Are the men staying at home?' asked Nadiya.

Her older sisters nodded.

'Tom was a bit miffed,' said Vera, 'but he's come round because he doesn't want Lydia and Simon to go yet. He thinks they're too young.'

Nadiya raised her eyebrows. Vera's daughter was seventeen and her son sixteen. She looked at Lyuba.

'Adrian's the same,' she said, 'and despite Valeria being at uni, he also thinks she's too young.'

'But it's safe surely?' asked Nadiya.

'I think it must be,' said Vera. 'But Tom and Adrian are English. They're not drawn to it in the same way we are.'

'I really want to see where Mama grew up,' said Lyuba.

'It won't be the same,' said Taras. 'The Bolsheviks did a lot of damage.'

'But people are re-building.'

'Yes, they are, but don't expect it to be like it is here. Just before the Germans came, when the Russians had run away, it was like the Wild West. People settling old scores…'

'*Tatu*, that was in 1941.'

'People don't forget. They'll still know who the *syksoti* were.'

'Well, there can't be any traitors there now. Ukraine's independent.'

'So they say,' said Taras.

'We'd better get on with this *koshyk*,' said Vera, 'or it won't be ready for church.'

Lyuba emptied the shopping bags of the items to be blessed while Vera went to fetch their mother's basket. It was wide and shallow, perfect for displaying each of the items. She and Lyuba began to fill glass bowls with soft white cheese and butter, decorating them with crosses formed with cloves. A pot was filled with salt with a smaller cross of cloves. Meanwhile, Nadiya took the secateurs into the garden and snipped small lengths of myrtle from the bush Natalya had encouraged for exactly this purpose. She took the cuttings indoors and began to decorate the rim of the basket while Taras chose the best piece of horseradish and scrubbed it clean.

Lyuba went into the sitting room to fetch a clutch of *pysanki* from the display cabinet. Natalya had painted the eggs and her daughters kept this reminder of her in the *koshyk* rather than creating their own new ones. Meanwhile, Vera went out to her car to fetch the sweet loaves she had baked. Each one was decorated with a different pattern of leaves and flowers, while the biggest loaf had a cross at its centre. It would take pride of place in the basket, surrounded by a ring of salami.

'The *paska* looks lovely, Vera,' said Nadiya.

'Yes, I think it's worked out a bit better than last year's,' she said, remembering her disappointing first attempt to imitate her mother's *paska*.

'Mama would be proud of you,' said Lyuba.

'She would be proud of all of you,' said Taras.

'Are you going to get shaved before church, *Tatu*?' asked Nadiya.

'Yes, yes. I won't let her down either,' and he went upstairs to the bathroom.

The sisters paused in their work.

'Do you think he's alright?' asked Nadiya.

'This is how he is now,' said Lyuba. 'Vera and I have the week covered between us. One of us calls in to see him every day. Adrian or Tom…'

'Lydia and Simon come after school,' said Vera.

'Valeria joins the rota when she's home from uni.'

'He tells me who's been when I phone him, but you know what he's like on the phone.'

'As brief as possible,' smiled Vera.

'I worry about him being lonely,' said Nadiya.

'Well, we can't change that. He adored Mama.'

'I wish he'd come to Ukraine with us, though.'

'You heard him. I don't think he'll change his mind this year.'

'Maybe when we've been we'll be able to tell him we had a good trip.'

'That's assuming it is a good trip,' said Lyuba.

'It will be,' said Vera, laying Natalya's embroidered cloth over the basket.

***

The visit had been planned for August to coincide with Lyuba's holiday from teaching. Vera and Nadiya booked their dates accordingly and the three sisters met again at their father's house to plan their trip.

'What do you think we should we take them, *Tatu*?' asked Vera.

'Assume they have very little,' said Taras, 'and people always need warm coats for winter.'

Lyuba reached for a notebook and began to write a shopping list. 'Coats for the aunties…'

'Good ones,' said Nadiya. 'Maybe cashmere.'

Lyuba raised her eyebrows.

'They should have nice ones, shouldn't they, *Tatu*?'

'Yes. Your mother always sent them good quality things.'

'And the boys…or I should say, men. Michaylo and Andriy are a bit older than us, aren't they?' asked Lyuba.

'Yes, they're in their forties,' said Taras. 'We should get them sheepskin jackets.'

'What about Michaylo's wife, Tanya?'

'And Zoya?'

'Coats, too, I think.'

'But different ones to the aunties.'

'Yes, something more modern,' said Nadiya.

'Good. Now for the children,' said Lyuba.

'Toys definitely,' said Nadiya.

'Children always need shoes,' said Vera, 'but we don't know their sizes.'

'I want you to give them some money from Mama and me,' said Taras. 'Then, although the quality won't be very good they can buy them there.'

'We can take a note of their sizes and send them shoes later,' said Lyuba.

'But they'll be disappointed if there are no gifts when we go,' said Nadiya. 'Let's get them some fun things while we're out shopping.'

'One more thing,' said Taras. 'I want you to take a gift for the church. People tell me that they're rebuilding the churches everywhere.' Taras produced an envelope and, taking out a piece of paper, read aloud:

In the name of Natalya, Lyuba and Vera Palmarenko, I send you $1,000 with my daughters Lyuba, Vera and Nadiya Sidorenko to help rebuild the church in Krasivka.

May God guide you in this holy work.

Taras Sidorenko

'Are you sure you want to give as much as that, *Tatu*?' asked

Nadiya.

'Yes. Your mother would have wanted it and $1,000 will go a long way over there.'

'Won't they think we're showing off?'

'No. They will expect it in the village. They think we're all rich over here.'

'Well, by their standards we are,' said Vera.

'What about the aunties?' asked Lyuba.

'I think they'll just be glad to see us,' said Vera, 'judging by their letters.'

'They will,' said Taras. 'But be careful in the house. They will eat well because they grow much of their own food. They keep a cow and chickens…But they probably won't have much money.' He turned to his youngest daughter. 'Nadiya, put a jar of coffee in your luggage.'

'Don't they have coffee there?'

'Yes, but it will be expensive.'

'There must be some money coming in,' said Lyuba. 'Doesn't Andriy work away?'

'Yes, but we don't know how much he gives his mother. Michaylo works too and gets paid apart from cultivating their fields, but they will still be much poorer than us.'

'Do the women work?' asked Lyuba.

'All the time,' said their father. 'But only Tanya and Zoya will work at the *kolhoz* for a wage.'

There was a pause as the sisters tried to picture this way of life, but Taras did not leave it there. 'You should also know that the conditions will be more primitive than you're used to…the toilets and so on.'

'I wonder how they'll squeeze us in,' said Lyuba. 'The aunties' house is small, isn't it, *Tatu*?'

'Yes. Whatever arrangements they make, you can be sure they will give you the best of everything while they will make do.'

'I feel guilty already,' said Lyuba.

'No, *donechko*,' said Taras, 'I am telling you these things so that you're not disappointed.'

'We won't be,' said Vera. 'We'll take everything as it comes.'

Chapter 38

Vera took the loaves from the oven and placed them on the cooling rack which Michaylo had made for her. She went to the cottage door as Lyubka came up the garden path with a small basket of eggs.

'Are there many?'

'Enough,' said Lyubka. 'How much more baking are you going to do?'

'Just a honey cake.'

Lyubka shook her head. 'You know he won't eat any of it.'

'I know,' said Vera, 'but I want him to see I'm glad to have him home.'

Andriy had been working in Moscow and was coming home for a break. Michaylo had gone to Ternopil to pick him up at the station.

'I know he hasn't got his father's sweet tooth,' said Vera.

Lyubka stopped herself from saying that she wished that was all he had failed to inherit from Kripak.

The women entered the cottage as Zoya came out of the second room, her arms full of bed linen. She had grown into a tall, slender woman whose long dark braid hung down her back. Lyubka marvelled again that no one in the village had ever commented in their hearing that she was the image of her father.

'I've made his bed, Mama,' she said.

'Thank you. Lyubka, are you sure you'll be able to sleep on the settle?'

'Of course.'

Lyubka had slept alone in the second room since Vera's boys had grown up and left home. Zoya slept with Vera as she had ever since her arrival in their home. Michaylo had not gone far either. He had managed to get the cottage next door where he and his wife were raising their three children, who were, at that moment, keeping guard in the lane to announce the arrival of their uncle. Or they were supposed to be. The twin girls and their younger brother were currently giving all their attention to a game of jacks, which they were playing with pebbles from the roadside.

The sound of a car backfiring made Danylo glance up. 'They're coming,' he shouted.

The girls looked up and then ran for their grandmother's house. '*Baba*, *Baba*, Uncle Andriy is here.'

Vera and Lyubka hurried from the hot kitchen and out into the lane where Michaylo's Lada had just sputtered to a halt. The passenger door creaked loudly and Andriy unfolded his thin frame from the low seat. He stretched and groaned as Vera hurried towards him. He turned to look at his mother.

'What happened to your face?' she asked, her loving greeting forgotten.

He shrugged. 'Some big mouths on the train.'

'Did they beat you up?' she asked, taking hold of his chin and turning his face this way and that to see where the bruising was beginning to appear.

'Don't worry, Mama. I gave as good as I got,' he said, pulling his head back out of her hand.

Vera looked at Michaylo who also shrugged. 'What can we do with him?'

She took Andriy's arm. 'Come into the house. I'll bathe it for you.'

'Don't make a fuss,' he said, reaching into his pocket for a packet of cigarettes. He withdrew one and lit it.

'Come in, anyway,' she said, still holding his arm. 'Have you been eating at all?'

'Mamo!'

'Alright, I know,' but she did not let go of his arm. She led him into the house and drew him to a chair. 'Sit and I'll get you something to eat now.' She turned her head away from the sour smell of his body, telling herself that it was only because he had had a long journey that he had not been able to wash.

Lyubka had already filled a bowl with soup. She approached and placed it before her nephew. 'There you are, Andriyu. Eat up. Your Mama's right. You look as if you need feeding up.'

'Thanks, *Teta*.' He lifted the spoon and ate the soup, alternating mouthfuls with drags on his cigarette.

Michaylo's children stood in the doorway, staring at their uncle.

'Let me through,' said their father as he brought in Andriy's suitcase. He took it into the bedroom they had shared as boys and placed it beside the bed. '*Teta*,' he said to Lyubka as he came back into the main room, 'you might be more comfortable at my house. You can have the big bed.'

'No, thank you, dear. I'll be fine here.'

Andriy looked up from his bowl. 'Why? Is the cuckoo still here?'

'Andriyu!' said his mother.

'Or should I say, Mama's shadow? Where are you hiding, little shadow?' He pretended to look about him and then his eyes fell on Zoya. 'Oh, there you are. Got nothing to say?'

'Welcome home, Andriyu,' said Zoya.

'Thank you.' He lit another cigarette from the stub of the old one. 'Don't worry, I won't be here long.'

'You can stay as long as you like,' said Vera. 'You know I like to have you home.'

'Well, we'll see.'

'Come and take a look at this wretched car with me,' said Michaylo.

Andriy rubbed at the bristles on his cheeks and then ran his hands over his shaven head. 'Maybe later. I'm going to have a sleep first.' He pushed back his chair with a clatter and stumbled across to his bedroom. He flung himself face down on the bed and could soon be heard snoring.

Michaylo righted the chair and turned to his children. 'Come, you can help me.' He watched as they ran out to the car, hoping their father might have picked up a bag of sweets in the big town. He turned to Vera. 'Don't worry, Mama. He'll be better after a sleep.'

Vera shook her head but would not let her tears fall. She picked up Andriy's empty bowl but Zoya took it from her saying, 'I'll wash it, Mama.'

'Thank you, *donechko*.'

Andriy awoke several hours later and stumped into the kitchen.

Vera turned to him from the stove. 'What can I get you?'

'Some water.' He mimed washing his face.

Before Vera could fill the basin for him, Zoya had already done it. He took the bowl without speaking to her and bent to wash his face and head vigorously. As he straightened up, Zoya passed him a towel. 'Proper *naymichka*, aren't you?'

Vera sighed. 'Andriy, please don't speak to Zoya like that.'

'Why not? She behaves exactly like a servant.'

'She's helping, that's all.'

Andriy threw the towel down. 'She's always helping.'

'Are you hungry?' asked Vera.

'Yes. I'll have some more of that soup.'

After he had eaten, he got up from the table and made for the cottage door.

'Where are you going?'

'Out.'

'Where?'

'Out, Mama. There are bound to be some of the boys about.'

'Take your coat. The nights are still cold.'

'I don't need a coat,' he said, going out into the evening air in his shirtsleeves.

Vera turned to Lyubka. 'Who does he mean, "boys"?'

'Grown men as daft as him,' said Lyubka.

Zoya tidied away the bowl and towel and then sat by the table with her sewing. Lyubka and Vera were silent, unable to think of anything but Andriy who had gone out to seek cheap vodka. The village had a shop which carried a few groceries by day, but which by night became a haven for the thirsty. Its vodka was cheap and strong and his mother and aunt knew Andriy would be opening a bottle whose cap was not designed to close again, merely to be removed.

The women sat through the long evening, avoiding any talk of Vera's youngest son. Eventually, Lyubka said, 'It's getting late. We might as well go to bed.'

'Yes,' said Vera. 'He won't come home until he's ready.'

The women made themselves ready for bed, leaving one light burning for the prodigal. They dozed fitfully until the knock they had been waiting for came. Lyubka opened the door to one of Andriy's cronies.

'You'd better come and fetch him, missus. He's in the lane,' he said before staggering away.

Vera was already pulling on her coat over her nightdress.

'Wait,' said Lyubka, 'I'll go with you.'

'Zoya, call Michaylo,' said Vera, going out into the night. She went into the lane but could see no one. 'Where did he say he was?' she asked Lyubka.

'He didn't. Let's go towards the shop.'

They walked slowly along the dark lane and were soon caught up by Michaylo wheeling a wheelbarrow.

'What are you doing with that?' asked Vera.

'Well, if he could get home on his own two feet, we wouldn't be going out to look for him, would we?'

They walked forward slowly and, coming to a corner where a narrower lane led to the river, Michaylo peered into the darkness.

'Wait, I think he's there.'

They hurried forward to see a body slumped against a garden fence.

'Oh God, is he hurt?' asked Vera.

Michaylo lifted his brother's chin. 'No. Just drunk.'

He had disturbed what little balance Andriy had achieved and the younger man now slid onto his side and lay on the ground.

Vera leaned over her son, closing her nostrils again to the sharp stink of alcohol. 'Andriyu,' she shook his shoulder, 'we're going to take you home.'

Andriy groaned and opened one eye.

Michaylo took his mother's arm. 'Mama, come away while I try to lift him.'

Vera stood back and Lyubka took hold of the wheelbarrow's handles to hold it steady. Michaylo put his hands into his brother's armpits and heaved him up into a sitting position, then he stood behind him and attempted to lift him into the barrow. Vera took her son's legs and between them, they managed to drag Andriy into the wheelbarrow. He lay like a large skinny baby facing Michaylo who now took the handles to wheel his brother home.

Andriy's head lolled but he was able to speak. 'You should be ashamed of yourself,' he said to Michaylo.

'Me, ashamed?'

'Yes. Call yourself a man? You couldn't even carry me home.'

Michaylo shook his head and laughed. 'Oh, little brother!'

Lyubka took her sister's arm and they walked behind Vera's sons back to the cottage. They lifted Andriy out of the wheelbarrow and carried him like a corpse across the living room to his bedroom where they dropped him onto the bed. Vera took off his boots and Lyubka fetched a bowl to place beside the bed. Zoya brought in an enamel cup of water and placed that beside the bed too, then they withdrew, closing the door behind them.

'Will you be alright?' asked Michaylo.

Lyubka nodded. 'Yes, thank you, Michaylo. He'll sleep now until midday. You go and get some rest.'

'You, too,' he said. He kissed Vera's forehead. 'Try to sleep, Mama.'

Vera simply nodded.

Michaylo left, closing the cottage door as the women prepared to return to bed.

Vera spoke to Zoya. 'You go to bed. I'll be there soon.' She went to kneel before the icon in the corner. She put her hands together in prayer, bowed her head, and began silently: '*Hail, Mary, full of grace…*'

***

Lyubka had been correct. Andriy did not stir the following day until after the three women had finished their morning's work. He came into the kitchen stretching and scratching just as Lyubka was about to serve lunch.

'Morning, Andriyu,' she said.

'Morning.'

'Your mother will be in a minute. She's been working in the garden.'

Andriy made no comment.

'There's no need to make her life hard,' continued Lyubka. 'She's had enough troubles already.'

Vera's youngest son made no comment but sat down at the table. Lyubka approached her nephew and, placing her hand on his bony shoulder, said, 'Be kind to your Mama.'

He might have nodded in reply.

Lyubka sighed and went back to the stove.

Vera and Zoya could be heard washing their hands in the

bucket outside. As they entered the cottage, Andriy spoke: 'Good morning, Mama, Zoya.'

'Good morning, my son. Have you had a good sleep?'

'Yes, thank you.'

When they were all seated and eating the soup Lyubka had made from the dwindling store of root vegetables, Andriy said, 'Where's Michaylo?'

'He's gone to fetch Tanya. Her mother hasn't been well and she's been looking after her.'

'The children will be glad to have their Mama home,' said Lyubka.

'How long has she been gone?'

'Two weeks.'

The soup finished, Andriy got up and went out into the yard to smoke. He saw two spades leaning against the cottage wall. He finished his cigarette and, picking up the larger spade, walked into the vegetable garden. He could see where his mother and Zoya had been digging that morning so he took up where they had left off. He set to, his skinny arms belying his strength, as he made swift work of turning the rich, black soil.

'There's no need to do that,' called Vera, coming into the garden.

'I can see where you two have been messing about,' he said, without pausing.

Vera smiled. 'Well, I'll leave you to it then.'

Andriy did not return to the cottage until he had finished digging over the plot. 'You can get on with your planting now,' he said.

'Thank you,' said his mother. 'Zoya and I would have managed but you have been a great help. I've heated some water. You can have a bath if you want to.'

'Alright.'

Vera and Zoya hefted the zinc tub into Andriy's room and, after filling it with hot water from the stove, they left him to bathe alone. He emerged some time later, skin shining, wearing a clean white shirt.

'That's better,' said Vera. 'Are you going to have supper with us?'

'No, I'm going out. Don't wait up for me. I think we're going to Buchach.'

'Alright,' said Vera, but she turned away to hide her disappointment.

'Do you want me to empty the bath before I go?' asked Andriy.

'No. Zoya and I will do it.'

'Then I'll be off,' he said. He kissed Vera's cheek and left, calling goodbye to Lyubka as he passed her in the yard.

'Has he gone already?' she asked Vera as she came into the cottage.

Vera nodded.

Zoya came out of Andriy's bedroom, carrying two buckets of dirty water from his bath. She took them into the yard and emptied them. She continued to empty her half-brother's bath while Vera took a honey cake from the oven.

'I know he won't eat it,' she said as she saw Lyubka preparing to speak. 'I'll take it next door for Tanya. She'll be tired when she gets home.'

Vera's daughter-in-law arrived a little later looking pale but smiling as her children leapt from the car to shout to their grandmother: '*Baba*! *Baba*! Mama's home.'

Vera embraced Tanya. 'Welcome home, *donechko*. How's your Mama?'

'A little better. *Tato* says he can manage on his own for a while.'

'Good. You'll need to rest a little.'

'Oh, I'm alright.'

'Well, don't do too much. There are plenty of us here to help you.'

'Mama's right,' said Michaylo, as Tanya was embraced by Lyubka and Zoya.

When Tanya had had time to be shown all the wonders of her clean home by the children, she returned to Vera's cottage. 'Thank you for cleaning the house. Everything's done. Even the laundry!'

'Don't thank me. Thank Zoya. She did it all,' said Vera.

Tanya turned to Zoya and hugged her. 'Thank you, *sestrichko*, you are such a help to me.'

Zoya smiled at her sister-in-law. 'The children helped.'

Tanya laughed. 'Hmm.'

***

The two households lay in darkness when the calm of the night was shattered by the sound of a car horn being repeatedly pressed.

Vera sat up in bed. 'He'll wake the whole village.' She got out of bed and went to peer out of the cottage door.

Andriy was staggering up the path, shouting, 'Goodnight, goodnight.'

'Shh, Andriyu. Come in quickly.'

As he reached her, Vera pulled him by the arm to draw him into the house.

'I'm alright,' he said as he bumped his shoulder against the door jamb.

Vera closed the door quickly behind him.

Andriy swayed in the centre of the room, surveying Lyubka and Zoya in their nightdresses. 'So we're all up.'

'For shame, Andriyu,' said Lyubka. 'Just simmer down and go to bed.'

'Aah, *Teta*, ever the peacemaker.'

'She's right,' said Vera, 'take yourself off to bed.'

'Yes, Mama.' He turned towards Zoya. 'Got nothing to say?'

'Listen to Mama,' said Zoya.

'Oh, "Mama" is it?' She's not your Mama though, is she?' He swayed towards Zoya until they stood almost nose to nose. 'You with your simpering goodness. What is it you really want?' He reached around her shoulder and grabbed her braid in one hand while pulling her towards him by her nightdress with the other. 'Is this what you want?' he sneered as he pressed his mouth to hers.

'No!' shouted Vera as she and Lyubka rushed towards the pair. Both women needed all their strength to pull Andriy away from Zoya.

'Let me go! I'll show her…'

'No, Andriyu,' said Vera. 'You can't.'

'Oh, but I can,' and he lunged for Zoya.

'She's your sister,' cried Vera.

'No, she's not my sister,' he shouted at his mother.

'She is,' cried Lyubka, pulling at his arm. 'For pity's sake!'

He tore himself away from Lyubka and hurled himself towards Zoya.

'Andriy! Stop! You had the same father,' sobbed Vera.

Andriy staggered and turned to look at his mother. 'You're lying.'

She shook her head, the tears streaming down her face. 'No, I'm not.'

Andriy looked at Lyubka.

'It's true,' she said.

He turned to look at Zoya. 'No, it's not,' he said and fled from the cottage.

Zoya stood as if turned to stone. She stared at Vera as if she had never seen her before.

Lyubka put her arm around Vera's shoulders. 'Come and sit down.' She led her sister to a chair and guided her into it. Then she did the same for Zoya. 'Sit, *donechko*,' she said.

Zoya obeyed her but she shook her head, making the tears

flow down her cheeks. 'I'm not your daughter,' she said in reply to Lyubka while looking at Vera.

Vera's shoulders sagged as she tried to explain. 'You always knew I was not the mother you were born to, Zoya.'

'But I didn't know why you had taken pity on me.'

'You were a baby with no family…but you had the same father as Michaylo and Andriy.'

'Why didn't you tell me?'

'Perhaps I should have. I just thought it would bring us more grief.'

The three women bowed their heads, each brimful of their own sorrow as they looked at the past. They sat unmoving until Lyubka said, 'We should try to get some sleep.'

Vera rose stiffly from the chair and put out her hand to Zoya.

But Zoya shook her head. 'You're not my mother. I can't sleep there.'

'I am your mother. I have cared for you and loved you since the doctor brought you to this house.'

Again Zoya shook her head. 'Andriy's right. I am a cuckoo.'

'He also said you were your Mama's shadow,' said Lyubka. 'Don't throw all that love away.'

'I want to sleep on the settle,' said Zoya.

Lyubka looked at Vera who nodded. 'Alright.'

Zoya went over to the settle and drew the woollen blanket up to her chin.

Vera went over to her but Zoya pushed her face into the pillow. Vera stroked her head instead. 'Goodnight, *donechko*. Try to sleep.' She returned to her own bed and climbed in beside Lyubka. They lay down together, then turning on their sides, Lyubka spooned her younger sister.

***

The women rose the following morning nursing the bruises of the night's revelation. Vera went to milk the cow, Lyubka let out the hens, and Zoya made the *kasha*.

Michaylo came into the kitchen. 'Did I hear him come home?' he asked Zoya.

She nodded but continued to stir the *kasha*.

Michaylo approached her. 'Is he still in bed?'

'He's gone.'

'Where?'

She shrugged but then looked Michaylo fully in the face. 'Did you know?'

'Know what?'

'About my…our father?'

He sighed. 'I guessed.'

'How?'

'You look like him…but prettier.' Michaylo tried to smile.

'When did you guess?'

'I don't know. When we were growing up.'

'Why didn't you say anything?'

'Because I guessed that Mama and *Teta* knew, so I thought they would choose when to tell us.' He stroked her shoulder. 'It only made me feel closer to you. I really am your brother.'

'I know but Mama is not my Mama.'

'But you always knew that.'

'Yes, but I didn't know that she had taken me in as her husband's bastard.'

'Well, she did take you in and she has never treated you as anything but her daughter.' He saw the tears overflow onto her cheeks and took her in his arms. Rocking her, he said, 'Zoya, my dearest sister, don't upset yourself with what isn't there. Just carry on as before. Mama loves you, as do we all.'

'Andriy doesn't love me.'

'I'm afraid you can't have everything.'

'Do you think I should leave?'

He stood back from her but continued to hold her shoulders. 'Why would you want to leave your family?'

'Who's leaving?' asked Lyubka as she came into the cottage.

'Zoya's thinking of it,' said Michaylo.

'I hope you told her to stop this nonsense,' said Lyubka.

'I did.'

Lyubka looked at Zoya. 'It would break your Mama's heart if you left,' she said, 'not to speak of mine and Michaylo's and Tanya's. Don't be so selfish. Think of the children.' Then she took her in her arms and gave her a tight hug. 'No more of this now.'

'What's going on?' asked Vera from the doorway.

Zoya hung her head as Vera approached.

'Zoya?'

'I think I should leave.'

'I can't make you stay, Zoya. You're a grown woman.'

Zoya looked surprised.

'I think we should eat our breakfast before anymore leaving takes place,' said Lyubka.

'Yes. I'm going home for mine,' said Michaylo. 'Call me when he comes back.'

However, Andriy did not return that day. Towards noon on the following day, he strode into the cottage and went to his room where he threw his belongings into his suitcase and turned to leave. Zoya had been in the kitchen when he arrived but she had gone out into the garden to call Vera and Lyubka. They came hurrying up the path as Andriy came out of the cottage.

'Andriyu,' said Vera, 'where are you going?'

He looked for a moment as if he might ignore her but then he said, 'Work.'

'Where?'

'Moscow.'

'But I thought you didn't like it there,' said Vera approaching him.

296

He shrugged.

'When will you come home?'

He shrugged again as a car drew up in the lane. 'I have to go.'

'Kiss your Mama first,' said Lyubka.

He suffered his mother and aunt to kiss him and, as he was about to get into the car, Michaylo appeared.

'Hey, were you going without saying goodbye?'

He hugged his younger brother and whispered in his ear, 'Come home soon. Mama needs you.'

Andriy pulled himself away from his brother and got into the car. The family waved goodbye but Andriy only gave the smallest of nods.

'Did he say when he might come back?' asked Vera.

Michaylo shook his head. 'No, but hopefully not when our cousins from England are here.'

Chapter 39

Lyuba, Vera and Nadiya stood in the queue which had not moved in the ten minutes since they had joined it. They waited with all of the other "foreigners" to be processed and allowed to pass through the barrier into the Arrivals Lounge at Kyiv airport. Lyuba peered around the people in front of her to the glassed-in cubicle where a Customs official sat in his pale blue uniform shirt wearing a ridiculously large cap. The circumference of the crown overlapped his head so far that it looked like an ominous halo. His expression was grim as he checked every detail on each passport before allowing any visitor into his country. When Lyuba's turn came she held herself still and waited to be allowed in. He stamped her passport with a grudging click and flicked it back at her without making eye contact.

She hurried through the barrier and waited for Vera and Nadiya, hoping her youngest sister would not give him a piece of her mind. She put her hand luggage between her feet while she waited and turned her back on a second glass barrier to Arrivals to avoid looking at a hoard of desperate-looking men. She hoped they were only taxi drivers.

When Vera and Nadiya had finally been processed, the three sisters went out into the barrage of noise and bodies in the Arrivals Lounge.

'*Takshi? Takshi?*' was shouted at them from all sides.

Vera scanned their faces and chose a middle-aged man who resembled their father. '*Voksal?*' she asked. Taras had told them to ask only for the central train station in Kyiv and although they had several hours before their train left for Ternopil, the women would go straight there to wait.

The taxi driver nodded. '*Tak, Voksal.*'

He took two of their huge suitcases and set off at a speed

which belied his age, while Lyuba, Vera and Nadiya tried to keep up with him. He trundled the cases across the bumpy tarmac of the car park to a battered Lada which did not look as if it would survive the journey into the city.

He hurled their cases into the boot as if they were empty and then hooked the lid down with an elasticated tie. He gestured to the car doors and they climbed in, heaving their hand luggage onto their laps. The driver got into the car and tried to start the engine which caught on the fourth attempt. He pulled out of the car park onto a wide empty road which allowed him to veer between the potholes.

Lyuba tried to take her mind off the drive by fixing her eyes on the woods which slid past on either side, the birches stretching up their ghostly trunks into a haze of green leaves. She drank in the glow of the setting sun, its dusky rose pouring into the blue evening sky.

'It's so beautiful,' she breathed.

'It is,' said Vera.

The woods fell back as they approached a bridge and crossed the Dnipro, the almost mythical river which they had been taught was the greatest in all of Ukraine, if not in the whole of Europe. It seemed impossible that they were seeing it with their own eyes.

As they twisted this way and that through narrowing streets of the urban sprawl, Lyuba turned to look at her sisters. Vera shrugged but they all watched for clues to the whereabouts of the station. Suddenly they turned onto a wide avenue and almost immediately drove onto the enormous forecourt of the Voksal, its Soviet-style facade dwarfing the people below as they hurried about their business.

The driver pulled up as close to the entrance as he could. '*Voksal*,' he announced.

'*Dyakoyu*,' said Vera, but he ignored her thanks to untie the boot lid, then he lifted out their luggage as if it belonged in a doll's house.

Lyuba took out her purse. '*Funti chy dollyari?*' she asked. The sisters had not been able to purchase any *karbovantsi* outside of the country but their father had thought they would be able to pay for their taxi with foreign currency. He was right. The driver chose dollars over pounds and Lyuba did not haggle with him over the price.

'Even if he overcharged us, it was still cheap,' she said as they made their way into the teeming concourse of the station.

They queued at the Bureau de Change and after several minutes came face to face with a stocky woman behind the glass screen.

'What do you want?' she barked in Ukrainian.

'I would have thought that was obvious,' muttered Nadiya as she counted out the dollars to be exchanged for *karbovantsi*. She waited, pretending to be patient. The woman checked Nadiya's passport and then flicked the beads of her abacus before counting out the flimsy *kuponi* in a variety of colours, having failed to ask what denominations Nadiya might want.

'Looks like Monopoly money,' she said to her sisters as she tucked her share into her handbag.

'Tickets next,' said Vera and they joined another queue.

'Does no one in this country smile?' asked Lyuba, looking at the middle-aged cashier behind the glass of the ticket booth.

'Perhaps they've not had much to smile about,' said Vera.

'Probably not,' said Nadiya looking at the woman's acrylic sweater with its bobbly patches across her large breasts.

'It's not all about clothes,' said Vera, catching the direction of her younger sister's glance.

'No, but would she wear that if she could get something better? And look at her hair.'

The cashier's greying skull cap lay in harsh clumps around her jowls. Almost as if she had understood what they were saying, she looked up at the three sisters with a hostile glare.

'*Tri billyeti na Ternopil?*' asked Lyuba.

'*Shcho?*' barked the woman.

Lyuba pointed to herself and each of her sisters in turn then raised three fingers. 'Ternopil.'

'*Paperi,*' demanded the woman.

'I think she wants our passports,' said Vera.

'Why?' asked a flustered Lyuba. 'We're not crossing any borders.'

'I don't know but let's give it a try.'

They passed over their maroon and gold British passports.

'Ternopil,' repeated Lyuba for a third time.

'*Tak, tak,*' said the cashier. She imitated the Customs officer in examining each passport minutely but gave the sisters only a cursory glance to see if their faces matched their photographs.

'Do you think she's pretending to be able to read?' muttered Nadiya.

Vera nudged her. 'It's little people with a little power. This may be the only area of her life over which she can show some control.'

The cashier looked up at Lyuba. '*Tam I nazad?*'

Lyuba nodded. '*Tak,*' and then gave the date of their intended return to Kyiv.

The cashier hammered some numbers into a large calculator then scribbled a figure on a scrap of paper. She turned the paper to face Lyuba and showed it to her wordlessly. Lyuba counted out the sum in the brightly coloured *karbovantsi* and slid them beneath the glass screen. The cashier counted them again before passing over the tickets and passports.

As the sisters began to put their passports away, the cashier waved her hand at them impatiently. They looked behind them to see the long queue and stepped aside, although they took a moment to stow their valuables safely under the avid eyes of the other passengers.

They examined the Departures board and compared the

times with their tickets. No platform was shown yet as they still had two hours to wait until their train left at ten in the evening.

'Let's see if we can get a drink,' said Nadiya.

Lyuba looked around the crowded concourse. 'We should find somewhere to wait first.'

Vera pointed towards the huge archway which led to the trains. 'Maybe through there?'

She was right. The area beyond the archway was filled with rows of seats and around the perimeter were stalls selling refreshments. However, as they passed each full row, the women began to lose hope of getting any seats at all, let alone three together.

In the end they found one empty seat so they made their way towards it. Remarkably the old lady next to it heaved her striped plastic bag from the seat on the other side, placed it on the floor and moved up for them.

'*Dyakoyu, pani*,' said Lyuba.

The old woman nodded and gave them a half smile.

'Well, it's a start,' said Nadiya. 'Why don't you two sit here with the bags and I'll go and get us a drink.'

'Something non-alcoholic,' said Vera. 'We need to keep our wits about us.' She glanced around the waiting area which was not only full of people waiting for their trains but there were also groups of men drinking beer at the stalls. It seemed as if all eyes were on the little group of foreigners. Lyuba and Vera shifted the suitcases to form a solid barrier surrounding the hand luggage while they kept a firm grip on their handbags with their valuables.

'Get some water for the train,' said Lyuba. 'We've no idea what might be available.'

She and Vera watched anxiously as Nadiya strolled over to the food stalls. She walked slowly past each one, ignoring the men making comments about her. She passed a group of three men wearing collarless shirts and dark trousers. The tallest had

had his head shaved but his beard was coming through again. He curled his lip at her when she ignored him. Nadiya returned to the first stall and bought some water and a bag of pastries. She returned to her sisters. 'Drinks for now and breakfast.'

Vera nodded. 'Good idea.'

Their train would arrive in Ternopil at five-thirty the following morning.

'It's a pity we won't be able to see the countryside we pass through,' said Lyuba.

'Yes, but I don't think we'll get much sleep either.'

'Not if any of these desperate characters is on our train,' said Lyuba.

'They're just curious,' said Nadiya. 'You must admit we're a bit noticeable.'

'If they can't get hold of any Western goods, everything we have is saleable,' said Vera. 'You can't blame them looking.'

'Let's hope that's all they do.'

The girls sipped their water and tried not to stare back at what should have been their fellow Ukrainians.

After an hour or so Vera went to check the Departures board and, as she came back, there was a flurry of activity around the sisters.

'Is this us?' asked Lyuba.

Vera nodded. 'Platform 10.'

They gathered their luggage and began to follow the press of people making their way to the platform, but as they got closer they realised that they would have to haul their luggage down a long metal staircase to the train. They half-dragged, half-carried their bulky suitcases onto the platform, trying to keep together but unable to help one another. When they reached the bottom of the stairs they were jostled as they tried to see which direction to take.

'This way,' called Nadiya over the noise. She pointed to the numbers on the end of each carriage. They trundled their cases along the platform to the door of their carriage.

'Oh no,' said Lyuba as she saw the vertical flight of four steps up into the train.

'I'll go up,' said Nadiya, 'and you pass the cases to me.'

She climbed up the steps then Vera and Lyuba pushed the heavy cases up to her. With a strength belying her slender figure, Nadiya heaved up the cases and pushed them along the corridor ahead of her. Vera climbed up after passing up her hand luggage to Nadiya and then she turned to take Lyuba's heavy bag.

'Come on, Lyuba,' she called. 'We're all in now.'

The women struggled along the narrow train corridor ignoring the grumbling behind them and almost fell into their compartment when they reached it. They heaved their suitcases onto the high luggage rack and slid the door of the compartment closed.

'Thank goodness for that,' said Lyuba as she sank onto the bench seat.

'It won't be so bad on the way back,' laughed Vera. 'We'll have empty suitcases.'

'I wonder if someone else will join us,' said Nadiya, looking at the fourth space.

Just then the door was pulled back and a thin young woman entered followed by a young man. Vera moved along the bench seat automatically and they both sat down. They were carrying no luggage. The sisters looked at one another.

Nadiya pointed to the seat numbers on the plaques screwed to the walls. '*Chotyry osib,*' she said.

The couple looked at her blankly.

Nadiya waved four fingers at them and repeated, 'Four persons,' pointing in turn at the five people now seated in the compartment.

The couple shrugged.

'We don't seem to be getting anywhere,' said Nadiya. 'I think I'll go and see if I can find the conductor.'

'Be careful,' said Lyuba.

Nadiya slid the door open. 'You be careful too. These two don't look as if they could have afforded the fare. I'll leave the door open.'

When Nadiya had gone, the woman attempted a smile at Vera and said in Russian, 'Where are you travelling to?'

Vera replied in English. 'I don't understand.' She looked across at Lyuba. 'What do you think they're up to?'

'I don't know,' she said, examining the man from his pallid complexion down to his plastic shoes.

A barrel of a woman in a navy blue uniform appeared in the doorway of the compartment holding a battered clipboard.

'*Bilyeti!*' she barked.

Lyuba and Vera reached for their tickets and watched as the young couple took out theirs. The guard checked all of them then spoke to the young man.

Vera leaned towards Lyuba. 'Can you understand what she's saying?'

'Not really. They're speaking Russian.'

The sisters watched as the conversation continued but felt no confidence in its outcome. Nadiya hovered behind the guard unable to get past her broad figure. The guard consulted her clipboard and turned to Nadiya. '*Bilyet?*'

Nadiya pointed past her and squeezed into the compartment. She took her ticket from her handbag and showed it to the guard.

They all waited in silence while she scrutinised the numbers. She turned to Lyuba and Vera offering a stream of what might have been an explanation.

'*My ne rozumiyemo,*' said Vera shaking her head.

The guard shrugged but then spoke in Ukrainian. 'They have tickets for this compartment too.'

'Then there must be some mistake,' said Vera.

'Yes, a mistake.' The guard waited.

'She wants a bribe,' said Nadiya. 'Offer her a fifty and see what happens.'

Lyuba looked alarmed while Vera reached into her bag for her wallet. She removed a note from it while still concealing it in her handbag, then she proffered the green note. The guard shook her head and raised two fingers.

Vera held her gaze and passed her the note saying, '*Nyi*!'

There was a moment's pause then the guard took the note and jerked her head at the couple. They rose from the seat and followed her from the compartment. The guard slid the door closed.

'They were all in on it,' commented Nadiya.

'How disappointing,' said Lyuba.

'It's real life,' replied her youngest sister. 'They have very little and they see us as fair game.'

'But we're all Ukrainians.'

'Not to them we're not. We're rich foreigners.'

'It's not what I expected.'

'They've had almost fifty years of Soviet rule,' said Vera. '*Tato* told us to assume they have nothing and they haven't.'

'Except a determination to survive,' said Nadiya.

'Mama had that too although we're visiting a country she might have struggled to recognise,' said Lyuba.

***

Lyuba woke as the clattering of the train changed its rhythm and bright lights lit up the compartment. The train slowed to a halt. She held the blind back to peer out at a deserted station.

'Where are we?' asked Vera.

'I don't know. There doesn't seem to be a sign.'

When they moved off after a couple of moments, Lyuba saw a slender female guard swinging her lamp. 'They employ a lot of women,' she said.

'Soviet hangover,' said Nadiya. 'We would all have been equal.'

The train clanked up a gear and the sisters were lulled by its rhythm as they sped southwest towards Ternopil.

'Mama might have been on a train for days when she left home, and in a cattle truck,' murmured Lyuba.

'Goodnight, Lyuba,' said Vera.

But Lyuba couldn't sleep. She lay on her back on the narrow bunk. She thought of her mother standing in the dark of the cattle truck, having no idea where she was going or what she might find on her arrival. But Lyuba reminded herself that she and her sisters did not know what they would find either.

The women woke one another about an hour before they expected to arrive in Ternopil. Nadiya went out to use the lavatory but came back saying, 'If you can wait till we reach the station that might be a good idea.'

They tidied themselves with the wipes they had brought from home and made themselves presentable. Then they breakfasted on the stale pastries and water.

'Do you think there'll be coffee at the station?' asked Nadiya.

'I don't know but I hope Michaylo will be there to meet us,' said Lyuba.

'Let's have another look at his photo,' said Vera.

They peered at the photo of the cousin who was to collect them.

'He looks really strong,' said Nadiya, taking in his broad shoulders and barrel chest. Beside Michaylo stood his wife and their three children.

'Isn't it strange that we don't know our own family?' said Lyuba.

'We soon will,' said Vera.

***

When the train slowed in its approach to Ternopil station, the sisters were standing with their heavy luggage by the carriage door. The guard bustled in among them, smiling and nodding.

'If she thinks she's getting a tip, I shall tell her she's already had it,' said Nadiya.

The train screeched to a halt and the guard flung open the door. Lyuba stepped out first, finding the descent of the vertical steps even harder than the ascent, then she held a hand out to Vera. Before they could receive the first suitcase from Nadiya, they were jostled aside by a large man.

'*Skoro divchata*!' he said as he swung their suitcases onto the platform. 'Be quick, girls!'

Lyuba and Vera peered at him. 'Michaylo?'

'*Tak, tak! Skorenko*!' He continued to fling their luggage towards them.

All became clear as Nadiya stepped down.

The guard slammed the door shut and the train departed immediately. They stared at Michaylo as he explained, 'The train only stops for a few moments. You have to be quick.' Then he grinned at them. He opened his arms wide and they entered into his embrace. '*Moyi sestrychki*!'

All three sisters felt their eyes pricking with tears at this uncomplicated welcome. To them, their cousin Michaylo was still a stranger but here he was, welcoming them as his sisters. They kissed one another and then all four stood back to smile at each other.

'Let's go,' he said as he hefted a bag of hand luggage over each shoulder and then took hold of two of the suitcases. 'Can you manage the rest?'

The sisters laughed as they took the final pieces of luggage.

'How far is it to the village?' asked Nadiya.

'About two hours' drive.'

'Can we get some coffee first?'

He nodded. 'Yes, outside. The station café isn't open yet.'

They trundled through the small station into the car park where a van was selling refreshments in the early morning light.

Michaylo led them to another battered Lada and once they had stowed their belongings, he waved at the coffee stand.

'I'll wait here,' he said.

'No, come and have some coffee with us,' said Lyuba.

He jerked his head at the bulging boot of the car. 'There's too much temptation here for thieves.'

'We'll bring you one over then,' said Vera.

The coffee was thin and spoiled by powdered milk but it was hot. The sisters stood beside their cousin and his aged Lada and drank it gratefully.

They set off through a maze of streets lined with peeling and dilapidated buildings before reaching a wide pot-holed avenue which led out of the city. Michaylo tried to avoid the holes, nursing his car along, but even so the sisters found themselves being bounced about on poor suspension and worn-out seats.

When they overtook their first horse and cart, Lyuba exclaimed over its picturesqueness, although its load of stone belied this.

'Cheaper than petrol,' said Vera.

'And slower,' said Nadiya.

They passed people standing in small groups by the roadside, waiting for buses according to Michaylo.

'Those nests,' said Nadiya.

'Which ones?' asked Vera peering through the car window.

'Those on top of the poles.'

'Oh yes.'

'What are they, Michaylo?'

'Storks' nests. People say if you see a couple of storks flying then there's going to be rain.'

'Is there any truth in that?' asked Lyuba.

'None at all,' said Michaylo.

The road bisected fields of sunflowers which spread away over undulating hills as far as the horizon on one side and the dark border of a forest on the other. Despite the earliness of the hour and their sparse breakfast, the sisters gazed at the beautiful landscape which they had heard praised since childhood.

Michaylo broke into their thoughts. 'Not far now, girls.'

'Is there somewhere we can buy flowers?' asked Vera.

'Yes, but what do you want them for?'

'A gift for our aunties.'

'Alright. There is a place we can stop but can I suggest you buy flowers for your grandmother's grave instead?'

'We can do that as well,' said Lyuba.

As the road approached a wide bend, Michaylo did not follow it but took the left-hand fork which led immediately into another grubby, peeling town. They drove down a very steep hill and he parked precariously outside a shop which on closer inspection appeared to be selling flowers. There were no bright buckets of blooms on the pavement outside, only some faded plastic flowers behind a dirty pane of glass.

'Is this it?' asked Lyuba.

'Yes.'

'There would be flowers outside the shop in England.'

Michaylo gave a short laugh. 'They would be stolen here.'

The girls got out of the car and approached the shop. Nadiya pushed open the brown painted door and they entered the gloomy interior. A woman hurried from a back room.

'We'd like to buy some flowers,' said Lyuba.

'Fresh ones,' said Nadiya.

'Yes,' said the woman. 'I have these.' She pointed to buckets of roses and gladioli.

'Roses I think,' said Nadiya.

The sisters chose mixed colours for *Teta* Vera and *Teta* Lyubka, but Natalya's favourite yellow ones for their grandmother's grave. Then they returned to the car for the final leg of their journey. After only a little time, they turned right up a lane signposted to Krasivka.

When they entered the village, Michaylo drove slowly, taking a careful line between the potholes and playing children, who drew back to stand and stare at the foreigners he was bringing with him. The sisters peered through the windows, trying to recognise the cottage they had seen in the photographs their aunts had sent to England. The houses were all white-washed with corrugated roofs and each one seemed to have a burgeoning garden.

Michaylo turned right and bumped to a stop beside a cottage like all the others in the village with its paling fence holding in the hollyhocks. Two girls were playing in the road but almost immediately there was a cry from one of them, then they fled down the path to the house shouting, '*Baba, Teta*, they're here!'

Lyuba and her sisters opened the creaking doors of the Lada and got out stiffly.

The girls ran back towards them closely followed by a plump old woman wearing a brightly coloured headscarf round a face like a wrinkled apple. She reached Vera first and with no greeting, took Vera's face in her hands and kissed her.

'*Moyi dorohenki*,' she said as she hurried around the back of the car to Nadiya, who received the same treatment. 'My dearest ones.' Then it was Lyuba's turn.

'*Teta?*' asked Lyuba.

Her aunt nodded vigorously and turned to her sister who was running down the path towards them. Natalya's daughters stood together to greet her and she bowled into the three of them where she was swallowed in their embrace. Each of them was taller than their aunt but she whirled around in their midst, planting kisses and talking non-stop in between.

'Oh my girls! At last you're here. You look like your Mama…Oh this one is pretty… And this one…'

The sisters laughed while *Teta* Verochka tried to intervene.

'Lyubka, let them come into the house.'

But *Teta* Lyubka was still in the throes of delight. 'Can you believe it? Can you see Natalya's daughters?'

'Yes, yes. Come on now.'

Vera had extricated herself and had reached into the car for the two multi-coloured bouquets. 'These are for you, *Teta* Lyubka, and these are for you, *Teta* Verochka.'

There were cries of, 'There was no need!' 'You shouldn't spend your money like this!' but when *Teta* Verochka said, 'We'll save them for Mama's grave,' Lyuba was able to produce the yellow roses.

'These are for *Baba*.'

The aunties smiled. 'Natalya's favourite colour.'

Lyuba's eyes prickled with tears to find her mother so vividly present. But there was no time to reflect as they were introduced to women of their own age.

'This is my wife, Tanya,' said Michaylo, 'and my sister, Zoya.'

The younger women stepped forward more shyly, but they too embraced their cousins from England before their guests were ushered towards the house preceded by the three children.

As they approached the cottage, Vera noticed a collection of shoes on the doorstep and realised the family removed their dusty outdoor shoes when they went indoors. She bent to take off her own shoes muttering to her sisters to do the same, but was stopped by Zoya. 'No, there's no need to take your shoes off. That's just for these messy people,' she smiled, looking at her nephew and nieces.

The children stared and Nadiya said, 'Oh, you're Oksana and Olena,' to the two girls, who looked down at their feet.

'I'm Danylo,' said the boy.

'Of course you are,' said Nadiya.

The children smiled toothy smiles at being correctly

identified and the girls continued to stand close enough for their shoulders to be touching.

The sisters turned to see both aunts returning from the kitchen. *Teta* Lyubka held a round loaf on a tray covered with a *rushnyk*. There was a pot of salt beside the bread.

The aunts stood on the threshold of their home with Zoya beside them, while Michaylo and Tanya gathered the children.

'With this bread and salt we greet you,' said *Teta* Verochka.

Taras had told his daughters to expect the traditional welcome. 'The bread represents hospitality,' he had said.

'And the salt?'

'Eternal friendship because salt never sours and is never corrupted by time.'

Lyuba broke off a small piece of bread, dipped it in the salt and bowed her head in thanks, just as her father had instructed her to do. Vera and Nadiya followed suit.

'Welcome home,' cried Lyubka and Verochka.

Historical Note

In 1947, Britain became the host nation to tens of thousands of Ukrainians, Lithuanians and Byelorussians among others, who could not return to their homeland. Washed up in Europe, without documents, they became European Voluntary Workers and came to Britain to work on farms and in factories. Although given the title "Voluntary", the Ministry of Labour imposed rules concerning where they could live and work, at least for the first year of their residence. However, they did choose to come west, rather than to return home to Stalin's certain punishment of deportation to Siberia or execution. In the immediate aftermath of the Second World War, Stalin had ordered the NKVD to teach the Ukrainians a lesson. There was to be no hope of an independent state and any notion of such a state was crushed by summary executions and mass deportations to Siberia. The Ukrainian population had been decimated by both the Red Army and the Nazis leaving only a ravaged country of old men, women, and children to struggle to survive against the bullies.

In Britain, the exiles took jobs, shared houses, eventually buying their own homes, and brought up their children to love the homeland. After the death of Stalin in 1953, the tentative exchange of letters between the emigrants and their families in Ukraine began. This led to financial support in the form of parcels of fabric and clothing being sent to the families left behind. One valuable form of currency was the flower patterned headscarf which could be bought in the UK and sold in Ukraine without its value being depleted by the Soviet customs process, so it became a popular item to send.

The exiles' dream of returning home was not realised until

after Ukraine achieved independence in 1991. My father was able, like many others, to return to his village after an absence of fifty years and, in time, was able to show his children and grandchildren the land from which their family came. The story of my characters, Natalya and Taras, is based on the oral histories of family and friends. Indeed the letter from the British police, mentioned in Chapter 30, is a direct quotation from one received by my father in the 1950s. I also consulted my grandmother's letters to my father which opened a window on the closed world behind the Iron Curtain.

As ever, while working on "Bread and Salt", I read much that was interesting and some that was directly useful. In the context of this novel, I strongly recommend:

Iron Curtain: The Crushing of Eastern Europe by Anne Applebaum

The Soviet Police System edited by Robert Conquest

The Cold War by John Lewis Gaddes

Changing Identities: Latvians, Lithuanians and Estonians in Great Britain by Emily Gilbert

Stasiland by Anna Funder

A full bibliography can be found on my website: mariadziedzanauthor.com

Author Biography

MARIA DZIEDZAN was born in Grimsby in 1951. She studied Philosophy at Nottingham University before becoming an English teacher. She taught for several decades in Nottinghamshire and then retired from teaching to focus on her writing. *When Sorrows Come* was her first novel. It won The Big Bingham Book Read in 2015 and was one of the finalists for The Historical Novel Society Indie Award 2016. *Driven Into Exile* was the second book in Maria's *My Lost Country* series. *Bread and Salt* is its sequel.

Other books by Maria

 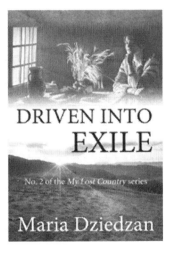

Acknowledgements

Writing this novel without my father, Ivan Semak, has been like having the stabilisers removed from my bicycle. His death in January 2017 not only left the family bereft, but I had no one to ask the hundred and one questions which crop up when writing. I do have notebooks full of material from our conversations but who could tell me how much a second-hand bike cost in the 1950s? So I am grateful to my godfather, Stefan Sianchuk for his patience (and answers). I am also indebted to Vida Gasperas, who generously shared her memories of arriving in Britain at the end of the war as a young girl from Lithuania and to Dr Charles Clayton who answered some very unusual questions about toxicity and other medical matters.

My thanks, as ever, go to those kind readers who give me their time to read and comment upon the various drafts. I am grateful for the nudges towards a better book…and this one is better for your suggestions. So thank you Zig Dziedzan, Larissa Dziedzan, Alex Dziedzan, Sonia Iwanczuk, Emilia Iwanczuk; a very big thank you to Dr Joy Sullivan for helping me to resolve the problematic ending; and to Steve Taylor who read several drafts and encouraged me from the earliest days of writing *Bread and Salt*. I am grateful to Helen Slade, not only for her reading but for her continued support with the mysteries of the website and to Julia Marriott who also multi-tasked, proof-reading and analysing. Writing is a lonely business, so I would like to thank my fellows at Fosseway Writers for their support. Special thanks go to Nick Rowe for his encouragement.

Finally, I must give credit to the invaluable services of Jonathan Veale at www.writeaway.co.uk, the best of editors, and to the skill of Brian Stephens at www.moulinwebsitedesign.com.

Credits

The back photo of the woman offering bread was taken by - Vyacheslav Logvynyuk

39481287R00193

Printed in Poland
by Amazon Fulfillment
Poland Sp. z o.o., Wrocław